WOMEN, WORK, AND FAMILY

WOMEN, WORK, AND FAMILY

Louise A. Tilly and Joan W. Scott

Holt, Rinehart and Winston

New York   Chicago   San Francisco   Atlanta   Dallas
Montreal   Toronto   London   Sydney

Library of Congress Cataloging in Publication Data

Tilly, Louise A.
  Women, work, and family.

  Bibliography: p. 259
  Includes index.
  1. Women—Employment—Great Britain—History.
2. Women—Employment—France—History. 3. Family—
History. 4. Family—Economic aspects. I. Scott,
Joan Wallach, joint author. II. Title.
HD6135.T54   301.5'1   74-19821
ISBN 0-03-033326-1
ISBN 0-275-85180-X

The popular impression seems to be that women today are taking a larger share of the world's work than they have ever done before—that this is a new departure, the outcome of the factory system. As a matter of fact the share taken by women in the work of the world has not altered in amount, nor even in intensity, only in character.

Ada Heather-Bigg, 1894

CONTENTS

PREFACE

Historians, asserted Hayden White in 1966, are trapped in nineteenth-century notions of art and science. Unwilling to join the intellectual revolution of the twentieth century, they lost their place at the cutting edge of scholarship. In literature the historian increasingly became a figure of scorn, shriveled and impotent. Within serious science and social science, the historian simply became irrelevant.

Though much—indeed perhaps most—written history still remains intellectually trapped in an antiquated positivism and stylistically unable to break out of a traditional narrative mode, White's devastating critique no longer applies to a significant and increasing portion of the profession. Influenced especially by developments within the social and behavioural sciences, historians have explored new questions with novel sources and methods. As a result, they have begun to revise the nature of historical inquiry: its methods, interpretations, and, even, its underlying questions.

Social and behavioral scientists, it must be stressed, should not be portrayed as the intellectual heroes of the twentieth century. Increasingly abandoning its early grounding in historical analysis, social science itself developed a peculiar indifference to time and context. Sociological theory, for instance, too often offered general explanations of social organization which rested on implicit and untested assumptions about the past. Research, on the other hand, accumulated data about contemporary situations on the assumption that particular social patterns could be explained in terms of their present characteristics, without reference to their past. These theoretical and methodological features of social science increasingly have come under attack from critics both within and without the social and behavioural sciences. As a consequence, contemporary research in sociology, psychology, economics, anthropology, and demography reveals a reawakened appreciation of the potential of historical analysis.

A great deal of the most interesting interdisciplinary history or historical social science remains inaccessible to students or to general readers. It exists in the form of journal articles, specialized monographs, or privately circulated research papers. The purpose of the *Interedisciplinary Social History Series* is to make some of this new research available in a readable, comprehensible, and scholarly manner.

The emphasis of the series is on social history, a field whose boundaries are difficult and controversial to define. In the rough definition guiding my delimitation the field comprises primarily the history of social structure and domestic organization, the explanation of demographic patterns, and the origins and development of social institutions and social movements. The field is delimited, thus, partly by its subject matter. As well, it is defined loosely by approach. That approach does not rest necessarily on any particular sources or methods. Rather, it is characterized by its emphasis on systematic analysis: the deliberate, self-conscious attention to assumptions, theory, and methodology. Negatively, it is an approach defined by its rejection of the methodological and theoretical unself-consciousness of most historical writing. As such, contemporary social history focuses more on questions than on events; it is more interested in structures or patterns than in simply telling a story.

Each book in the *Interdisciplinary Social History Series* introduces readers to a key area of concern to contemporary social historians. Though organized in whatever way their authors' wish, each book has three components: (1) a review of the literature in the field; (2) examples of the authors' research; (3) a general interpretation of the major issues.

Women, Work and Family by Louise A. Tilly and Joan W. Scott provides an ideal beginning for the series. Lucid, beautifully organized, the book combines the authors' own extensive research into primary sources with a commentary on the major literature in the field and a striking, convincing interpretation as crucial to understanding the position of women today as in the past.

Concerned primarily with the popular classes in England and France, Tilly and Scott offer an interpretation based upon the material influences on the lives of women during the last 250 years. They demonstrate the way in which the mode of production, the mode of reproduction, and the lives of women have intersected over time. Their interpretation and method of analysis are particularly important in four ways.

First, they advance a significant thesis which refutes many commonly held ideas about the history of women during industrialization. They show clear continuities between the type of work women did prior to, during, and after the development of industrial capitalism. Their book should bury effectively the notion that industrialization brought about the participation of a larger proportion of women in the workforce.

Second, they construct a model with which to analyse systematically the relation between women, family, and work in general, not just in the historical cases with which they are concerned. They plot, that is, the dimensions which must be part of any attempt to understand why and how the activities and position of women differ in various contexts.

Indeed, their comparison of the differences in the work patterns of women in Britain and France should serve as a model of systematic explanation.

Third, the book contributes to the theoretical analysis of the relationship between the family and social change. The authors offer a materialist explanation which avoids the dangers of simple reductionism. They show clearly that a close relation exists between the organization of the family and the mode of production at any given time. Yet, they also show that the relationship is very complex. Domestic organization does not change quickly or easily. Families adopt complex strategies which enable them to preserve elements of customary practices in altered circumstances, and the family patterns that emerge represent adaptations, complex compromises between tradition and new organizational and social structures.

Fourth, *Women, Work and the Family* is essential reading for anyone concerned with the position of women today. It offers a sophisticated framework that should be applied to the analysis of contemporary relations between women and their domestic and occupational lives. And it shows in what ways women's position today is a product of their past.

Michael B. Katz

ACKNOWLEDGMENTS

1. Louise Tilly

Many people and institutions have helped me in the long process which the completion of this book culminates. Natalie Davis first suggested that I write a separate paper on women workers as I completed my dissertation on the working class of Milan. My colleagues at Michigan State University gave me helpful comments on my first presentation of the paper which extended my ideas on women's work to nineteenth century Europe as a whole. A Rockefeller Foundation Population Policy Research Grant supported a year's leave, travel to France and England, and research expenses for my project on "Women in the Growth of an Urban, Industrial Economy in Europe." This financial support gave me the chance to sketch out a model, the wherewithal to collect the data to test it, and to analyze that data. The material on cities in this book is only a small part of that research, which will be reported on elsewhere. A Rackham Faculty Research Grant is helping me do further work in three French cities. European historians such as Olwen Hufton, Eric Hobsbawm, Dorothy and Edward Thompson, Michelle Perrot, Pierre Pierrard, and Jean Piat gave me valuable advice and support. Miriam Cohen, Michael Hanagan and Elizabeth Pleck gave useful and important comments on the completed manuscript. Graduates and undergraduates at the University of Michigan have helped me with library work, coding and programming, questions and ideas. Claudia Kselman and Paul Saba helped with bibliography and footnotes. Terri Palma and Martha Martell typed and retyped portions of the manuscript. Charles Tilly and our children have patiently listened and responded as I formulated and tested my explanations.

Joan Scott has been an ideal collaborator, from the time we first started to talk about women's work in Europe, in December, 1972, through our decision to collaborate on a paper, in March, 1973, to the present book. We've never lived in the same town, so our communication has produced a dossier of letters several inches thick and some astronomical phone bills. This method imposed by geographical distance has kept us honest. Ideas and evidence have been put forward, examined and discussed in a way that has never lacked in frankness and freshness. Our book is the measure of the fruitfulness of our collaboration.

2. Joan Scott

This book owes a great deal to my students at Northwestern University and the University of North Carolina at Chapel Hill. Their enthusiasm and their questions led to the development of new insights and to the refinement of some of the arguments. Their interest in the subject and their patience with my groping for new ideas was a continuing and important source of support and inspiration. Some of my colleagues at Chapel Hill, among them Richard Soloway, Stephen Baxter, and Peter Filene, offered useful suggestions, ideas and information. I appreciate the services provided by the Institute for Research in the Social Sciences at University of North Carolina. A fellowship from the National Endowment for the Humanities made it possible for me to do research in France and freed me from teaching responsibilities during the academic year 1975–76. Much of the writing of the manuscript was done during that year. Its argument, of course, in no way represents the views of the NEH.

I am particularly appreciative of the discussions I have had with Olwen Hufton, Herbert Gutman and Susan Rogers. Each has sharpened my understanding at various points in the process of shaping and writing this book. Dolores Janiewski read the completed manuscript and helped us clarify some definitions and arguments. John Cell read an early version of the manuscript. We have not been able to deal with all of his criticisms, nor meet his very high standards. But his questions and suggestions have improved the book a great deal. We are grateful for his time and help. Rosalie Radcliffe not only typed the manuscript cheerfully and expertly, but she offered some valuable suggestions and criticisms. Dan Hughes prepared the index. We appreciate his careful and conscientious effort. Charles Tilly was a demanding and helpful critic. Donald Scott has read and listened to this manuscript many times and throughout it reflects his advice, criticism and historical understanding.

The experience of collaborating with Louise Tilly has been a rare and unusual one and I have learned a great deal from it. People often ask us how we divided the labor and our response is that we shared it. The listing of the authors is an arbitrary one, for we find it impossible to assign greater weight to either of our efforts. The book represents a collaboration in the best sense of the term, for it is the product of a joint effort. Our different abilities and different styles always complemented one another. This is a different and a better book than either of us would have written alone.

Introduction

Women, Work, and Family reexamines an old problem from a new perspective. The problem is the impact of industrialization on women's work. Since the nineteenth century discussions of this subject have been fraught with controversy. In the twentieth century, commentators continue to debate the old questions: Is work good for women? Does earning wages enhance female status, power, and consciousness? Does women's work increase family prosperity or lead to the breakdown of "normal" family relationships? Has industrialization created the housewife or the liberated woman? Has women's lot improved or deteriorated as a result of industrial development?

The range of answers offered in the 1970s does not differ significantly from those given a hundred years ago, although we have become used to the factories and technology which were then still a novelty. Some nineteenth-century commentators welcomed the new factory system. It provided jobs for women "appropriate to their strength which, without tiring them, allow(ed) them to earn a small supplementary wage and increase the well-being of their families."[1] The sight of women working at the Imperial Printing House in Paris obviously pleased Jules Turgan: "The workrooms have a charming air," he wrote, "because they are filled almost exclusively with women, sometimes pretty, often young and always graciously coquettish."[2] Other observers, however, were alarmed at the sight of women tending machines. And they were disturbed even more about the social consequences of women's work away from home. Writing in 1861, the French politician Jules Simon pointed to a "terrible vice in our economic organization . . . the suppres-

1

sion of family life." It resulted above all, he said, from the fact that women went out to work. The promiscuity of factory life destroyed female morals and maternal sentiment. "A woman who becomes a worker," Simon warned, "is no longer a woman."[3] Friedrich Engels disagreed. Writing in 1884, Engels defined the family Simon wanted to save as the cause of women's "social, legal and economic subordination." "The first condition for the liberation of the wife," he wrote, "is to bring the whole female sex back into public industry . . . this in turn demands that the characteristic of the monogamous family as the economic unit of society be abolished."[4]

The range of opinion was very wide indeed. And the assessment of the impact of industrialization on women's work depended on the perspective of the observer. That has remained true in histories of women's work and in discussions of public policy and the Equal Rights Amendment. As long as one asks whether work for women is good or bad, differences of opinion will continue and the discussions based on these differences will confuse rather than enlighten us about women's experience in the past. Before we can evaluate the impact of industrialization on women's work, we must know what the nature of that impact actually was.

In this book we examine the historical record of women's work in England and France, from about 1700 to 1950. The two nations had different economic histories during the eighteenth, nineteenth, and twentieth centuries. England industrialized rapidly after 1750. France had a very different form of industrialization and the rate of change was slower. A comparison of the two countries permits us to isolate the influences on women's work and to determine which are historically specific, which are more general. We focus almost exclusively on those social groups which involved large numbers of women in productive activity at home and in the labor market. These groups include peasants, artisans, small shopkeepers, skilled and unskilled laborers—members of the working or popular classes.

Although we focus on two European nations for our examples, the conceptualization and methodology we use is applicable equally to the history of women in the United States or in other countries. The definitions and the important variables in our explanation are relevant to the history of women's work elsewhere. Of course, the experience of women and families in countries undergoing industrial growth and demographic change varies. Nevertheless, in all such countries the level and character of industrial development determine the demand for women as workers, as reproducers, as child rearers. The supply of women available for these activities is shaped in part by demographic factors such as sex ratios, mortality, the age and rate of marriage, and levels of fertility. These factors establish the structural context within which women, as individuals or as members of groups, formulate attitudes and make choices.

Work is defined as productive activity for household use or for exchange. The meaning, location, and nature of work, of course, have changed over time. During the nineteenth century what we have termed work usually meant wage earning, as it does today. But in earlier centuries the jobs women performed to help support their families did not always or necessarily bring in money. Growing vegetables, raising animals, preparing food, making clothing, and helping with farm or craft work served household needs. These activities had economic value, but it was more often what economists call "use value" than "exchange value." Furthermore, this kind of work merged imperceptibly with women's household or domestic chores. As a result our use of the term *work* for the early modern period of the seventeenth and eighteenth centuries encompasses all of these activities. For the period of industrialization, however, work denotes only market-oriented, or wage-earning, jobs. This definition is somewhat arbitrary, for it excludes domestic activity, the useful, economically valuable housework that women perform for their families. We do not deny that unpaid household labor is work. Indeed, we suggest that its value to families was often seen as greater than the value of woman's wage labor. To avoid confusion, however, we have found it useful to refer to housework as domestic activity in order to distinguish it from wage-earning or "productive" activity. Similarly, reproduction—the bearing and raising of children—is a kind of "work" with economic value to society and to the family. Nonetheless, it is not included in our use of the term *work*. Since the three forms of female activity became increasingly distinct during industrialization, we felt it was important to use different words to describe them.

Our analysis of women's work approaches the subject from two sides. First it looks at the jobs women did and asks: What were the particular economic and demographic factors that influenced women's work? Aggregate descriptions and statistics are used to compare women's work on the national level in England and France. In addition, we compare women's work in rural and urban areas and we contrast their occupations in cities with different economies. Our purpose is to understand the specific circumstances which created jobs of different types for women.

The second part of the analysis examines the women themselves. Who worked? How many women worked in a given period? What were the age and marital status of working women? Why did they work? These questions inevitably lead to the family and household setting in which women were embedded as daughters, wives, and mothers. By looking at women within a household context we can talk not simply about women's work, but about women's domestic activities as well. How did married women, for example, allocate their time among productive and domestic and childbearing activities—all of which had value for the family? What was the impact on women's work of changes in their domestic and reproductive activity?

To answer these questions we had to assemble a great deal of information about economic structure, women's employment patterns, and family and household organization. We also had to define our terms carefully so that we could examine work in the context of women's other activities. The analyses of anthropologists, demographers, historians of the family, and economists helped us conceptualize our approach to this study. Their insights enabled us to formulate questions and find answers that have deepened our understanding of the history of women and their work.

We began by defining the term *women*. There is, of course, no historically meaningful, homogeneous social category of "women." Some studies of women's work recognize this, distinguishing among women of different classes and occupations. Yet too often the history of a particular group of women becomes the basis for a generalization about all women. Extrapolating from the experience of middle-class women late in the nineteenth and early in the twentieth centuries, some historians have argued that new jobs created by industrial expansion enabled women to leave their "traditional place" at home and develop the consciousness and organization that ultimately led to political enfranchisement.[5] This is not an accurate characterization of the history of working-class women in that period.

Beyond the question of class and occupation, the word *woman* encompasses a series of social and biological categories which must be specified by historians. The biological given of sex (female) is made specific by social connections with men, which are also sexual links. The sexual-social links can be taken into account by looking at women in terms of their life cycles. Females start life as daughters, virgins. They become sexually mature and leave their families of origin for husbands or lovers; they become mothers of children. If they live long enough, the mothers see their own children leave and marry, and they become mothers-in-law and grandmothers. The death of their husbands makes them widows. Anthropological investigations have established the important differences each of these life-cycle stages have for the work, status, and power of women. In some societies, for example, the passivity of the young unmarried women is exchanged for the activism of a mother and then for the domineering authority of a mother-in-law.

Every woman in the past did not live this "normative" life cycle, tied to biological time. Some girls were orphaned and never lived with their own parents. There were women who never married because they died young. There were also women who lived out a long unmarried life because the circumstances of their lives or the choices they made precluded marriage. The fact that they were single, however, had an important influence on their position. Social-sexual references—single, married, mother, widow—then, as well as class and occupational designations, are important for any historical understanding of women's experience.[6] The absence of even the simple distinction between married and single women has confused many an interpretation of the impact of industrialization on women.

The anthropological perspective suggests that the position, activities, and statuses of women are related to their household and family position. These at once influence and are influenced by women's productive activity as well as by other public roles they may perform. By family we mean the kin group living in a single household. These are usually, but not always parents and their children. The sharp distinction historians have often made between work and family seems to be inaccurate.[7] The distinction was based on the concept that work could be understood only in reference to wages paid in return for it. The woman at home was said to be economically nonfunctional. Thus Alice Clark began her book *The Working Life of Women in the Seventeenth Century* with a disclaimer:

> For the purposes of this essay, the highest, most intense forms to which women's productive energy is directed have been excluded; that is to say, the spiritual creation of the home and the physical creation of the child. Though essentially productive, such achievements of creative power transcend the limitations of economics and one instinctively feels that there would be something almost degrading in any attempt to weigh them in the balance with productions that are bought and sold in the market or even with professional services.[8]

Yet some economists have suggested that, both before and after industrialization, the household division of labor is based on an economic calculus. They argue further that this calculus covers all family activities, including reproduction.

> Women allocate time in a more complex variety of ways than men. . . . While men's work consists almost exclusively of paid time in the market, women's work often consists of unpaid, non-market work which is assigned no value in economic data, but which may have immense value to the individual woman or family.[9]

In a family, a mother's time spent with children is given more or less weight depending upon "the value of children," the manner in which offspring are perceived as resources for the family. The value of the time devoted to children must be weighed against the gains a woman's paid work brings to the family. Moreover, families or households allocate the time of different members differently. The way any particular member uses his or her time is determined both by opportunities available to him or her and by the activities of other household members. The important point is that the family or household is the unit of decision making for the activities of all its members, and that decisions are made which implicitly assign economic value to all household tasks.[10] Thus, changes in the importance of children and in the time required for their care, like changes in work opportunities, have important consequences for women. An interpretation which assumes that only paid work is important, or that it is the only source of respect and status, neglects not only the domestic and reproductive activities of women, but the implicitly economic function of those activities within families. (Reproductive activity is used here as a shorthand for the whole set of women's household activities: childbearing, child rearing, and day-to-day management of the consumption and production of services for household members.)

Interest in the household and the stress on the economic value of women's domestic and childbearing functions lead us to ask what the impact was of changes in household and family organization on women's work. Many of the early histories of women's work, while taking into account female domestic and reproductive activities, did not consider them germane to the history of work itself. (Engels was the exception. He suggested in *The Origin of the Family, Private Property and the State* that the reproductive regime of a society was connected directly to its organization of production. But he never fully elaborated this insight.) Most authors acknowledge that factory jobs created problems for women with children, that the separation of home and work resulting from industrial development was a hardship for women who had to work. But in these studies, women's reproductive and family roles were considered an unchanging fact; unlike work they were assumed to have no history. This was a reason Clark excluded "the creation of the home and . . . the child" from her study. She assumed these were enduring functions, not susceptible to historical consideration, because she had neither a method nor a conceptualization which enabled her to view family roles historically. For Clark, women's domestic and childbearing activities transcended the limits not only of economics, but of time.

The history of reproduction has been conceptualized and studied under the rubric of family history. Only recently have social historians and historical demographers begun to treat the history of the family as a subject worthy of serious investigation. The work of Philippe Ariès, Pierre Goubert, E. A. Wrigley, and Peter Laslett (to name only a few) has important ramifications for interpretations of the history of women's work. Ariès suggested in his *Centuries of Childhood: A Social History of Family Life* that during the seventeenth and early eighteenth centuries a change in attitudes toward children took place among upper-class families. Using school records, paintings, diaries, and memoirs, he concluded that children assumed an increasingly central emotional role in family life. At the same time, families became more private, insulating their members from the sociability of public life. While Ariès was careful to restrict his comments to developments in upper-class families, he nonetheless suggested that the evolution he described affected lower-class families at a later date. The important point was that the organization, structure, and interior relationships of families had a history which could be discerned by a careful observer of the "artifacts of a society."[11]

Using demographic evidence, for the most part, especially records of marriage, birth, and death, Goubert, Laslett, Wrigley, and others have shown how sensitive populations were to changes in food supply and food prices, to occupational opportunity and to mortality rates.[12] Couples adjusted their ages at marriage, for example, and, once married, their fertility at different times and in different circumstances. By examining data on marriage, birth, and death, the historical demographers have been able to describe long-term trends in the experience of local communities. They have shown that there are historical and class patterns of marriage, of the size and organization of households, and of rates of fertility and mortality.

The intimate and mundane life experiences of men and women are not universally and at all times the same; rather these have changed over time. An unfortunate division of labor among scholars has prevented a full examination of the implications of these facts. Studies of demographic history often neglect the subject of women's work, while studies of women's work neglect the history of the family. Yet the implications of each area for an understanding of the history of working women are important. The age at which a woman marries, the number of children she bears, the size of the household in which she lives, and the value of children to the family all directly affect her working life. The amount of time required for household and childbearing activities affects the amount of time spent in productive work. A history of women's work must therefore also be a history of the family.

This book is a history of the economic, demographic, and familial influences on women's work. We assume that both the mode of production and the structure of the family shape the productive and reproductive activities of women. The economic system of a society constrains and shapes production and reproduction and eventually modifies family organization. But, at any point, the family is the institution which mediates between the system and individuals. It is the locus for decision about the activities of all its members—men, women, and children.

The book does not consider questions about the connections among women's work, status, power, and "consciousness." Nor does it deal with the cultural and ideological determinants of the position and activities of women. Although there are occasional references to the status and power of women in their families and to the continuity of familial values, these are not dealt with fully or at length. To treat those issues would have involved a great deal more research than we were able to do. And it would have detracted from our major purposes, which were to set straight the historical record on women's work and to analyze the interrelationships among changes in the economy, in women's work, and in the organization and structure of working-class family life.

PART I

The Family Economy in Early Modern England and France

You cannot expect to marry in such a manner as neither of you shall have occasion to work, and none but a fool will take a wife whose bread must be earned solely by his labour and who will contribute nothing towards it herself.

"A Present for a Servant Maid" (1743), quoted in Ivy Pinchbeck, *Women Workers and the Industrial Revolution*, pp. 1–2.

1

Economy and Demography

In the cities and the countryside of eighteenth-century England and France economic life was organized on a small scale. The visual image one gets from reports of the period is of small farms dotting the countryside and of small shops lining the crowded narrow streets of cities.

During his journey in France, the English journalist Arthur Young observed in the region of the Pyrenees "many small properties . . . the country mostly inclosed and much of it with thorned hedges." He described the vineyards of the Garonne as "one of the most fertile vales in Europe . . . the towns frequent and opulent; the whole country an incessant village."[1] In poorer regions, too, Young noted the prevalence of small farms, isolated or grouped in scattered hamlets and villages. In parts of northern England, the picture was similar:

> From Wooburn to Newport Pagnell the soil has great variety; for some miles it is quite a light sand, and then a gravel with some light loams: About Wanden the soil is chiefly sand, but few of their farms are very large. . . .[2]

An English clergyman writing in 1795 recalled that

> Formerly many of the lower sort of people occupied tenements of their own, with parcels of land about them, or they rented such of others. On these they raised for themselves a considerable part of their subsistence. . . .[3]

The center of life for rural people, whatever the size of their holding, was a farm. The center of the farm was the household in which they lived and around which work was organized.

For those engaged in rural and urban manufacturing the household was both a shop and a home. This handloom weaver's recollection of his uncle's house could have been written by many a craftsman or small shopkeeper in England and France:

> The row of houses in which my uncle lived faced the morning sun; a nearly paved footpath, and a causey for carts, lay in front of the houses from one end of the row to the other. My uncle's domicile, like all the others, consisted of one principal room called "the house"; on the same floor with this was a loom-shop capable of containing four looms, and in the rear of the house on the same floor, were a small kitchen and a buttery. Over the house and the loom-shop were chambers; and over the kitchen and buttery was another small apartment, and a flight of stairs. . . .[4]

In the craftshop and on the land most productive activity was based in a household, and those laboring often included family members. This form of organization is often referred to as the household or domestic mode of production. It had important consequences for family organization. The labor needs of the household defined the work roles of men, women, and children. Their work, in turn, fed the family. The interdependence of work and residence, of household labor needs, subsistence requirements, and family relationships constituted the "family economy."

The specific form of the family economy differed for craftsmen and peasants. And in the city and the country there were important differences between the prosperous and the poor, between those families with property and those who were propertyless. Nonetheless, in all cases production and family life were inseparably intertwined. And the household was the center around which resources, labor, and consumption were balanced.

RURAL ECONOMIES

Most people lived in rural areas and worked in agriculture during the eighteenth century. Estimates based on scattered local studies show that in 1750 agriculture employed about 65 percent of all English people and about 75 percent of the French population.[5] The forms of agricultural organization differed in France and England.

In France, the most typical rural household in the eighteenth century was the peasant household. In the course of the century the pressures of increased population and of high rents and taxes drove many families off the land or left them severely impoverished. Young's description conveys the hardship of their lives:

> The farmers, in the greater part of France, are blended with the peasantry; and, in point of wealth, are hardly superior to the common labourers; these poor farmers are *metayers*, who find nothing towards stocking a farm but labour and implements; and being exceedingly miserable, there is rarely a sufficiency of the latter.[6]

Some families barely subsisted on their land, others not only produced for themselves but marketed a crop of grapes, grains, olives, and the like. Some families manufactured cloth or clothing to supplement their earnings. Others hired themselves out as part-time laborers as well as tilled their own soil. Whatever the expedients they adopted to make ends meet, these rural people remained peasants, and the family's life ultimately was organized around the property, no matter how small the holding.[7]

The composition of the peasant household could vary considerably over the years. At any time those living and working together constituted a "family" whether or not they were related by blood. "The peasant concept of the family includes a number of people constantly eating at one table or having eaten from one pot . . . peasants in France included in the concept of the family the groups of persons locked up for the night behind one lock."[8]

Although the terms *family* and *household* were often used interchangeably, and although servants took their meals with family members, the number of non-kin in the household of a propertied peasant depended on the composition of his own family. The propertied peasant had to balance labor and consumption. His resource—land—was fixed. The amount of work to be done and thus the number of laborers needed changed in the course of the family's life cycle. A young couple could adequately provide for its own needs, with the assistance perhaps of some day laborers at planting and harvest times. As children were born, they also had to be fed, and the availability of the mother to work away from the hearth decreased. The consumption needs of the family exceeded its labor power, and so at this point outside labor was recruited. Young men and women were added to the household as servants. They usually worked in exchange for room and board, rarely for cash wages. They were available for work because their own families either could not support them or did not need their labor. (One study suggested that 30 percent of all rural workers in England at the end of the seventeenth century were servants, and that 60 percent of all those fifteen to twenty-four years old in rural England were servants.) As the peasant's own children grew up, the need for outside help diminished. When several children lived in the household, there might be more labor available than the size of the landholding warranted. At this point, farmers might rent or buy additional land. More typically, in the land-poor regions of Western Europe, children would 'leave home to seek employment. They usually worked in other households as servants.[9]

In England some people still supported themselves on small farms during the eighteenth century, but they were a decreasing group. The growth of agricultural capitalism, particularly in the form of sheep-herding to produce wool for sale, led to the enclosure of large areas of land and the gradual, and violently resisted, dispossession of small farm-ers. Despite their protests and resistance, English farmers lost the strug-gle to retain their land and their right to farm it.[10] By 1750 land ownership was concentrated "in the hands of a limited class of very large landlords, at the expense both of the lesser gentry and the peas-ants. . . ."[11] One troubled observer described the process in 1795:

> The *land-owner*, to render his income adequate . . . unites several small farms into one, raises the rent to the utmost, and avoids the expence of repairs. The rich farmer also engrosses as many farms as he is able to stock. . . . Thus thousands of families, which formerly gained an indepen-dent livelihood on those separate farms, have been gradually reduced to the class of day-labourers. . . . It is a fact, that thousands of parishes have not now half the number of farmers which they had formerly. And in proportion as the number of farming families has decreased, the number of poor families has increased.[12]

The dispossessed became agricultural laborers working for wages on the large farms, or they turned to cottage industry. Those involved in cottage industry worked at home on account for a merchant entre-preneur. In England the typical form of cottage or domestic industry was wool and, later, cotton weaving. In both England and France, merchants brought raw materials to rural cottages and then picked up the woven cloth which they had finished in towns or large villages. By having cloth woven in the countryside, the merchants managed to escape the control of the guilds, organizations of urban craftsmen, which closely supervised production in the cities. Although cottage weavers, like agricultural laborers, worked for wages, they worked in their own households, controlling the pace and organization of produc-tion. The family was the unit of production and of consumption, the household was the locus of work and residence. The family economy thus existed in the cottages of domestic weavers (and hosiers and nail or chain-metal workers) as it did in the households of propertied peasants.

Agricultural laborers, on the other hand, left home to earn wages elsewhere.

> Thus an amazing number of people have been reduced from a comfortable state of partial independence to the precarious condition of hirelings.[13]

Family members often worked together. And the aim of everyone's work was to secure enough to support the family, both by bringing home some cash and by laboring in exchange for food. Among these families family membership meant shared consumption, but not shared production. In this case the family economy became a "family wage economy." The unit's need for wages, rather than for laborers, defined the work of family members.

WORK IN URBAN SOCIETY

Cities in both England and France had similar economic and occupational structures in the early modern period. They were essentially centers of consumer production and of commerce. The dominant form of activity differed from city to city. Yet city life differed markedly from life in the country. Gathered within city walls was a diverse population linked by an exchange of goods, services and cash.

The varieties of urban life can be illustrated by examining several cities. For the early modern period, we will describe *York*, England, and *Amiens*, France. Both these cities were typically "preindustrial" in economy and social structure. York was a Cathedral town, engaged in commerce, while the principal business of Amiens was small-scale, largely artisanal textile manufacture. York was known for its picturesque walls and beautiful buildings.

A nineteenth-century antiquarian wrote:

> Within these walls there grew into existence, century after century, a great and beautiful city. The larger portion of the population gathered around the Minster, which was the favourite side, not only for association's sake, but for safety. The area, however, was a very limited one for general use. The Minster, St. Leonard's Hospital, and other religious buildings, all lay within enclosures of their own, a series of stone pens which prevented the extension of the city.... Room and protection were wanted, and health

Map 1.1
England, Scotland and Wales, showing frequently mentioned cities.

and comfort were sacrificed to secure them. Many of the streets are called gates, or ways, a name which has come down from the old English people. Stone houses were of the utmost rarity. The domestic buildings were flimsy structures of wood, of post and pan work. . . . Before many a house was a clog, or stump of wood, on which its owner often sat and gossiped with his neighbors. . . . They traded under the most rigid rules. For the greater part of their goods they could only charge after the rate of assize laid down by the authorities of the city, and they were rigorously looked to by the masters and searchers of their own trade.[14]

Map 1.2
France, showing frequently mentioned cities. (Borders of
1815–1871,1918–1945.)

Deyon described the diversity which would strike a traveler to late-seventeenth-century Amiens:

> It was not a very agreeable looking city once one had penetrated the
> austere gates, . . . a humid and unhealthy city whose canals often doubled
> as sewers. But it was a buzzing city, where trade in wine, in wheat, in spices
> and in textiles made a perpetual bustle. Through the streets, . . . of the old
> town, the voyager descended towards the markets and the inns, into the
> midst of a half-peasant, half-urban crowd, speaking in *patois.* . . . It was a
> manufacturing town also, in the northern and western quarters, where the
> venturesome sightseer's senses would be assailed by the rattle of looms, the
> beating of the fulling mills, the smells of the tanneries and the sight of the
> shops of wool washers and combers.[15]

The specific jobs available to men and women differed according to
the economic structure of each city. In York, most manufacture involved luxury products: bell casting, glass painting, and pewter and
clock making were among those listed. The cocoa, chocolate, and confectionary business which was to dominate the late-nineteenth-century
economy of York had its origins in small eighteenth-century family
businesses. In addition, there were jobs connected with the river trade
from York to the seaport of Hull. Butter, grain, coal, salt, and wool were
regularly shipped through York. And, although the fortunes of the city
(once the "second capital" of English society) seemed to be declining
by the end of the eighteenth century, it remained a center of handi-
crafts and trade.

> York had no notable manufactures; its economy was based on its impor-
> tance as a market centre supplied by, and supplying a wide area around
> the city; and a large part of its population was engaged in producing and
> distributing both the basic needs of its inhabitants and the luxury goods
> and services demanded by the gentry for whom York was an important
> social center.[16]

In the provincial capital of Amiens most people were engaged in the
woolen trades. Various tax lists enable us to determine the occupations
of others in the city, although these lists give but a partial description,
since only the wealthier people in the city were taxed. Most artisans and
shopkeepers on the lists were in textiles, food, and the building trades.
A list from 1722 indicates a number of servants, too.[17]

Despite differences in specific trades in each city, the forms of organization were similar. Economic units were small, often overlapping
with households. The scale of production was also small, for the quality

and quantity of activity in commerce and manufacture were controlled by guild or other forms of regulation and by the availability of only limited amounts of capital. Life was more specialized in urban than in rural society. Food and clothing production, for example, was carried on in separate settings from the households of most urban residents. Rather than make most of what it needed, the urban family bought what it needed in the market or in shops. Shoemakers, for example, made shoes for sale, but they purchased their other clothing and food. Because of this division of labor, urban families were involved in many more consumer activities than their rural counterparts, and cash was regularly used as a means of exchange.

Manufacture and trade, however, were geared primarily to the demand of the local population. Hence the production of food and clothing and the construction of housing were the largest urban manufacturing sectors. Together they employed, according to one estimate, from 55 to 65 percent of a city's working population.[18]

In Amiens, as in York, guilds regulated the training and activities of skilled craftsmen. The number of workers in a trade was limited and, except in a few cases such as millinery and shawl making, the masters and apprentices were male. Craftsmen often worked at home or in small shops assisted by family members, apprentices and journeymen, and servants. Indeed, the dynamic of the self-employed artisan's household was much like that of the peasant's, for labor supply and consumption needs had to be balanced. An artisan had to produce and sell enough goods so that he could feed his family. Competition from others in the trade was controlled by guilds, which limited the numbers of those who became masters. Yet labor demands were variable within a trade; some work was seasonal, there were periods of great activity, other periods of slump. An artisan's family members often served as extra hands, as unpaid assistants in time of high demand. In addition, if family members alone could not furnish the necessary labor, an artisan hired assistants, who lived in the household as long as their labor was needed. On the other hand, if he could not use the labor of his family members at his trade, a craftsman often sent them off to find work elsewhere. His children joined another household as apprentices or domestic servants.

Although craftsmen produced most goods in workshops in their homes and used their families as labor units, the economy of the city provided many opportunities for work away from home. Men and women earned wages as servants or as street merchants, or as assistants to artisans or construction workers. The wage workers included journeymen who had no chance to advance to mastership, masters who had lost their small capital in bad times and now worked for others, daughters and sons of craftsmen whose shops could not absorb their labor, migrants to the city, unskilled workers, and widows with no capital but with a family to support.

Servants formed a substantial portion of urban populations in the seventeenth and eighteenth centuries. Their precise numbers are often difficult to determine since they were not always listed separately in tax and demographic records. Nonetheless, from those records which clearly identified servants, it has been estimated that perhaps 16 percent of those between the ages of fifteen and sixty-five in European cities in this period were servants. Hufton suggests that in eighteenth-century French cities, servants could represent as much as 13 percent of the working population. In Aix in 1695, some 27 percent of the working population were servants. The term *servant* designated a broad category of employment.[19] Any household dependent, whether performing domestic or manufacturing tasks, was a servant. There were servants in the households of the rich and in the households of craftsmen and petty artisans. They were young men or women who joined a family economy as an additional member. Indeed the language used to describe servants denoted their dependent and age status. "Servant" was synonymous with "lad" or "maid"—a young, unmarried, and therefore dependent person.

Wage laborers, on the other hand, lived in households of their own, bound together, like the families of agricultural laborers, by the need to earn money which would pay for their subsistence. Their presence in cities is attested to by the rolls of charitable organizations, which gave them bread when they could not earn enough, and by the complaints of guilds against their activity. Petty artisans, unskilled and casual laborers, carters, and street hawkers were commonly listed. In Paris in 1767, when an Order in Council enjoined the registration of non-guild members selling food, clothing, or lodging to the public, the list included "retailers and repairers of old clothes and hats, or rags and of old ironware, buckles and hardware . . . sellers of medicines for eyes, corns, and assorted afflictions. . . ." The inventory of lawsuits against non-guild members in York in 1775 included many of these same trades. [20] In the families of wage laborers, all members old enough to seek employment did so.

The work of each person brought little remuneration; the combined earnings of family members were often barely enough for the support of the group. In these families, individuals sold their labor power in order to support the family unit; they were "in fact if not in principle . . . proletarian[s]."[21] Theirs was a "family wage economy."

PRODUCTION AND CONSUMPTION

In both England and France, in city and country, people worked in small settings, which often overlapped with households. Productivity was low, the differentiation of tasks was limited. And many workers were needed. The demand for labor extended to women as well as men, to everyone but the youngest children and the infirm. Jobs were differentiated by age and by sex, as well as by training and skill. But, among the popular classes, some kind of work was expected of all able-bodied family members.

The work of individuals was defined by their family positions. An observer of twentieth-century French peasants described their household economy in terms which also portray peasant and artisan families in the seventeenth and eighteenth centuries: "The family and the enterprise coincide: the head of the family is at the same time the head of the enterprise. Indeed, he is the one because he is the other . . . he lives his professional and his family life as an indivisible entity. The members of his family are also his fellow workers."[22] But whether or not they actually worked together, family members worked in the economic interest of the family. In peasant and artisan households, and in proletarian families, the household allocated the labor of family members. In all cases, decisions were made in the interest of the group, not the individual. This is reflected in wills and marriage contracts which spelled out the obligation of siblings or elderly parents who were housed and fed on the family property, now owned by the oldest son. They must work "to the best of their ability" for "the prosperity of the family" and "for the interest of the designated heir."[23] Among property-owning families the land or the shop defined the tasks of family members and whether or not their labor was needed. People who controlled their means of production adjusted household composition to production needs. For the propertyless, the need for wages—the subsistence of the family itself—sent men, women, and children out to work. These people adjusted household composition to consumption needs. The bonds holding the proletarian family together, bonds of expediency and necessity, were often less permanent than the property interest (or the inheritable skill) which united peasants and craftsmen. The composition of propertied and propertyless households also differed. Nevertheless, the line between the propertied and propertyless was blurred on the question of commitment to work in the family interest.

One of the goals of work was to provide for the needs of family members. Both property owning and proletarian households were consumption units, though all rural households were far more self-sufficient than urban households. Rural families usually produced their own food, clothing, and tools, while urban families bought them at the market. These differences affected the work roles of family members. Women in urban families, for example, spent more time marketing and less time in home manufacture. And there were fewer domestic chores for children to assist with in the city. In the urban family, work was oriented more to the production of specific goods for sale, or it involved the sale of one's labor. For the peasant family, there were a multiplicity of tasks involved in working the land and running the household. The manner of satisfying consumption needs thus varied and so affected the kinds of work family members did.

When the number of household members exceeded the resources available to feed them, and when those resources could not be obtained, the family often adjusted its size. Non-kin left to work elsewhere when children were old enough to work. Then children migrated. Inheritance systems led non-heirs to move away in search of jobs, limited positions as artisans forced children out of the family craftshop, while the need for wages led the children of the propertyless many miles from home. People migrated from farm to farm, farm to village, village to town, and country to city in this period. Although much migration was local and rural in this period, some migrants moved to cities, and most of these tended to be young and single when they migrated. Indeed, in this period cities grew primarily by migration; for urban death rates were high and deaths often outnumbered births, a result largely of the crowded and unsanitary conditions that prevailed. Migrants came to the city from nearby regions. Deyon examined parish registers, apprenticeship contracts, and civil enfranchisement registers for Amiens and found that most migrants came from Picardy, the province of which Amiens was the capital. Village compatriots tended to live near one another. Young men and boys often migrated to be apprenticed to a craftsman who himself came from their village. Young women and girls followed their brothers to Amiens and became domestic servants.[24]

Migration increased in times of economic crisis, when food was scarce and when, even with everyone working, families could not feed all their members. The precariousness of life in rural and urban areas in the seventeenth and eighteenth centuries has been documented dramatically in studies such as those by Pierre Goubert and Olwen Hufton. These studies have shown that large numbers of ordinary people barely survived on the fruits of their labor. At the end of a lifetime of work, an artisan or peasant might have nothing more than the few tools or the small piece of land with which he began. Simply feeding one's family in these circumstances was a constant preoccupation. An increase in the price of bread, the basic staple in the diet of the popular classes, could easily make a family's earnings inadequate for its survival. Thus Goubert charts the fortunes of the Cocu family in terms of the price of bread:

> The family earned 108 sols a week, but they ate 70 pounds of bread among them. With bread at one half sol a pound their livelihood was secure. With bread at 1 sol a pound, it began to get difficult. With bread at 2 sols, then at 3.2, 3.3 and 3.4—as it was in 1649, 1652, 1662, 1694, 1710—it was misery.[25]

Even if the price of bread remained stable, other factors might unbalance a family's budget. Agricultural or trade depressions could severely strain a family's resources. At these times there were bread riots as people collectively sought food for their families. If matters did not improve, individual families might send children off to seek their fortunes away from home, as servants, apprentices, or vagrants. Sometimes the father of the family left home in search of work. He thereby relieved the household of the need to feed him, since he could contribute nothing to its support. He also left the family to an uncertain, but probably poverty-stricken, future.

If the adult members of the family could continue working, then young children were sent away to restore the balance between consumption and work. When families were desperate, parents might expose or abandon a last-born child. Older children, still too young to work productively, were sent off also, to whatever their fate might hold. Fictional characters such as Hansel and Gretel and Hop-O'-My-Thumb, children deliberately lost by parents who could not feed them, had real counterparts. Deyon's study of seventeenth-century Amiens indicates that during food shortages in 1693–94 and 1709–10 the number of abandoned children rose. These were not only infants, but children as old as seven.[26] Another recent study of the records of charity in eighteenth-century Aix-en-Provence reveals that children were regularly enrolled at an orphanage because their families could not feed them. Only a third of these were actually orphans. Once a child entered the orphanage, he or she was likely to be joined by a sibling. In other cases, a child would return home and be replaced in the orphanage by a sibling. Families used the orphanage as a temporary measure, enrolling a child and the withdrawing him or her as economic circumstances allowed. Hence one girl entered the Aix orphanage in 1746, "rejoined her family briefly in 1747, then returned ... later left again, and ... reentered ... in 1755."[27]

The location and organization of work differed among the households of rural and urban people and among the propertied and the propertyless. So did the levels of consumption vary and the manners of satisfying family needs. Yet in all cases the family was both a labor unit and a consumption unit, adjusting its size and assigning work to its members to meet its needs in both spheres.

DEMOGRAPHY: MARRIAGE

The demographic patterns of early modern England and France reflected the need to balance people and resources. Death frequently influenced these patterns. Perhaps the most sensitive indicator of the relationship between resources and population was the age at which couples married. The precise age at marriage varied from city to country and from region to region depending on inheritance laws and on specific conditions. Yet among the popular classes the crucial differences were between the propertied and the propertyless.

Marriage was, among other things, an economic arrangement, the establishment of a family economy. It required that couples have some means of supporting themselves and, eventually, their children. For peasant children this meant the availability of land; for artisans, the mastery of a skill and the acquisition of tools and perhaps a workshop. Wives must have a dowry or a means of contributing to the household. Among families with property these resources most often were passed on from generation to generation.

In England, inheritance by the eldest son prevailed. In France this custom of primogeniture was not universal. In some areas of France, particularly in the west, an heir and his wife lived with his parents, in a stem family arrangement. In northern France, on the other hand, a young man had to postpone marriage until a house was vacant. This meant until the death of one or both parents. Land was passed to one child—usually, though not necessarily, the oldest son. He paid his siblings a cash settlement which represented their share of the family land. A brother could use his money to buy some land of his own or to set himself up in a trade. A sister used her money as a dowry. Often the heir had to mortgage the property to pay off his sisters and brothers. Sometimes, too, the money was not available. Then the heir's siblings might remain on the family farm as unmarried laborers in their brother's household, working in exchange for room and board. "A peasant reckons this way; my farm can feed no more than one, at most two, sons; the others may have to remain unmarried or seek their fortune elsewhere."[28]

Among artisans, trade regulations prevented early marriage. Apprentices and journeymen were not allowed to marry until they had completed their training. In some cases, the duration of apprenticeship was as much a function of the artisans' desire to control workers' access to their trade as it was of the difficulty of the skills taught. Apprentices' and journeymen's associations reinforced the control by expelling from their ranks anyone who married. A young man was ready to marry only when he had an established niche in the system of production.

The need for a dowry meant that young women, too, often had to wait for the death of their parents to receive a settlement. In the weaving center of Manchester, for example, in the period 1654–57, more than half of the girls marrying for the first time had recently lost their fathers. Other girls, those who worked to accumulate savings for a dowry, had to spend many years gathering a small sum.[29]

The result of these requirements was a relatively late age at marriage in both England and France; women were generally twenty-four or twenty-five years old, men twenty-seven. The late age at marriage of women meant that couples had fewer children than they would have had if the woman had been nineteen or twenty at marriage. If she married at twenty-five, the woman was actively engaged in childbearing for only a portion of her fertile years. (There was little sexual intercourse outside of marriage, very low rates of illegitimacy. During the eighteenth century in France, the illegitimacy rate increased from 1.2 to 2.7 percent of all births.) Thus relatively late marriage functioned as a kind of birth control, in the sense that it limited the size of the completed family.[30]

Among the propertyless, there were no resources to inherit. When a young man and woman were able to earn wages, they could marry. Not only must an individual be able to work, however, but work which paid wages must be available. (Servants, for example, could not marry since a requirement of their jobs was that they live in the household they served, that they remain unmarried, and that they receive much of their payment in room and board, not cash.) One study has shown that in Shepshed, England, during the seventeenth century, the coming of domestic industry provided jobs and cash wages and led to a lowered age of marriage.[31] In other areas, the growth of commercial agriculture, and the consequent demand for agricultural laborers, may have had the same effect.

Among the poorest, marriage sometimes did not take place at all. The absence of property and the lack of any expectation that it would be acquired, made legalization of sexual relationships unnecessary. From seventeen-century Aix comes this comment on the urban poor: "They almost never know the sanctity of marriage and live together in shameful fashion."[32] These people, however, were exceptions. In general, those without property did marry. They married younger than their peasant and artisan counterparts, and as a result, their wives bore more children over the course of the marriage. But most expected to be able to live on the fruits of their labor. A couple marrying in Amiens in 1780 acknowledged their poverty, but wrote a contract anyway, agreeing that if they did manage to make some money, the future bride would have "by preciput 150 livres of the estate and the survivor would have the bed and bedclothes, . . . his or her clothes, arms, rings and jewels."[33]

Some people never married, of course. In general, permanent celibacy was more common in cities than in the country. There were examples of unmarried brothers or sisters remaining sometimes on farms with a married sibling. More commonly, however, these individuals migrated to a city in search of work. The occupational structure of particular cities often determined the marital fate of many of its migrants. In Lyons, for example, the women who came to work in the silk industry greatly outnumbered the men. As a result, during the eighteenth century, some 40 percent of adult women were still single at age fifty in that city. (In towns where men outnumbered women, more women were married.) In Amiens, with its mixed occupational structure, 20 percent of the women over forty in one wealthy parish were single at death. The rate was 13 percent in two poorer parishes. Domestic servants in the wealthy parish account for the difference. Cities housed most people whose occupations by definition precluded marriage—members of religious orders, soldiers, servants, and prostitutes were typically urban residents.[34]

BIRTH AND FERTILITY

Once a couple married, at whatever age, they began to have children. About half of all first babies were born less than a year after their parents' marriage. Studies of French villages indicated that subsequent children were then born about twenty-five to thirty months apart. This interval was apparently the result of two factors, post partum abstinence from intercourse, and nursing, which postpones the onset of ovulation. Among working-class families in cities, birth intervals were shorter because mothers sent their children to wet-nurses rather than nursing them themselves and because infant mortality was high. In both cases, women became fertile sooner than they would have if they had nursed an infant. In Amiens, for example, in a parish of small shopkeepers, artisans and workers, children were born about two years apart. In Lyons, where work in the silk industry demanded a great deal of a mother's time and where children were regularly sent to wet nurses, birth intervals were even shorter: births occurred there at the rate of one per year.[35]

There is some evidence to indicate that couples sometimes practiced deliberate birth control. One study, of the English village of Colyton in Devon in the seventeenth century, seems to show that couples were deliberately limiting the size of their families. Its author, E. A. Wrigley, suggests that a longer than usual interval between the next-to-last and last birth is an indicator of attempted fertility control. This first attempt of couples to avoid conception failed, of course, but the longer birth interval is evidence of their effort. Such control as there was was probably achieved by means of coitus interruptus, or withdrawal, the most widely known and widely practiced technique.[36] Most other studies, however, using the same kinds of data and the same method of family reconstitution, do not point to deliberate family limitation before the late eighteenth century. Yet completed families were not large: four or five children at most, more often only two or three who lived to adulthood. Why?

First, standards of nutrition and health were very low. Analyses of the diet of the popular classes in this period show consistent evidence of malnutrition, a factor which inhibited conception and which promoted miscarriage. Poor nutrition of a mother increased the likelihood that her infant would be stillborn or weak. And it affected the supply of milk she had to nurse it. In addition, poor nutrition made many women infertile before forty or forty-five—the usual age of menopause.[37]

Second, mortality rates were very high. If infants did not die at birth because of unsanitary or crude childbirth procedures, they died within the first year of life. Young children, too, died in large numbers. Finally, many marriages were shortened by the death of one of the spouses. Childbirth resulted in a high incidence of maternal death. In one fishing village in France, one-third of all marriages were broken by death within fifteen years. Men's opportunities for remarriage were usually greater than those of women. As a result, women did not engage in intercourse during all of their fertile years and hence did not bear children. Given the odds that death would strike a young child or a spouse, there was little need to employ birth control.[38] Death was the natural regulator of family size in early modern England and France.

DEATH AND MORTALITY

Premature death was a frequent experience of family life in this period. Death rates nearly matched birth rates, producing a very slow growth of population. The crude birth rate was about 35 per thousand; the death rate 30 per thousand. Moreover, until around 1730, there were years with dramatically high death rates, reaching 150, 300, and even 500 per thousand in some localities. These deaths were the result of widespread crop failures and consequent starvation, or of epidemics of diseases like the plague. The last plague epidemic struck in southern France in 1720–22,[39] but new diseases caused killing epidemics well into the twentieth century. Demographers usually place the end of extreme and widespread mortality due to disease and starvation in the early eighteenth century.

Yet even in relatively stable times, death rates were very high by modern standards—a rate of 30 per thousand is more than triple the present-day rate in Western Europe. Studies of French villages show that about one-quarter of all infants born alive died during their first year of life, another quarter died before they reached the age of twenty. Urban death rates were even higher. In Amiens, for example, during the seventeenth century, 60 to 70 percent of all burials were of persons under twenty-five. Although rates varied from parish to parish and among villages, the overall situation was similar in England and France. Goubert aptly summarized the mortality experience of preindustrial families: "It took two births to produce one adult."[40]

The life expectancy at birth for people in this period was thirty years. Of course, that figure included infant and child mortality. If a person lived to age twenty-five, the likelihood was much greater than at birth that she or he would live to fifty or sixty. Yet, although systematic evidence is hard to accumulate, it is clear that adult mortality was also quite high. The figures on orphans and widows are revealing in this connection. Laslett's analysis of the English village of Clayworth found that during the period 1676–88, "32 percent of all resident children [under 14] had lost one or both of their parents." A study of all children in households in nineteen English communities from 1599 to 1811 indicates that some 20 percent were orphans. For France, Jean Fourastié has drawn a hypothetical portrait of family life, for a man at the end of the seventeenth century. In that situation marriage would be broken by the death of a spouse after an average of twenty years. The average age of a child orphaned in this way would be fourteen years.[41]

Many children were left orphans when their mothers died in childbirth. Ignorance of the need for sanitary conditions, the crude attempts of midwives to force a baby from the womb, and the general poor health of pregnant women made for high rates of maternal mortality. Age-specific mortality tables drawn for small seventeenth- and eighteenth-century villages show women dying in larger numbers than men between ages twenty-four and forty—the childbearing years. In Amiens, in the parish of Saint-Rémy in 1674–76, fifty-three women and forty men aged fifteen to forty-five died. In another parish in 1665–68, deaths were recorded for ninety-one women and only fifty-two men in that age range.[42]

The death of a parent left not only orphans, but widows or widowers. The existence of these people is attested to by notices of second marriage, particularly of men, and by charity rolls and tax lists, on which widows' names predominated. Fourastié's calculations show that of 1,-000 men married at age twenty-seven and surviving to age fifty, nearly half would have lost their wives. Many of these men would have remarried and would have also lost a second wife. (The calculations for women would be similar except that fewer widows remarried.) Overall, in eighteenth-century France "at least 30 percent of all marriages were second weddings for one of the partners." Most parishes had many widows in them. In Châteaudun, at least half of the seamstresses and spinners listed on tax rolls in 1696 were widows. In eighteenth-century Bayeux, over 46 percent of all textile workers in the linen and woolen trades were widows.[43] The poor widow, struggling to support her children, was a familiar figure in the towns and villages of the period.

Early modern populations could do little medically to control mortality. Nutrition was poor, little was known about hygiene, and medical science had not developed. In 1778, a French demographer noted that "it is still a problem whether medicine kills or saves more men."[44] The result was that every person who survived to adulthood experienced the loss of close relatives: a father, mother, sisters, and brothers. Few children knew their grandparents, few grandparents lived to see the birth of a first grandchild. Orphanhood, widowhood, and the loss of children were common experiences. In calculations about family size, about fertility and household labor supply, the expectation of death played an important part.

These, then, were the economic and demographic characteristics of England and France during the seventeenth and eighteenth centuries. Agriculture was more important than manufacturing, and most people lived in rural areas. In France, small-scale property holding and artisanal manufacture were typical. In England, by 1750, there had been consolidation of agricultural holdings and a consequent increase in the size of farms, on the one hand, and in the proportion of people without property, on the other hand. Work in both countries was relatively undifferentiated and productivity was low. On the demographic side, fertility and mortality were both high, so population growth was very slow. A relatively high age of marriage and a degree of nonmarriage served to reduce fertility. From the perspective of the household, most aspects of life were affected by the need to maintain scarce resources and consumers in a delicate balance. Family life and economic organization were inseparably entwined. Premature death was a familiar experience in each household. Within this context were shaped the position and activities of women.

2

Single Women
in the Family Economy

Most single women belonged to households, either as daughters or servants. Most were young, but whatever their age, single women were regarded as dependents of the household in which they lived and worked. Under the domestic mode of production most work was organized around a household, the basic unit of which was a married couple. Girls either worked at home or for another family. If they were to escape this state of dependency, they had to marry, for single adult women were effectively children. The language of the day equated a girl with a maid, a maid with a servant. Age, marital status, and occupation were inseparably intertwined.

Single women were often effectively servants for their families, if not in the households of strangers. Those employed in other areas, textiles for example, usually lived with a family or with other women like themselves. Even in religious orders, single women joined a family of celibate sisters. Prostitutes usually lived in groups. Economically it was extremely difficult to be single and independent. In the best of jobs female wages were low, one-third to one-half of what men's were.[1] The only way for a woman to achieve a measure of economic security, as well as adult status, was to marry. If she did not marry, her position was anomalous. If she became a nun, of course, she gained protection and recognition, although her role and autonomy were limited. An unmarried woman outside a convent was vulnerable to material hardship and sexual exploitation.

Although aggregate figures are not available for this period, local studies indicate that in rural areas marriage took place at a relatively late age and nearly all women did marry. In urban areas, rates of celibacy among women could be higher because of differences in sex ratios and as a result of the concentration of specialized occupations for single women.[2] Most of these occupations, like domestic service or religious orders, involved a family-like dependency.

SINGLE WOMEN'S WORK

All women began their working lives as daughters, serving the family economy of which they were a part. The specific jobs they did were a consequence of their family's place in the productive process, of the nature of the enterprise in which it was engaged.

A daughter began assisting at home as soon as she was able to work. Indeed, at an early age, her role was no different from that of male children, and many accounts make no distinction when describing children's work. Girls and boys were given small tasks to do as early as four or five years of age. In rural areas they cared for farm animals and helped at harvesting and gleaning. In cottages where families engaged in rural industry, young children washed and sorted wool or learned to spin. Defoe, describing families of wool weavers in early eighteenth-century England, noted:

> The women and children carding or spinning, all employed from the youngest to the oldest, scarce anything above four years old, but its Hands were sufficient for its own support.[3]

As they grew older, girls usually assisted their mothers, boys their fathers. In agricultural areas, daughters helped with dairying, cared for poultry, prepared food, and made cloth and clothing. During planting and harvesting they joined family members and hired hands in the fields:

> The country of Hertford doth consist for the most part of tillage ... employing the female children in picking of their wheat a great part of the year and the male children by straining before their ploughs in seedtime and other necessary occasions of husbandry.[4]

When their mothers took on industrial work, daughters assisted them. In the villages around the silk-weaving center of Lyons in France, mothers and daughters cultivated silkworms with mulberry leaves. When industry kept the father from farm work, mothers and daughters took care of the farm. Female family members were farmers along the coasts of France, for example, because males were fishermen who were at sea for long periods of time.[5]

In cities also, daughters worked for their families. The craftsman's household was also his workshop and his family members were among his assistants, whether he wove silk or wool, sewed shoes or coats, made knives, or baked bread. In Beauvais in 1693, lived

> Jean Cocu, weaver of serges and his wife and three daughters, all four spinning wool for him, since the youngest daughter was already nine years old.[6]

If the father worked elsewhere, daughters assisted their mothers as market women, laundresses, or seamstresses. A seventeenth-century diary notation provides a clear illustration of the way daughters followed their mothers' trades:

> payed Mistress Cooke, in Shoe Lane, for a new trusse, and for mending the old one ... should shee dye, I am in future to inquire for her daughter Barbara, who may do the like for mee.[7]

When she worked at home a daughter served a kind of apprenticeship to her mother, learning the domestic, agricultural, or technical skills she would need as an adult.

Not all girls remained working at home until marriage, however. The labor needs of her family defined the type of work a daughter might do at home, but also whether or not she would remain there. Family labor was differentiated by age and sex. So, if a family had no need for a daughter's labor, she would be sent to a job somewhere else. Peasants with two or three working children and more than one daughter would send younger daughters away to earn their keep. Weavers, who needed several spinners to supply thread for their looms, jealously guarded their daughters at home, while bakers or shoemakers whose sons, male apprentices, and wives were an ample labor force, regularly sent their daughters away. Families thus adjusted their labor supply by sending off daughters not suited for certain work and taking on male apprentices in their stead.

The ability of a family to feed its children was another influence on where a daughter worked. For subsistence farmers with small holdings, the cost of maintaining a daughter might be greater than the value of her labor. It would be cheaper to hire and feed a few local laborers during the harvest season than to provide for one's own child all year long. Moreover, in time of economic crises, the numbers of "surplus children," those who could not be supported, would grow, and daughters and sons would be sent off to seek jobs as servants or apprentices.

Death was yet another factor which sent daughters to work away from home. The death of a parent often left the widow or widower less means to support the children. In the French town of Châteaudun during the sixteenth to eighteenth centuries, for example, daughters of winegrowers remained at home until marriage. They participated in all aspects of domestic and household work and were given ample dowries when they married. The death of a father, however, immediately changed the pattern. At that point, the mother took up a trade and sold the family holding or passed it to one of her sons. Daughters who were too young to marry or "who could not marry immediately became chamber maids in town or farm servants in the country." The luckiest of these found places at the homes of other winegrowers.[8]

The remarriage of a widowed parent could also result in the dislocation of the children of the first marriage, either because the step-parent resented feeding and caring for children who were not his or her own or because conflicts and jealousies became unbearable. Folk tales such as Cinderella and Snow White capture an aspect of these relationships. Rétif de la Bretonne tells of such a situation in his prosperous peasant family. When his father remarried, the new wife drove out four of her stepdaughters. One married, one went to Paris, and the two others moved in with their grandfather.[9]

Even if both parents were alive, however, the economic resources of the family might be insufficient for the establishment of more than one child with the means to live independently as a married adult. Daughters needed a dowry, and families customarily provided them with it. In rural areas, depending on laws of inheritance, a girl was given either a sum of money or movable property, usually household and farm furnishings. Again depending on local practices, she might receive a full settlement at her marriage or be promised a payment after the death of her parents. In cities, craftsmen gave their daughters household furnishings, cash, skills, or tools. In country and city, the size of the family contribution to a dowry or settlement was very small among the lower classes. Often, the family's contribution had to be supplemented. An artisan's daughter had an advantage over her rural counterpart in this situation, for the skills she had were highly valued. Unlike the heavy manual labor of a farm, trade skills guaranteed a lifetime of relatively high wage-earning possibilities or of assistance to one's husband at his trade. These were acceptable as substitutes for the dowry required of rural girls. But, in either case, if a dowry was needed for a woman's contribution to a marriage and the family (or some other source) could not provide it, a girl had to earn it herself.[10]

When for one or a combination of reasons daughters left home to work, they usually entered another household. In the country, domestic service was the typical occupation of a young girl. Of course, in areas of rural textile manufacture, particularly in England, in the early eighteenth century, spinners were in great demand. It took the work of four spinners to supply thread enough for one weaver. One Englishman complained about "Maid-Servants who choose rather to spin, while they can gain 9s/week by their Labour than go to service at 12d a week to the Farmers' Houses as before."[11] Spinsters lived either at home or in the weaver's household. But even in areas where spinning and lace-making jobs were available, girls sometimes went into service at age twelve or thirteen, after having done textile work as a child. Cities offered other opportunities and urban-born girls took advantage of them. Such girls might be apprenticed to a crafts- or tradeswoman. Others might work for wages in a local enterprise, usually related to textile or garment manufacture. In Caen, France, the lace industry employed girls between ages five and fifteen. They were first apprenticed for two months and their parents paid both for their training and for a place at the workbench. When the lessons were completed, the girls began to earn a daily wage. But in cities, as in the country, the main occupation for young girls was domestic service. In Ealing in 1599, for example, almost "three quarters of the female children [between ages fifteen and nineteen] seem to have been living away from their parents," most often as servants.[12]

In a period when most productive activity was organized within or around a household, service was the major occupation for young single women. Service involved a variety of chores, not only the ones the twentieth century associates with domestic work. A servant was a household dependent who worked in return for board and wages. The low cost of her labor, the availability of young, single women to work, the need in producing households for an extra hand, made the employment of a servant a fairly common practice. Service was the customary means by which households exchanged labor supply and balanced their own labor and consumption needs.

In upper class families a girl "in service" was a maid of one kind or another, a laundress, charwoman, serving maid, or nursemaid. In household productive units she was an extra hand, available to do whatever work was required. She might be a dairymaid or harvester on a farm; in textile towns she was "a resident industrial employee." In Lyons, for example, a *servante* did domestic chores and helped prepare the silk to be woven. As with a daughter, the nature of the family enterprise defined her work, except that a servant girl usually did the dirtiest and most onerous of the chores that needed to be done.[13] In return for her work she was fed, housed, and clothed and paid a wage at the end of her term, which usually lasted a year. This meant that a servant had little or no money to spend on herself during the year and was entirely dependent on her employers. The year term also meant frequent moves for a girl from one household to another. Moves might be even more frequent for some girls. Employers might fire them at any point, refusing to pay anything for their services. The failure of a small business inevitably sent the servant girl packing, with no payment of her wages, no matter how long she had worked.

When daughters left home to work they did not always sever family ties. Their parents often helped them find jobs, and provided homes for them between terms of service. One study suggests that female farm servants in England returned to their families far more frequently than did males.[14] Moreover, kin networks were a common means used by those seeking jobs. In the country, peasants and agricultural laborers sought work for their daughters at neighboring farms or in a nearby village or large town. On market days and at fairs, local women learned from other women of available positions for their daughters. In some areas, there were more formalized ways of securing jobs as servants. Young girls would come on their own to annual hiring fairs in search of employment. Sometimes, if a brother or father journeyed to another area, as Savoyard men did to Lyons or as men from Rouergue did to the Herault vineyards, a sister or daughter might accompany him. In some areas of eighteenth-century France, Hufton suggests, male family members seem to have set the patterns of female migrations.[15] In cities, artisans or their wives used trade, neighborhood, and kin connections to secure apprenticeships for their daughters. Unskilled laborers introduced their children to whatever jobs they did in the urban labor market.

A girl's ability to maintain contact with her family depended on how far she had journeyed from home. Some girls did travel alone from their country villages to large textile centers or regional and state capitals, becoming permanent urban residents. Rural-born girls migrated city-ward, while urban girls tended to remain closer to home, working and marrying in the city of their birth. In general, however, the continuing demand for cheap female labor in towns and on farms made it possible for most girls to remain within a short distance of home, sustained by occasional visits, by parcels of food, and by the expectation of returning there to marry.

The death of a girl's parents, of course, modified this pattern. Orphans were on their own, lacking family connections to help them find work or to sponsor their migrations. Without resources, with no one to turn to for help, orphans had to settle for whatever work they could find, throwing themselves on the mercy of an employer, a charitable organization, or the state. They were more vulnerable, more open to exploitation, more likely to end up in trouble as criminals, prostitutes, and mothers of illegitimate children. A sixteenth-century English magistrate described the "dells" of his day as delinquent girls on the road "through the death of their parents and nobody to look after them. . . ."[16] In a society where family membership was important for economic and social survival (as well as for social identity), the lack of a family had only negative effects.

The work of a young single woman was circumscribed by a limited range of occupational opportunities. The type and location of her work was defined by her family's needs. A daughter worked, as everyone did in lower-class families in this period, to help support the unit of which she was a part. In addition, her work prepared her for marriage, by giving her training and skills and sometimes also by enabling her to accumulate the capital she needed for a dowry.

COURTSHIP AND MARRIAGE

A girl was ready for marriage when she had accumulated some capital or received it from her family, when she was ready to help establish a productive unit, a household. The amount was not necessarily very large. In France, some cash, a bed, sheets, and some pots were frequently all a girl brought to her new household. An Irish ballad sung by a "lovely lassie in Bannion" went:

> Me mother says I can marry and she give me her bed when she die . . . Me father has forty-one shillings and the grass for a goat an a cow . . .[17]

Often a girl's small earnings supplemented the family contribution.

Unless she migrated far away, or unless she was an orphan, a girl's marriage usually involved her family in a variety of ways. First, her family's economic situation limited her choice of a husband to someone of roughly comparable means. The size of the dowry the family promised or provided was a reflection of its property holdings or trade prosperity. An artisan's craft position was itself an important consideration, for access to a tightly controlled craft might be gained for a son-in-law. Among property-owning peasants, parents often vetoed suitors whose family holdings did not measure up to their own. Marriage was a chance to extend or renew family capital. Less directly parental and community expectations imbued children with the idea that they would repeat their parents' experience. They usually did not expect to rise in the world, only to remain at their parents' level. Hence they sought partners among their social and economic peers.

Second, the parental community of residence and work was most often the one within which a girl found a husband. In rural areas, young women met young men in the village, at local social gatherings, or in the household of an employer. In France, the *veillée* offered young people a means of meeting one another, under the watchful eye of parents and neighbors and in activities which were usually segregated by sex. The *veillée* was the rural custom of gathering in the largest, warmest barn on cold winter evenings. The animals and the groups of people created warmth, and the company an occasion for socializing. "People sat on benches, chatting, laughing, complaining about taxes and tax collectors, gossiping about young men and women. . . ."[18]

In the city, a girl might marry an apprentice or journeyman in her father's shop, or the son of another craftsman. Networks of labor and trade were also important sources of marriage partners. In Amiens, such "corporative endogamy" was the rule. Young men in the same trades married one another's sisters with great frequency; apprentices married their master's daughters or widows.[19] But apprentices or journeymen might also choose a servant girl in the household. The small capital she had saved from her service brought to the couple the possibility of buying a loom and setting up a shop of their own.[20] Since social, occupational, and family life were so closely intertwined, one's associate at work often became a marriage partner.

Among the propertyless, of course, marriage crossed occupational lines, but geographic endogamy was the norm. Artisans and peasants as well as the unskilled and propertyless tended to marry others from the same parish or a neighboring one. One study of early-eighteenth-century Bayeux found that 63 percent of all women married in Bayeux came from there, or from one of fourteen neighboring parishes.[21] A community might also extend beyond the parish. Trade routes and paths of migration for laborers extended the boundaries of the effective social community. Local market systems probably were the largest social unit within which marriage partners were chosen.

Social and geographic endogamy had important implications for marriage and for premarital sexual behavior. It meant that family and communal ties, as well as the relationship between the two individuals, bound a couple together and governed their behavior. In many areas, engaged couples began sleeping or living together before marriage. Local custom varied, of course. In areas of France and England, studies have documented the practice. In addition, the fact that rates of prenuptial conception tended to be higher in cities than in rural areas suggests that such cohabitation was more common in cities. Premarital sexual activity was tolerated because marriage was expected to and usually did take place. Hence, although some brides were pregnant at the altar, bastards were relatively few. Using marriage and birth registers from seventy-seven parishes in rural England, from 1540 to 1835, P. E. H. Hair found that between one-third and one-sixth of all brides were pregnant at their weddings.[22] Indeed, pregnancy often seems to have precipitated a couple's marriage. In small village communities, or among groups of urban craftsmen, families could put a great deal of pressure on a young man who had begun to regret his choice of a mate and was hesitating about marriage. Such social pressure tended to ensure that marriage usually followed engagement, especially if pregnancy intervened.

The women who bore illegitimate children were often those with no ties to their families of origin. Several English studies have indicated that most illegitimate births came from the poorest and most vulnerable women in a community. One study suggests the existence of a subgroup of "bastard-bearers."[23] These were people whose sexual behavior was not that different from their more prosperous counterparts. The difference was that "the relatively more secure position [of the better-off] meant that their behavior was more certain of ultimate legitimation."[24] In other words, prosperous parents were in a better position to enforce the promise of marriage which had compromised their daughters. On the other hand, girls with no parents or those who were a long distance from home were most vulnerable. Servant girls in cities were often open to exploitation by their employers or by young men they met. Indeed, rates of illegitimacy and of child-abandonment were highest among domestic servants. These women could not appeal to parental, religious, or community authority to help them make a seducer keep his promise.

Young women were protected not only by their parents but by community institutions as well. In many rural areas, the rituals of courtship and marriage involved vigilant groups of young people who regulated the morals and sexual activity of the village. Adolescent boys particularly policed the behavior of courting couples, sometimes even influencing a man's choice of a mate. A wide discrepancy in the ages of the couple, for example, or promiscuity or adultery, could attract the ridicule of local youths. They would engage in elaborate rituals, following the couple, mocking them, singing profane songs under the woman's window. A bad-smelling bush planted before a girl's door indicated her low moral standing. A group of young men might fight or fine strangers courting local girls.[25] Unwed mothers as well as married men who seduced single girls would be "charivaried" or, in England, hear the sound of "rough music" at their door. In one of many variants,

> The youth assemble with horns, pots and cowbells, and make a terrible racket at the door of the man and of the girl. Two weeks later they summon all the inhabitants of neighboring villages together in a place of their chosing. The Court of Fools convenes. Two straw figures representing the man and the girl are juridically condemned to be burned by the master of proceedings, and this is done with a dreadful noise. Then the whole cortege and the accompanying court file through the streets of the village and in front of the door of the guilty parties.[26]

In the village community these proceedings had the effect of legal sanctions. The charivari set and enforced standards of acceptable sexual conduct. Natalie Davis has pointed out that they also regulated the activities of the youths themselves, preventing too-early marriage and premarital promiscuity.

Organizations of craftsmen, too, watched over the activities of journeymen and apprentices. The rules of journeymen's organizations included the requirement that members not marry until they had completed their training and were in a position to help support a family. Guilds also had rules which prohibited young men from seducing girls and which enforced their regulations with fines and expulsion.[27] Of course, those outside the guild structure were not subject to such rules. In general, the movement of people into, out of, and within cities made the regulation of sexual and social behavior more difficult, especially among the unskilled. Hence rates of illegitimacy were higher in cities, and concubinage was a more common practice.

A woman's courtship and her marriage involved her family in a number of important ways. A young man usually asked a young woman's family for her hand. Then the families of the engaged couple assembled to draw up a contract which specified the economic terms of the marriage. The wedding was celebrated by family and community members. In the country, whole villages turned out to eat, drink, and dance in celebration of the consecration of a union; in cities all the craftsmen of a particular trade (many of whom were also related) attended the festivities. Among the propertyless and the unskilled the wedding might be less elaborate, but dancing was free and people could clap and sing if there was no money to hire music. These rituals and festivities marked the couple's entry into adulthood, the creation of a new family, the beginning of an independent existence. Among property holders marriage might ally two families and join property holdings. In the lower ranks of society marriage was simply the establishment of a new family economy, the unit of reproduction and of work without which "one cannot live."[28]

The characteristics of marriage among the popular classes clearly were different from those in the upper classes. Among wealthy families there was strict parental control over marriage. Parents sought to preserve their status and wealth by allying their children with a limited group of similarly wealthy families. Children's marriages extended networks of power and influence. The lineage must be protected, the patrimony enlarged and transmitted from one generation to the next. In these cases property was the basis for status and political power, hence family control over children's marriages was vital for the preservation of the elite position of aristocrats or local notables. There was, for example, a close association between the transmission of wealth and political power in Vraiville, a French village studied by Martine Segalen. There all the mayors for ten generations were descendants of, or married to, one of the thirteen most eminent families.[29] The families carefully chose spouses for their children from among a very small group of large property holders.

Among the popular classes parental consent and family contracts did not mean the same thing. Within the social and economic limits already described, individual choice of a spouse was permitted. Parental consent functioned as a verification of the couple's resources. Parents wanted to be sure a child would find his or her new family situation roughly equal to that of the family of origin. Moreover, the contract involved not the acquisition of resources for the patrimony, but the surrendering of resources by families to the new family. Families, rather than the individuals to be married, drew up the contracts because they were the units of social identification and of membership for all individuals. The children were leaving one family to establish another and they were transferring their resources, their means of support, from one household to another. Relatively few persons, men or women, went through an intermediate stage of independence—economic or social—as they passed from their family of origin to their family of procreation. Individuality in the modern sense was socially and legally limited.

The age of marriage was constrained by the fact that family and social resources were limited. Like their husbands, wives were expected to bring a contribution to the marriage, in the form of capital, household furnishings, or marketable skills. Marriage itself signified the beginning of a new enterprise, of an economic partnership of husband and wife. It was "the founding of a family."[30] And it was the emergence of this new family, the re-creation of a social and economic unit, the beginning of a new enterprise that families and communities celebrated at a wedding.

During the time she was single a young woman usually worked in a household. Family labor and consumption needs determined whether or not she worked at home. But wherever she worked, she was dependent on the household in which she lived. Her work was both a means of contributing to her family's economy and a means of supporting herself. It also prepared her for marriage by helping accumulate the resources she would need to establish a family of her own.

3

Married Women
in the Family Economy

The married couple was the "simple community of work, the elementary unit" in the preindustrial household.[1] The contribution of each spouse was vital for the creation and survival of the family. From its outset, marriage was an economic partnership. Each partner brought to the union either material resources, or the ability to help support each other. Peasant sons brought land, craftsmen brought their tools and skill. Daughters brought a dowry and sometimes a marketable skill as well. The dowry of a peasant or artisan daughter was usually a contribution to the establishment of the couple's household. These might include "a bit of cash, furniture, linen, tools. Sometimes a loom, one or two skeins of wool, several pounds of wool and silk, a boat, a thousand eels for a fish merchant, sometimes a house or part of a house in the city, a meadow and some plots of land in the country."[2]

In Bayeux, a marriage contract from 1700 shows that the wife brought to her new household: "a bed, a half dozen sheep, an oak chest, a cow, a year old heifer, a dozen sheep, 20 pounds of linen, two dresses and a half dozen table napkins."[3]

Among the propertyless there was only the promise of work and wages. In Amiens in 1687, Francois Pariès, a mason, and Marie Hugues declared in their contract that they had no material possessions and that "they are mutually satisfied with their well-being and with one another."[4] The point was that the wife as well as the husband made an economic contribution (or a promise of one) which helped set up the new household. In addition, however, it represented a commitment to help support the new family. The resources brought to the marriage were only a beginning. The continuing labor of each partner was required to maintain the couple and, later, its children. In the course of a lifetime, the work of husband and wife was the major source of the family's support. Families were productive and reproductive units, centers of economic activity and creators of new life. Married women contributed to all aspects of family life and thus fulfilled several roles within their households. They engaged in production for exchange and production for household consumption, both of which contributed to the family's economic well-being. And they performed the reproductive role of bearing and raising children.

MARRIED WOMEN'S WORK

A married woman's work depended on the family's economic position, on whether it was involved in agriculture or manufacturing, whether it owned property or was propertyless. But whether labor or cash were needed, married women were expected to contribute it. The fact that a woman bore children influenced the kind of work she did, but it did not confine her to a single set of tasks, nor exclude her from participation in productive activity. The organization of production in this period demanded that women be contributing members of the family economy. It also permitted women to control the time and pace of their work, and to integrate their various domestic activities.

Within the preindustrial household, whether on the farm or in the craftshop, among property holders and wage earners, there was a division of labor by age and by sex. The levels of skill expected of children advanced with age, with young children performing the simplest and crudest chores. Certain kinds of heavy work were reserved for men, but women also did many heavy tasks which today are considered too arduous for females. Hauling and carrying were often women's tasks. Rural and urban wives sometimes had occupations of their own, or they shared their husbands' occupations performing specified tasks within the productive process. Indeed, the jobs women did reflected the fact that they performed several functions for the family. The normative family division of labor tended to give men jobs away from the household or jobs which required long and uninterrupted commitments of time or extensive travel, while women's work was performed more often at home and permitted flexible time arrangements.

RURAL WOMEN

On farms, men worked in the fields, while women ran the household, made the family's clothes, raised and cared for cows, pigs, and poultry, tended a garden, and marketed surplus milk, vegetables, chickens, and eggs. A French peasant saying went: "No wife, no cow, hence no milk, no cheese, neither hens, nor chicks, nor eggs . . ."[5] The sale of these items often brought in the only cash a family received. Women's participation in local markets reflected their several family roles. They earned money as an out-growth of activities concerned with family subsistence; and they might use the money to purchase food and supplies for their families. Their domestic and market activities overlapped, and both served important economic functions for the family. Moderately prosperous farm families owed their success to a variety of resources, not the least of which was the wife's activity. Rétif de la Bretonne, the eighteenth-century French writer, describing the peasant Covin and his wife Marguerite in mid-eighteenth-century Burgundy, attributed their good fortune to a combination of factors. In addition to the fact that they owned a house, "their two hectares of field furnish some wheat for their bread; their half hectare of vineyard gives Covin his pocket money and his wine; . . . The weaving the couple does puts a bit of butter on the spinach . . . Marguerite makes some money from her spinning, from the eggs of her six hens, from the wool of her seven sheep, from the milk, butter and cheese of her cow and from the vegetables in her garden. . . ."[6]

Wives of propertyless laborers also contributed to the family economy. They themselves became hired hands, "working in the fields and doing all kinds of hard jobs." Others became domestic textile workers. Still others alternated these activities. When Vauban, justifying his fiscal recommendations under Louis XIV, described the family of an agricultural laborer, he emphasized the importance of the wife's ability to earn money: "by the work of her distaff, by sewing, knitting some stockings, or by a bit of lace-making, according to the region."[7] Without this and her cultivation of a garden and some animals, "it would be difficult to subsist." Home work most commonly involved spinning or sewing. Lacemaking, straw plaiting, glovemaking, knitting, and needlework were the major areas of domestic manufacture. Pinchbeck estimates that lacemaking alone employed as many as 100,000 women and children in seventeenth-century England. About a million women and children worked in the clothing trades as a whole in England in that period.[8] And in France, as rural industry took hold in some areas, the numbers of women employed in spinning rose. Women earned low wages spinning, perhaps five sous a day in Picardy at the end of the seventeenth century.[9] Male weavers earned double that amount. Yet the individual wage a married woman could earn was less important than was her contribution to a joint effort. Spinning and weaving together were the complementary bases of the family economy.

When no home work was available, a wife marketed her household activities, shopping for others at the market, hawking some wares: extra pieces of linen she had woven or lengths of thread she had spun and not used. Rural women also became wet nurses, nursing and raising the children of middle-class women and of urban artisans who could afford to pay them. In the countryside around Paris and around the silk-weaving center of Lyons, for example, wet nursing was a common way for a rural woman to earn some additional money while caring for her own child. In areas around big cities in France particularly, this might be an organized enterprise. In Paris, for example, men or women (called *meneurs* or *messagères*) located rural nurses, recruited urban babies, then transported the infants in carts to the country, where they often remained until they were three or four years old, if they survived infancy. One late-eighteenth-century estimate places at about 10,000 the number of Parisian infants sent out to nurse. Maurice Garden suggests that close to a third of all babies born in Lyons (some 2,000 of 5,000–6,000) were carted off to the countryside. Until the late eighteenth century these included the children of the upper classes as well as of artisan and shopkeeping families.[10] Most often, however, the more prosperous families hired wet nurses who lived in the household. The wet-nurse "business" was most developed, it appears, in large preindustrial urban centers where married women played an active role in artisan and commercial enterprise. There was little supervision of the nurses in this period. The job could be fairly lucrative and demand was high, so some women "nursed" babies long after their own children had grown and their milk dried up.

Married women, then, would often alternate different kinds of work, putting together a series of jobs in order to increase their earnings or to earn enough to help their families survive. Indeed the absence of employment for the wives of wage earners was often given as the reason for a family's destitution.

Although women tended to work at or near home, they did not do so exclusively. On farms, the rhythm of the seasons with their periods of intensive labor brought women into the fields to sow and harvest, as well as glean. Here is an account from mid-seventeenth-century Yorkshire which describes women and men together harvesting grain and peas. Jobs were allocated according to physical strength:

> Wee allwayes have one man, or else one of the ablest of the women to abide on the meow, besides those that goe with the waines. . . . It is usual in some places (wheare the furres of landes are deepe worne with raines) to imploy women, with wain-rakes, to gather the corne. . . . Wee use meanes allwayes to gett eyther 18 or else 24 pease pullers, which wee sette allwayes sixxe on

a lande, viz, a woman and a man, . . . a woman or boy and a man, etc., the wakest couple in the fore furre. . . . It is usuall in most places after they gette all pease pulled, or the last graine downe, to invite all the worke-folkes and wives (that helped them harvest) to supper.[11]

The situation might also be reversed, with men joining women as extra hands for the harvest, while the women carried on all the farm work in the fields and the house during most of the year. In areas where small property holders worked as agricultural laborers or as tradesmen, women tended the family plot and men worked away from home "except for about a week in hay harvest, and for a few days at other times, when the gathering of manure or some work which the women cannot perform" required the men's assistance.[12] In the vineyards of the Marne "the wife [was] really the working partner of her husband: she share[d] all of his burdens," cultivating the grapes.[13]

On the other hand, there was household work which included the entire family. In villages in France, for example, the kneading and preparation of bread (which was baked in a communal oven) "mobilized the energies of everyone in the house every other week in summer and once a month in winter."[14] And the winter slaughter of a pig took all family members and sometimes some additional help. When the farm or the household needed labor, it incorporated all hands, regardless of sex, in periods of intensive activity. At other times, though work roles were different, they were complementary. The family economy depended upon the labor of both husband and wife.

URBAN WOMEN

Wives of skilled craftsmen who worked at home usually assisted their husbands, sharing the same room, if not the same bench or table. The wife sometimes prepared or finished materials on which the husband worked. Thus wives spun for their weaver husbands, polished metal for cutlers, sewed buttonholes for tailors, and waxed shoes for shoemakers. Sometimes a wife's work was identical to her husband's, as this romanticized portrait of two broadloom weavers makes clear:

Or if the broader mantle be the task
He chooses some companion to his toil
from side to side, with amicable aim
Each to the other darts the nimble bolt.[15]

If the wife was not her husband's constant companion at the loom, however, or if spinning was her customary job, she still must be able to take his place when he had other tasks, when he was ill, or when he died. Pinchbeck cites a long poem from eighteenth-century England, which included a discussion between a clothier, departing to buy wool, and his wife, who protests at the additional work she will have when he is gone. She calms down, however, when he reminds her of the importance of the trade.

> Bessie and thee mun get up soon
> And stir about and get all done
> For all things mun be aside laid
> When we want help about our trade.[16]

The fact that all family members worked together and benefited jointly from the enterprise meant that some jobs were learned by both sexes and could be interchangeable. It meant, too, as the verse suggests, that the family's joint economic activity was the first priority for everyone.

If the products made at home were sold there, then a craftsman's wife was usually also a shopkeeper. She handled transactions, kept accounts, and helped supervise the workers in the shop. Many of these women hired servants to free them from "the routine of domestic drudgery." When work pressed, as it did in the Lyonnais silk trade (where the typical female occupation was silk spinning or assistance with weaving), mothers sent their infants off to nurses rather than break the rhythm of work in the shop.[17]

Yet, if a wife was her husband's indispensable partner in many a trade, and even if her skill equaled his, she remained his assistant while he lived. Married women were granted full membership in certain guilds only after their husbands had died and then so long as they did not remarry. Occupational designations in all but the food and clothing trades usually were male. Women were referred to as the wives of the craftsmen, even when they were widows and practicing the trade on their own. Hence, Mrs. Baskerville, a widow of a printer and letter founder, "begs leave to inform the Public, . . . that she continues the business of letter-founding, in all its parts, with the same care and accuracy that was formerly observed by Mr. Baskerville."[18] The practice reflected a family division of labor which undoubtedly took into account a woman's domestic tasks: her other activities might claim her time while the husband could be a full-time craftsman. In addition, in the most skilled trades, an investment in long years of training might be unwise for a woman in the light of the lost time, the illnesses, and the higher mortality of women usually associated with childbirth.[19] The exclusion of women also represented a means of controlling the size of a craft. Only when labor was scarce were women permitted to practice certain trades. The press of numbers, however, led to their exclusion from goldsmithing, for example, in England by 1700. (Women were employed, however, as unskilled assistants—often called servants—in large shops. But these were usually young, single women.) By and large, in the home-based skilled trades, married women were part of the family labor force.

Some women did have crafts or trades of their own in the cities of England and France in 1700. Most of these were associated with the production and distribution of food and clothing. The all-female *corporations* in seventeenth-century France include seamstresses, dressmakers, combers of hemp and flax, embroiders, and hosiers. In addition, there were fan and wig makers, milliners, and cloak makers.[20] Lists from English cities are similar.

In many of these trades women regularly took on apprentices. In millinery, for example, an apprenticeship lasted from five to seven years and required a substantial fee. The women ran their enterprises independently of their husbands, whose work often took them away from home. The Customs of London provided in the seventeenth century that:

> Married women who practise certain crafts in the city alone and without their husbands, may take girls as apprentices to serve them and learn their trade, and these apprentices shall be bound by their indentures of apprenticeship to both husband and wife, to learn the wife's trade as is aforesaid, and such indentures shall be enrolled as well for women as for men.[21]

Women were represented, too, in the retail trades, assisting their husbands and running their own businesses as well. In England, brewing once was a female monopoly. It was no longer by the eighteenth century, but women still practiced the trade. Women were also bakers, grocers, innkeepers, and butchers. At least one woman butcher in eighteenth-century London "lived by killing beasts in which ... she was very expert."[22]

By far the most numerous group of married women working independently were the wives of unskilled laborers and journeymen. They were women in precarious economic situations, since their husbands never earned enough money to cover household needs. These women had no skills, nor did they have capital for goods or a shop. No family productive enterprise claimed their time. So they became petty traders, and itinerant peddlers selling such things as bits of cloth or "perishable articles of food from door to door" accompanied by their children.[23] The street was their shop; their homes were their workplaces; and their work required no investment in tools or equipment. On the list of

non-guild members in Paris cited in Chapter 1 there were 1,263 women
and only 486 men. The women were lodging-house keepers and retailers or "repairers of old clothes and hats, of rags and old ironware,
buckles and hardware."[24] When they did not sell items they had sca-
venged or repaired, they sold their labor, carting goods, water, or sew-
age, doing laundry, and performing a host of other unskilled services
which were always in demand in the city and usually outside the control
of the guilds. Their work was an aspect of "the economy of makeshift"
which characterized their entire lives. As such, the time spent earning
wages was sporadic and discontinuous:

> a poor woman . . . goes three dayes a week to wash or scoure abroad, or
> one that is employed in Nurse keeping three or four Months in a Year, or
> a poor Market woman, who attends 3 or 4 mornings in a Week with her
> Basket. . . .[25]

The writer advocated spinning as a means of continuously employing
these women at home and of making them "much more happy and
cheerful." His description nonetheless captures the variety of jobs that
might be done by a poor woman as she sought ways of contributing to
the family fund.

The time required of women differed greatly in different situations.
During harvesting and planting, wives worked day and night in the
fields. Wives of urban butchers and bakers spent many hours in the
family shop. Lyons' silk spinners paid others to nurse their babies.
Women doing casual labor had to spend long hours earning a few pence
or sous. Yet the work of most married women permitted a certain
flexibility, some control over the time and pace of work. Some studies
estimated that in the course of a year, a woman probably spent fewer
days at cash-earning activities than did her husband. While a man
worked about 250 days a year, a woman worked about 125 to 180 days.
The studies, based on contemporaries' analyses of family budgets of
French weavers in 1700 and agricultural laborers in 1750, assumed that
a married woman worked less "because of the supplementary demands
of her sex: housekeeping, childbirth, etc."[26] In the fields, women could
stop work to nurse a baby or feed a young child. In craft and retail shops,
they could allocate some time for domestic responsibilities. In addition,
they could include young children in certain aspects of their work,
teaching them to wind thread or clean wool. Those who walked the
street, selling their wares, were invariably accompanied by their children. Yet rather than "working less," as contemporaries described it, it
seems more accurate to say that demands on women's time were more
complex. In this period, the type of work women did meant that even

if home and workplace were not the same, a woman could balance her productive and domestic activities.

WIDOWS

We have described so far a "normal" situation, in which both husband and wife were alive. Yet mortality statistics indicate that quite frequently death changed this picture. The death of a husband disrupted the family division of labor and left the wife solely responsible for maintaining the family. Sometimes, of course, there were children to assist her, to run the farm or earn some wages. But often they were too young or too inexperienced to contribute much.

In the best of circumstances, a widow gained the right to practice her husband's craft. She became legal representative of the family, and her mastery and autonomy were publicly recognized. Advertisements from eighteenth-century English newspapers capture a certain sense of the strength and competence a widow could have:

M. Hawthorn, Widow of the late John Hawthorn, Watchmaker of this town, tenders her grateful thanks to the friends of her late husband; and begs to acquaint them and the public, that she will carry on the said Business (having engaged able workmen therein) and hope for the continuance of their favours, which she will at all times studiously endeavour to merit.[27]

Widowhood, however, was usually a more difficult situation. Deprived of a husband's assistance, many women could not continue a family enterprise and instead sought new kinds of work. In the French town of Châteaudun, for example, wives of vineyard owners, who had managed the household side of the family enterprise while their husbands lived, took in sewing and spinning when they died. The wife could not do the heavy work of harvesting the grapes herself. And she could rarely afford to pay hired help. The few opportunities for her to earn money—usually as a seamstress—were poorly paid and were insufficient to keep up the activities of the vineyard.[28] In cities, women who did the most onerous jobs were often widows whose need led them to take any work they could find. Many of these women were unable to support themselves despite their work, for wages were so low. The jobs available to these women—as seamstresses, or unskilled workers— were notoriously poorly paid. Hence it was impossible for women and their families to live on earnings alone. So they often sent their children off to charitable institutions, or to fend for themselves. Widows and orphans made up the bulk of names on charity lists in the seventeenth and eighteenth centuries. In Châteaudun most of the women on the lists of those with no resources were widows. In Le Puy, "17 widows, 12 of them lacemakers, had dependent upon them 49 people. . . . There were a further 32 households of 93 people who were given over to cadging a livelihood: 21 of these were headed by widows (62 people). . . ."[29]

Remarriage was clearly the happiest solution for a widow, since an economic partnership was the best means of survival. Widows and widowers did remarry if they could. One study of the Parisian region found that in the sixteenth, seventeenth, and eighteenth centuries men remarried within a few months or even weeks of their wives' deaths.[30] Among the lower classes, the rates of remarriage were much higher than among the upper classes, who were protected from penury by the money or property specifically designated for widowhood in marriage contracts. Prosperous widows were sometimes prevented from remarrying by children who did not want their inheritance threatened. If she could find a husband, a second marriage for a widow of the popular classes meant a restoration of the household division of labor. If she had a craftshop or some land, a widow might attract a younger man eager to become a master craftsman or a farmer. (As the husband of a master's widow a man was legally entitled to take over the mastership.) But if she had no claim to property or if she had to relinquish those claims because of the difficulty of maintaining the enterprise alone, she would marry a man whose economic situation was considerably worse than her first husband's. In these instances, farm wives, for example, would become agricultural field laborers or, perhaps, spinners.[31]

In most cases, however, widows failed to find new spouses and they had to manage on their own. Widowers more often chose younger, single women as their second wives. A widow's advanced age or the fact that she had children lessened her chances of finding a husband. (Sometimes the price of remarriage was the abandonment of her children, since a prospective husband might be unwilling or unable to contribute to their support. But even this alternative might be preferable to the precarious existence of a widow on her own who might have to abandon her children anyway.) The charity rolls and hospital records of the seventeenth and eighteenth centuries starkly illustrate the plight of a widow with young children or of an elderly widow, desperately struggling and usually failing to earn her own bread. "Small wonder," comments Hufton, "the widow and her brood were common beggars. What other resource had they?"[32]

Although there were fewer of them (they either remarried or simply abandoned their children), widowers too were on the charity lists. Like the widows, these men had great difficulty supporting themselves and their dependent children. Such men and women were eloquent testimony to the fact that the line between survival and starvation, between poverty and destitution, was an extremely thin one. They clearly demonstrate as well that two partners were vital to family survival. The family division of labor reflected an economy based on the contributions of husband and wife. The loss of one partner usually meant the destruction of the family economy. Although the jobs they performed may have differed, the work of husband and wife were equally necessary to the household. It was this partnership of labor that struck one observer in eighteenth-century France:

> In the lowest ranks [of society], in the country and in the cities, men and women together cultivate the earth, raise animals, manufacture cloth and clothing. Together they use their strength and their talents to nourish and serve children, old people, the infirm, the lazy and the weak.... No distinction is made between them about who is the boss; both are....[33]

It is not entirely clear that a partnership of labor meant there existed a "rough equality" between husband and wife in all areas of family life.[34] It is clear, however, that the survival of the family depended on the work of both partners. The household division of labor reflected the biological differences between husband and wife. But tasks performed were complementary. The differentiation of work roles was based in part on the fact that women also had to bear children and manage the household, activities which were necessary, too, to the family economy. The family economy reproduced itself as the basic economic unit of production. Children were important as well for the sustenance of aged and dependent parents.

MARRIED WOMEN'S DOMESTIC ACTIVITY

The wife's major domestic responsibility was the provision of food for the family. The work of all family members contributed directly or indirectly to subsistence, but wives had a particular responsibility for procuring and preparing food. In a peasant family, "the duties of the mother of the family were overwhelming; they were summed up in one word: food."[35] In the unskilled laborer's home, too, the wife raised chickens, a cow, a pig, or a goat. Her garden supplemented the miserable wages she earned sewing and those her husband made in the fields. Urban wives frequented markets, where they haggled and bargained over the prices of food and other goods. Some also kept small gardens and a few animals at home. Whether she grew food or purchased it— whether, in other words, she was a producer or consumer—the wife's

role in providing food served her family. A wife's ability to garden and
tend animals, or to bargain and to judge the quality of items for sale,
could mean the difference between eating decently and not eating at
all. In more desperate circumstances, women earned the family's food
by begging for it or by organizing their children to appeal for charity.
They supervised the "economy of makeshift," improvising ways of
earning money or finding food, and going without food in order to feed
their children. One curé in Tours compared such women to "the pious
pelican of the *Adoro Te,* who gave her blood to feed her young." Hufton's careful study of the poor in eighteenth-century France has led her
to conclude that "the importance of the mother within the family
economy was immense; her death or incapacity could cause a family to
cross the narrow but extremely meaningful barrier between poverty
and destitution."[36]

Food was the most important item in the budgets of most families.
Few families had any surplus funds to save or to spend on anything
other than basic necessities. A French artisan's family, for example,
whose members earned 43 sols a day, spent in 1701 approximately 36
sols on food: bread, herring, cheese, and cider. Poorer families ate less
varied fare. Rural and urban wage earners in eighteenth-century
France could spend more than half of their income on bread alone.[37]

The fact that she managed the provision of food gave the wife a
certain power within the family. She decided how to spend money, how
to allocate most of the family's few resources. She was the acknowledged manager of much of the monetary exchange of the family and
her authority in this sphere was unquestioned. Legally, women were
subordinate to their husbands. And some were clearly subject to physical mistreatment as well. Recent studies of criminality, violence, and
divorce among the lower classes during the seventeenth and eighteenth centuries indicate that wife beating occurred and that women
were at a disadvantage in seeking redress in court.

The law tolerated male adultery and punished it in females; and it
also tolerated violence by men against their wives.[38] The studies, of
course, focus on examples of family breakdown and disharmony which
reached the criminal courts. They do not, therefore, adequately describe the day-to-day dealings of husband and wife, nor do they detail
distribution of power within the household. Yet it is precisely the
distribution that is important. Men had the physical and legal power,
but women managed the poor family's financial resources. Within the
households of the popular classes there seem to have been not just one,
but several sources of power. Men did not monopolize all of them.
Wives' power in the household stemmed from the fact that they
managed household expenditures for food. Among families which spent

most of their money on food this meant that the wife decided how to spend most of the family's money.

WOMEN IN POPULAR POLITICS

The wife's role in providing food could lead to her involvement in public, political actions. Household concerns and economic issues overlapped in this period; the family was a public as well as a private institution. The politics of the disenfranchised popular classes was a politics of protest. Groups of people gathered to complain about what they considered unjust prices or taxes. And, lacking any other means of influencing the elites who governed them, they often took matters into their own hands, refusing to pay high prices or taxes, and burning tolls and fiscal records. Women and men engaged in these disturbances, the most typical of which was the bread or grain riot.

The bread riot was usually a protest against the adulteration of flour by millers, the hoarding of wheat and bread, or what the crowd considered unjust prices. These demonstrations were often led by women, and women formed a large proportion of their participants. George Rudé and E. P. Thompson have analyzed bread-and-grain riots at length. They have shown that the demonstrations were a means used by the popular classes to protest the introduction of laissez-faire capitalist practices. When local authorities reduced their customary attempts to control the price of grain and bread, as was done in England and France in the eighteenth and early nineteenth centuries, prices soared, especially in time of shortage. People rioted in the name of traditional justice, demanding that prices once again be fixed so that the poor, too, might eat. The rioters were not the abject poor but representatives of the industrious classes, peasants and artisans, tradesmen and their wives. Women frequently began the protests as they waited outside a bakery to buy their families' bread or as they arrived at the market and learned that the price of grain had increased, or that no grain was available. Crowds of women and their children, joined by men, then descended on the miller or the baker, seizing his supplies and selling them at a "just price," punishing him by damaging machinery or simply distributing available flour or bread. Thompson cites a number of examples in England:

In 1693 we learn of a great number of women going to Northampton market, "with knives stuck in their girdles to force corn at their own rates." ... The mob was raised in Stockton (Durham) in 1740 by a "Lady with a stick and a horn." At Haverfordwest (Pembroke) in 1795 an old-fashioned

J. P. who attempted, with the help of his curate, to do battle with the colliers, complained that "the women were putting the Men on, and were perfect furies. . . ." A Birmingham paper described the Snow Hill riots as the work of "a rabble urged on by furious women."[39]

And, in 1800, in protest against an act which forced millers to make only whole-meal flour, in Sussex,

> A number of women . . . proceeded to Gosden wind-mill, where, abusing the miller for serving them with brown flour, they seized on the cloth which he was then dressing . . . and cut it into a thousand pieces, threatening at the same time to serve all similar utensils he might in future attempt to use in the same manner. The Amazonian leader of this petticoated cavalcade afterwards regaled her associates with a guinea's worth of liquor at the Crab-Tree public house.[40]

Natalie Davis has argued that in the sixteenth century women's preponderant role in these and other disturbances reflected popular views which saw women as inclined to passion and disorder. They were also legally exempt from punishment, hence not responsible to the authorities for their behavior. She suggests, too, that women, particularly if they were mothers, were understood to have a moral right to speak the truth and denounce injustice.[41] In addition, of course, the bread riots flowed from the concrete and collective experiences of women as they carried out their family role of consumer and food provider. These women were responsible for marketing, and they best knew the consequences for their families of higher prices, of products of inferior quality, and of deprivation. Englishwomen protesting the Brown Bread Act of 1800 said the bread was "disagreeable to the taste . . . utterly incompetent to support them under their daily labour, and . . . productive of bowelly complaints to them and to their children in particular." Yet though the specific issue was particularly compelling for women, the form of protest was the same as that employed by men.[42] The market riot, and the tax riot, grew out of routine assemblies of people going about their everyday business and pursuing their household and community concerns.

CHILDBIRTH AND NURTURE

The role of food provider was an important aspect of a married woman's productive economic activity and it was also tied to her reproductive role. For it was she who bore and nurtured children, she who clothed and cared for them. Children were the inevitable consequence of marriage; childbearing was an exclusively female activity. Married women expected to spend much of their married lives pregnant or caring for young children. High infant mortality rates and ensuing high fertility meant that at least two-thirds of a wife's married years involved reproductive activity. For women the risks and pain of childbirth, the need to spend some time nursing an infant, the supervision and feeding of children were all part of the definition of marriage.

The activities surrounding childbirth were almost exclusively performed by females. Midwives sometimes assisted at the birth of a child. These were usually local women who had "inherited" the few skills they had from their own mothers or from another woman in the community. But a midwife's services cost money and often women simply helped one another, with no previous training or experience. Their lack of knowledge contributed to maternal and infant disability and death. An eighteenth-century account details what could occur:

> If we consider their technique . . . we see that they do not hesitate to lop off with a kitchen knife an arm—should the arm appear first in the passage. They . . . attach the mother to a ladder, feet in the air in order to push the child back should the presentation be irregular. If the child emerges buttocks first they use a hook, and they do not hesitate to cut the mother barbarously to facilitate the exit of the child . . .[43]

The presence of another woman was helpful to a mother for a practical and legal reason also. If the baby died, she could serve as a witness that it had not been deliberately murdered by its mother. In the seventeenth century, in both England and France, male doctors began to take an interest in childbirth. They developed new methods of assistance and regulated the practice of midwifery. Books of instruction were prepared, and investigations of local practices were made. In France, regulation of midwives was partly a consequence of a drive by church officials to increase the custom of baptism. One clergyman, Mgr. Rochefoucauld, visited every parish in the diocese of Bourges early in the eighteenth century. He found many women helping one another in childbirth and urged all women to get together and elect one or two "official" midwives, who would be trained and certified by the state and church. In the villages and towns he visited, some women apparently followed his instructions. But the reforms did not change the practice in most regions.[44] Well into the nineteenth century babies were delivered by untrained women. As Hufton has put it, "The actual birth of the child was surrounded by a 'complicity' of females."[45] Childbirth created a bond among women. They not only shared the experience, but also assisted and nursed one another as best they could.

Yet after the birth of a baby, in the list of household priorities the care of children ranked quite low. Work and the provision of food for the family had first claim on a married woman's time. In the craftshop or on the farm, skilled or unskilled, most labor was time-intensive. Men and women spent the day at work, and what little leisure they had was often work-related. Hence in the rural *veillée* people would gather in barns on winter evenings to keep warm, to talk, but also to repair farm tools, to sew, to sort and clean fruit and vegetables. In cities when women were not formally employed or when their paid work was through, they put in long hours spinning, buying and preparing food, or doing laundry. Household tasks were tedious and no labor-saving technology lightened the chores of a working woman. She simply did not have time to spare to devote specifically to children. The demands of the family enterprise or the need to earn wages for the unskilled could not be postponed or put aside to care for children who, in their earliest years, represented only a drain on family resources. Busy mothers in French cities sent their babies out to be nursed by wet nurses if they could afford it. Silk spinners in Lyons, as well as the wives of butchers and bakers, entrusted newborn infants to strangers rather than interrupt their work to care for them, even when this increased the likelihood that the infant would die.[46] Indeed, death rates among children put out to nurse were almost twice as high as among infants nursed by their own mothers. Even infants who remained at home, however, did not receive a great deal of care. The need for special attention for young children simply was not recognized. As Pinchbeck and Hewitt have put it, "Infancy was but a biologically necessary prelude to the sociologically all important business of the adult world."[47]

Philippe Ariès' pathbreaking book on family life demonstrated that ideas about children and the experience of childhood have had an important history. Before about the eighteenth century, children were not central to family life. They were dressed as miniature adults almost as soon as they could walk, and they were included in all aspects of adult activity, work as well as games. While childhood was understood as a stage of dependency, there nonetheless was no special treatment prescribed for children, no notion that their physical and emotional needs might differ from those of adults. New ideas about childhood began to spread among the upper classes by the latter half of the seventeenth century, but Ariès indicates that these did not reach the popular classes until late in the nineteenth century. So in seventeenth- and eighteenth-century working-class and peasant families, children from infancy to about age seven were dependent beings, but their presence in no way altered family priorities. Children were incorporated into ongoing activities, and had only a minimal claim on material resources and parental time.

The position of children in a family was the result of several factors: high infant and child mortality rates and a relative scarcity of both time and material resources. The likelihood was great that a child would die before it reached maturity. Parents' treatment of their children clearly took these odds into account. They often gave successive children the same name, anticipating the fact that only one would survive. Since the life of any child was so fragile, there was no reason to try to limit or prevent pregnancy. Moreover, as two historians have put it:

> The high rates of mortality prevailing amongst children inevitably militated against the individual child being the focus and principal object of parental interest and affection.... The precariousness of child life also detracted from the importance of childhood as an age-status. In a society where few lived to grow old, age was of less significance than survival.[48]

The needs of the family economy and not children's individual needs or the needs of "childhood" determined whether or not children remained at home from infancy onward. If they were not put out to a wet nurse, children might be sent into service or apprenticeship at age seven or eight. They were expected to work hard and were sometimes subjected to harsh treatment by their masters and mistresses. (Court records are full of accounts of young servants and apprentices fleeing from cruel employers.) On the other hand, if the family needed their labor, children worked at home.

Children were a family resource only if their labor could be used. In propertied families, of course, one child was also important as an heir. As soon as they were able, young children began to assist their parents in the work of the household. In time of scarcity, those not working might be abandoned or sent away, for they were of limited usefulness to the household as it attempted to balance labor and food.

As family laborers, children were accorded no special treatment. They simply worked as members of the family "team." Their interest and their needs were not differentiated from the family interest. The mother's services to the family were therefore services to them as well. Although she spent time as a childbearer, a mother allocated little time to activities specifically connected with child rearing. Children were fed and trained to work in the course of the performance of her other responsibilities. Married women allocated their time among three major activities. The organization of production in this period permitted them to integrate their activity, to merge wage work, production for household consumption, and reproduction.

Production was most often located in the household, and individuals for the most part controlled the time and pacing of their work. Production for the market was often an outgrowth of production for household consumption. Although household chores were time-consuming, they did not demand a broad range of skill or expertise. Childbirth interrupted a woman's routine and claimed some of her time, but after a few days, a woman was usually back to work, taking time out only to nurse the infant. Views of children and standards of child care were such that children were either sent away at a young age or were incorporated into adult routines and adult work. Hence it was possible for a married woman to earn wages or to produce for the market, to manage her household, and to bear children. Each activity influenced the others, but no single activity defined her place nor claimed all of her time. In the course of her lifetime, indeed in the course of a year or a day, a married woman balanced several types of activity and performed them all. She was the cornerstone of the family economy.

PART II

Industrialization and the Family Wage Economy

"I never was married. I went out to service when I was younger, and to waistcoating after quitting service; so that I might be at home with mother and father, and take care of them in their old age. . . ."

London garment worker (1850), quoted in E. Yeo and E. P. Thompson, eds., *The Unknown Mayhew*, p. 125.

"After we were married . . . I worked on as hard myself as ever I had done . . . [doing] straw-work . . . charring or washing . . . and I have taken in needlework. This was before any of my children were old enough to work."

Lucy Luck (1848–1922), quoted in John Burnett, ed., *The Annals of Labour: Autobiographies of British Working Class People, 1820–1920*, p. 77.

4

Industrialization

Industrialization involved the movement of labor and resources away from primary production (agriculture, fishing, forestry) toward manufacturing and commercial and service activities. The scale of production increased and the factory replaced the household as the center of productive activity. In the terms we have been using, the industrial mode of production replaced the domestic mode of production. The process of industrialization was gradual, and it affected different groups of people at different times. Over the long run, the decline of small units of production meant a decline in the numbers of propertied peasants and craftsmen and an increase in proletarians, propertyless people working for wages. The family wage economy, which had characterized the family organization of propertyless people in the past, became an increasingly common form of family organization among the working classes.

PATTERNS OF INDUSTRIALIZATION IN FRANCE AND BRITAIN

One of the enduring images of industrialization, created by contemporaries and transmitted by historians, is of the female factory worker. She is the prototype of the wage-earning woman. Typically, she is a young "mill girl" or a married "operative," torn from her family by the need to earn wages. A member of the British Parliament offered this observation in 1838:

Amongst other things I saw a cotton mill—a sight that froze my blood. The place was full of women, young, all of them, some large with child, and obliged to stand twelve hours each day. Their hours are from five in the morning to seven in the evening, two hours of that being for rest, so that they stand twelve clear hours. The heat was excessive in some of the rooms, the stink pestiferous, and in all an atmosphere of cotton flue. I nearly fainted. The young women were all pale, sallow, thin, yet generally fairly grown, all with bare feet—a strange sight to English eyes.[1]

Whether or not they judged factory work too harsh for women, many observers saw cotton mills as synonymous with industrialization, and they talked of the impact of industrialization on women largely in terms of work in textile factories. Moreover, they argued that the numbers of women engaged in productive activity for the market dramatically increased with the appearance of cotton mills.

This kind of interpretation is understandable, for textile factories did employ many women in new locations. The concentration of large numbers of persons working together, the time-discipline required by moving machinery and by large labor forces, and the use of inanimate power to move complex machines attracted observers' attention. The mills quickly became the symbol of the benefits and dangers of economic and social change.

The interpretation is nonetheless misleading. Industrialization did mean that many more women had to help their families earn wages. Instead of contributing their labor to household production, they had to sell their labor power and bring in cash. Textile factories did create jobs for women. But these factories were neither the only nor the predominant form of female wage-earning activity during the nineteenth century in England and France. The impact of industrialization on women's employment was more varied and far less dramatic then the standard image of the mill girl implies.

England was the first nation to industrialize. The transformation took place there after 1750, first in the cotton industry and much later in iron and steel. New technology, changes in the organization and scale of production, and their social consequences were so dramatic, that nineteenth-century commentators referred to the process as an Industrial Revolution.

By 1850, as Figure 4–1 shows, manufacturing was clearly the dominant form of economic activity in Britain, agriculture was declining, while "service" grew.[2]

In contrast, France's economy remained predominantly agricultural throughout the nineteenth century (Figure 4–2). Although French

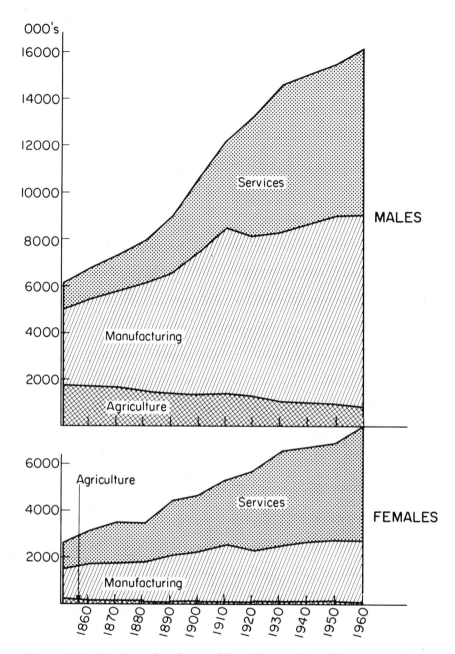

Figure 4.1　Number of males and females employed by sector, Great Britain, 1851–1951

Source: Deldycke, *La Population active et sa structure*. (Unless otherwise noted all figures for France and Britain in this book are based on statistics contained in Deldycke.)

manufacturing grew in the early nineteenth century, it did so only slowly. By the mid-nineteenth century, estimates show a per capita income for the United Kingdom of £ 32.6 in 1860, £ 21.1 for France in 1859.[3] Other indicators of economic growth listed in Table 4–1 dramatically illustrate the gap between English and French economic development.

In England, the cotton textile mill was the early symbol of industrialization. Large numbers of women and children, particularly, worked in these mills at highly differentiated, low-skilled, repetitive jobs. The employment of machines and of women and children resulted in increased output at substantial savings to manufacturers. By the mid-nineteenth century, iron and steel production and the manufacture of machinery and heavy equipment became more important than textile production. These industries employed male workers almost exclusively. The railroad, with its need for iron and steel for track and rolling stock, replaced the cotton mill as the symbol of British industrialism.[4]

TABLE 4–1. Selected Indicators of Economic Growth: France, United Kingdom, 1810–1900

	1810	1840	1860	1880	1900
Raw Cotton consumption per inhabitant					
France	0.3	1.5	2.7	2.6	4.5
United Kingdom	2.1	7.3	15.1	17.1	18.1
Cast iron produced per inhabitant in kilos (five-year averages)					
France	4	12	25	46	65
United Kingdom	20	54	130	220	220
Coal consumption per inhabitant in kilos (five-year averages)					
France	40	130	390	740	1,200
United Kingdom	600	1,110	2,450	3,740	4,070
Motor force in horsepower per 1,000 inhabitants (excluding transport)					
France		1	5	14	46
United Kingdom		13	24	58	— [†](1907: 220)

[†]Figure for 1900 not given. Bairoch gives only 1907.
SOURCE: Derived from Paul Bairoch, "Niveaux de développement économique de 1810 à 1910," Annales, E.S.C., 20e Année (November–December 1965), pp. 1102, 1104, 1107, 1108.

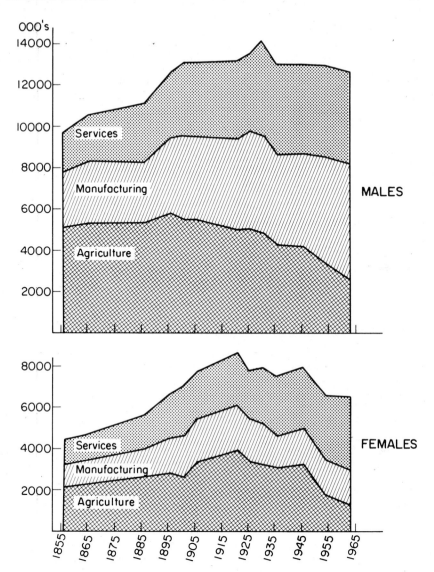

Figure 4.2   Number of males and females employed by sector,
France, 1856–1954

In France there were cotton textile factories in the cities of Mulhouse,
Lille, Roubaix, and Tourcoing and in areas of Normandy and Picardy
by the 1850s. In the two decades after 1840, railroads were built and
the exploitation of iron ore and of coal intensified. Yet, for the most part,
French manufacturing still took place on a small scale in the households

of peasants and craftsmen or in workshops of four or five workers. France's laboring population lived scattered throughout the country in rural as well as urban areas, "so that the distinction between industrial and agricultural work is often artificial."[5]

Aggregate levels of women's employment in the two countries, based on data which are available only from 1850 on, did not reflect the enormous differences between their economies. Throughout the nineteenth century France had a small-scale organization of production in agriculture and manufacturing. England, on the other hand, was already well industrialized and had a large-scale organization of production. Yet, as Figure 4–3 shows, both countries had about the same proportion of working women. Indeed, in France, women consistently accounted for a slightly higher proportion of the labor force than did women in England during the nineteenth century (Figure 4–4). Moreover, while the British figures remained fairly stable, in France the proportion of the female population in employment increased until the 1920s. Figures 4–3 and 4–4 indicate that there was no simple or uniform evolution in women's workforce participation as a result of industrial development.[6]

When we look beyond the aggregate figures at the kinds of jobs women held, we find many differences between England and France. Yet we also find a striking similarity. In both countries, women tended to be concentrated in unmechanized, "traditional" sectors of the economy, except for the the textile industry. The mechanized textile industry's growth in these countries marked the entry of women into wage labor in factory settings. Nevertheless it was only part of the picture. In the economy outside of textiles, the smaller the scale of organization, the larger the size of the female work force.[7]

In England in 1851, 45 percent of all women workers were in manufacturing. But of these, only half were textile operatives. A full 40 percent of those in manufacturing were in the nonmechanized, home-based garment trades. Overall, textile workers represented 22 percent of the female labor force. In contrast, domestic service claimed 40 percent. In France, in 1866, agriculture accounted for the largest proportion of employed females, 40.2 percent. In the manufacturing sector, those in the garment trades outnumbered those in textiles. Moreover, not all textiles were produced by factory industry. Wool and linen, for example, continued to be spun and woven at home. Finally, some 22.5 percent of working women were domestic servants.

The differences in the proportions of women in domestic service are important. Domestic service was the typical form of female employment outside of agriculture before industrialization. In England, it apparently expanded as an occupation as the country industrialized. As

TABLE 4-2. Percentage of Female Labor Force in Economic Sectors of England and France

	England, 1851	France, 1866
Manufacturing	45	27.3
Textiles	22	10
Garment	17	11
Commerce	—*	5.1
Domestic Service	40	22.5
Agriculture	8	40.2
Other	7	4.9

*No women are listed in this category in Deldycke. There surely were women in commerce in England, but no figures are available for this category in 1851.
SOURCE: Deldycke et al., La Population active et sa structure, pp. 174, 191.

agricultural employment for women declined, manufacturing did not absorb all potential women employees, and they became servants. Moreover, a large portion of women workers in rural areas were household servants. The service sector of the economy was large as a consequence, but not (as is usually argued) because modern white-collar jobs (in the distributive trades and the professions) increased. Instead, the more traditional area of service employment—domestic service— dominated in this sector until the end of the nineteenth century. Figure 4-5 illustrates the continuing importance in England throughout the nineteenth century of domestic service as a proportion of all service activities. Until 1880, 50 percent of all service employees were domestic servants in England. In France, on the other hand, domestic service represented a much smaller proportion both of the service sector and of the female labor force. This was because women continued to be employed in agriculture. Indeed, employment on small farms seems to have been the structural equivalent for French women of domestic service in Britain. Clara Collet, an acute observer of British labor-force statistics, noted in 1898 that "diminished opportunities for remunerative or economical work at home resulted in a large number of young women going into domestic service."[8] In France, where the decline of employment in the agricultural sector was very slow, there was no increase in domestic service.

Not simply the size of the agricultural sector, but its organization affected the numbers of women working. Figure 4-6 shows that the ratio of male to female workers in British agriculture far exceeded the French ratio. Not only was British agriculture a smaller sector of the economy, it also employed fewer women in proportion to its size. By

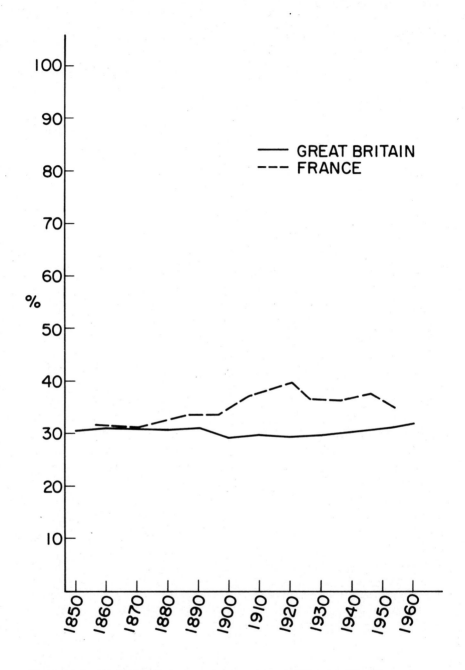

Figure 4.3 Working Women as percentage of Total Labor Force;
Great Britain and France, 1851–1961

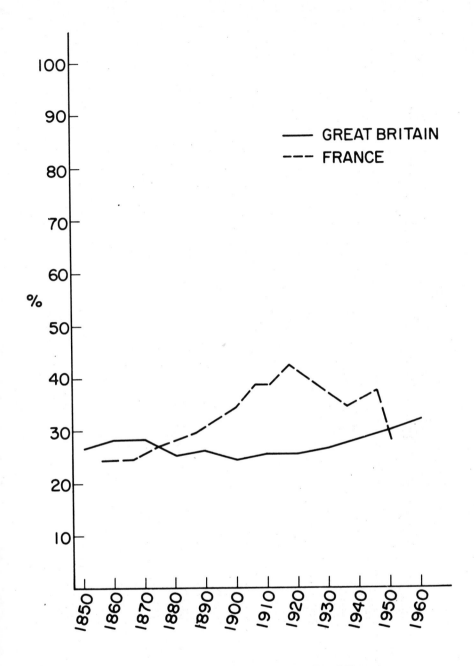

Figure 4.4   Working Women as percentage of Total Female
Population; Great Britain and France, 1851–1961

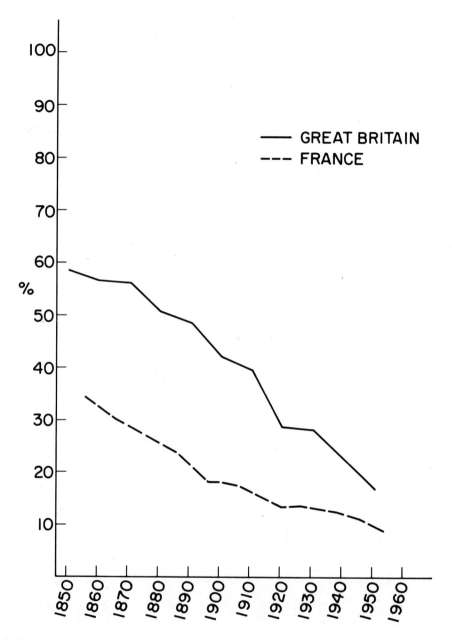

Figure 4.5   Domestic Service as Percent of Total Services; Great Britain and France, 1851–1956

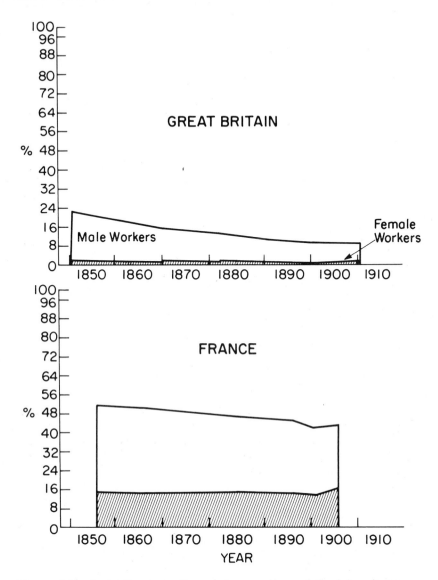

Figure 4.6 Agricultural employment as a share of the labor force. Great Britain and France, 1851–1911

the 1850s, the organization of British agriculture was "industrialized." As a result of the eighteenth-century enclosure movement, relatively few people owned land. Farms were large and employed non-land-owning workers. These farms were highly market-oriented. The following verse depicts the changing fortunes of some farmers in the course of a century:

1743

Man, to the Plow
Wife, to the Cow
Girl, to the Yarn
Boy, to the Barn
And your Rent will be netted.

1843

Man, Tally-ho
Miss, Piano
Wife, Silk and Satin
Boy, Greek and Latin
And you'll all be Gazetted.[9]

   The leisure of the farmer's family was made possible by higher productivity rising from economies of scale. Within the household, the
farmer's wife delegated her work to domestic servants. In the fields,
agricultural laborers tilled the soil. There were, in other words, a few
wealthy owners and many dependent wage earners in the British countryside. Most of the fieldworkers were men, many of whom lived in
cottages on a farmer's estate. Women might work at harvest time, as
members of roving agricultural gangs, but they were occasional workers and were not listed as employees by census takers. Girls, too, were
absent from field work. "I remember formerly," a witness told a parliamentary commission in 1843, "when girls turned out regularly with the
boys to plough, etc., and were up to the knees in dirt, and in the middle
of the winter, in all kinds of employment. Now you never see a girl
about in the field."[10] By the 1860s farmers needing additional labor
might compel a man to bring his wife along to work as a condition for
hiring him. But the permanent agricultural work force in England was
predominantly male.[11]
   In France, in sharp contrast to Britain, the small family-run farm
predominated. There were regional variations, to be sure. In the north
of France, the condition of the soil and the geography of the countryside contributed to the development of large-scale farming during the
nineteenth century. There, as well as in areas of the south and west
typified by small holdings, subsistence peasants and propertyless laborers hired themselves out to work on larger farms. Overall, however, after the Revolution of 1789, "there was a clear tendency for an
increase in the number of small owners whose assets consisted of no
more than a house, a garden and one or two fields. . . ." At the height
of this development in the 1880s, there were 3.5 million farms in
France.[12]

Despite the small size of French farms, new methods of farming led to increased productivity during the nineteenth century. From about 1850 to 1873, agricultural prices rose and peasant producers prospered. Nonetheless, the period of prosperity did not fundamentally transform the organization of the French countryside. At midcentury, Marx had described "the great mass of the French nation" as an "agglomeration of autonomous units . . . A smallholding, a peasant and his family; alongside them another smallholding, another peasant and family. . . ."[13] In 1959, a British historian could still write: "In the last resort, and at bottom, France is a Peasants' Republic."[14] Unlike the wealthy British farmer, the French peasant had to depend on the labor of his family, so wives and daughters living and working on small family farms were an important part of France's agricultural workforce. This fact is reflected in the census listings, which designated female family members engaged in farm work as "employed."

A similar contrast between Britain and France prevailed in commerce, a rough category that includes business, sales, and secretarial/-clerical positions. While in France about 5 percent of women worked in commerce in 1866, no women were listed in that field in England in 1851. This undoubtedly reflects some difference in occupational designation, for there surely were women involved in commerce in England in 1851. It also undoubtedly reflects the fact that small family businesses, run by couples, typified French business organization. The more numerous, larger-scale British enterprises tended to employ male clerks.

Apart from agriculture and domestic service, garment making and textiles were the major employers of women in both countries during the nineteenth century. The rise of ready-made clothing production involved a twofold transformation of the old skilled tailoring and shoemaking trades. First, piecework, given out to women particularly, replaced workshop organization. Large numbers of women sewing at home, receiving a pittance for their work, swelled the ranks of what skilled workers referred to as the "slop" trades. "The trade is falling into the hands of an inferior craft," a skilled shoemaker told Henry Mayhew in 1850. "All the money at present embarked in the shoe trade, or nearly all, is on the low-priced [slop] system."[15] As a result, the numbers of jobs for women in this low-skilled, "traditional" work increased. The garment industry mechanized very slowly; factories appeared only after the 1850s in England and late in the 1880s in France. Even then, however, manufacturers found that large supplies of cheap female labor justified the continuation of the putting-out system. Well into the twentieth century in both countries, garment making was organized in sweatshops or as home production.[16]

In the localities where the cotton-spinning industry developed, large numbers of women worked in factories. Indeed, it was only in textiles that mechanization and large-scale organization created employment for women. In 1835 in England close to half of all cotton-textile workers were women and girls, and their numbers increased during the century. In France, the transfer of female and child workers into spinning factories began in the late 1820s in the Alsatian city of Mulhouse. (But in France, mechanization was far slower and textile production continued in the old way for a much longer period.) From Lancashire and Alsace came reports of insufficient work for men, abundant opportunity for women and children. The early factories used the labor of women and children in unskilled jobs, often as assistants to male spinners. Dr. Andrew Ure, one of the admirers of the new system, described its benefits in 1835:

> It is, in fact, the constant aim and tendency of every improvement in machinery to supersede human labour altogether or to diminish its cost, by substituting the industry of women and children for that of men; or that of ordinary labourers for trained artisans. In most of the water-twist, or throstle cotton-mills, the spinning is entirely managed by females of sixteen years and upwards. The effect of substituting the self-acting mule for the common mule, is to discharge the greater part of the men spinners, and to retain adolescents and children. The proprietor of a factory near Stockport states, . . . that, by such substitution, he would save 50 £ a week in wages, in consequence of dispensing with nearly forty male spinners, at about 25s. of wages each.[17]

Yet we must be careful to distinguish the concentration of jobs for women in certain areas from an overall increase in women's employment. Ivy Pinchbeck has pointed out that the consolidation of spinning in factory towns actually deprived large numbers of women in other areas of this age-old occupation. And although we have no way of estimating their numbers, we do have descriptive evidence which indicates that some women found themselves "unemployed" when spinning became a factory industry.

Yet another area involved women in market activity during the nineteenth century. This was employment in what has been termed the urban "secondary labor force," the unskilled, casual service sector of an urban economy. The women workers in this sector are often hidden from the historian's view because they are not listed on censuses or other official tabulations of work-force participation. Descriptive accounts make it clear, however, that the women carters, petty traders, hawkers, street merchants, laundresses, and boardinghouse keepers of eighteenth-century cities were still numerous among growing urban populations as industrialization proceeded.

The aggregate view indicates that industrialization did not change the type of work women did, nor did it greatly increase the amount of time that women in the aggregate devoted to productive work for market exchange. Indeed over the course of the nineteenth century, women's work-force participation varied very little. Early industrialization did concentrate some women in factories, but the majority of working women remained in household settings, as family farm workers, shopkeepers, and servants in France, as servants in Britain, as garment workers and casual laborers in both countries. Indeed, throughout the nineteenth century in England and in France, the majority of working women performed jobs with low levels of skill and low productivity similar to those that had characterized women's work for centuries.

The labor forces of both England and France were segregated; that is, women tended to be concentrated in certain jobs, while other jobs remained primarily male. This had been the case in the past, but under the household mode of production different jobs were performed by the different sexes in the same location. Increasingly, under the industrial form of organization, men's jobs took them away from their own households. So, if women worked at home, they worked less often in the company of men. The same was true if they worked in factories because most occupations were segregated by sex.[18] In France, such segregation was less typical because of the continuation of small farms and shops. In England, where locations of work changed more quickly and decisively, segregated jobs were the norm.

Another important change did occur, though it is not reflected in the figures we have discussed. Women tended, more often than in the past, to earn wages for their work. The decline of the household mode of production meant that even if they worked at home, women were no longer part of a family production team. Instead, they worked for an employer who paid them a wage. This development which we have referred to as proletarianization had important ramifications for women's family activities. Indeed it was proletarianization, of which factory labor was but one example, that changed patterns of women's work in nineteenth-century England and France.

URBAN GROWTH

Aggregate figures indicate that, overall, industrialization did not transform the levels of women's work or the kinds of work they did. Yet within certain cities dramatic changes did take place. Indeed, it was precisely the vision of Manchester or Roubaix that led English and French observers to their generalizations about the impact of industrialization on women. But if Manchester was the "symbol of an age," it was not typical of urban economic organization; rather it was only one of several types of nineteenth-century cities. The growth of cities was an important part of the development of England and France, and differences in the national patterns of urbanization were linked to differences in industrial development. Yet within each country there existed a variety of urban types with different occupational opportunities for women.

Britain and France both experienced dramatic increases in the number and size of their cities during the nineteenth century. England urbanized more rapidly, while the persistence of agriculture in France accompanied a lower level of urbanization. Table 4–3 shows the comparative importance of urban populations in England and Wales as compared with France at three points during the nineteenth century. By 1891, 72.1 percent of the English population lived in places of over 2,000 inhabitants; about 32 percent lived in cities of over 100,000. In France, on the other hand, the comparable figures were 37.4 percent and 12 percent. Over the course of the century, French urban population (in cities over 10,000) increased 2.7 times, English urban populations increased 2.9 times. France's urbanization proceeded at a rate

TABLE 4-3. Percentage of Total Population Living in Cities, 1801–1891

Date	City Size	France	England/Wales
1801	100,000+	2.8	9.7
	20,000+	6.7	16.9
	10,000+	9.5	21.3
1851	100,000+	4.6	22.6
	20,000+	10.6	35.0
	10,000+	14.4	39.5
1891	100,000+	12.0	31.8
	20,000–100,000	9.3	21.8
	20,000+	21.1	53.6
	10,000+	25.9	61.7
	2,000+	37.4	72.1

SOURCE: A. F. Weber, *The Growth of Cities in the Nineteenth Century* (Ithaca, N.Y.: Cornell University Press, 1967), p. 144.

only slightly lower than England's, but since it started at a much lower level, it ended the century at a lower level as well. While 79 percent of the French population lived outside of cities of over 20,000 people in 1891, only 41 percent of the English population did.[19]

Yet within the two countries, cities with similar economic organizations had similar patterns of employment. In both England and France industrial development created new types of cities. Other cities were barely affected by changes experienced elsewhere. Still others were transformed by increases in population and the expansion of older forms of economic activity. Visitors to both countries often remarked on the diversity of the cities they visited and on the differences in the occupations and activities of the inhabitants from one city to another. In cities with different economies, there were very different occupational opportunities for women. It is useful to examine some of these cities to gain a closer look at patterns of women's employment in specific economic contexts. We are also struck with the variety of work experiences that nineteenth-century urban women could have.

COMMERCIAL CITIES: YORK AND AMIENS

York and Amiens continued in the nineteenth century, as in the past, to be centers of commercial and administrative activity. York was isolated from changes which took place elsewhere in England. Even its appearance changed little. The city corporation resolved in 1799 to take down the old stone walls of the city to permit urban growth. Yet not all citizens agreed that this was a good idea, and those whose ancient privileges gave them certain rights sought to block the action. By 1807 work on the demolition had begun despite litigation; but the archbishop intervened and work ceased. The project was resumed after his death, only to be blocked again by local citizens who raised money to restore the walls. The picturesque stone gates to the city were never torn down; they still stand. At the end of the nineteenth century, the city of York retained its walls, one of the few English cities to preserve the physical symbol of urban separatism.[20]

York's economy changed as little as its physical appearance. Its occupational structure at midcentury was still "preindustrial." From the mid-nineteenth century on, our information about urban occupations is based on population censuses which listed occupations for individuals. In 1851 43 percent of all male workers were employed in artisanal trades and in commerce; another 12 percent were in the building trades. Only 9 percent were in modern manufacturing, such as iron casting, linen production, and glassmaking. The female labor force was even less "modern." In 1851 26.5 percent of the female population was employed. Sixty percent of working women were domestic servants (as compared with the national figure of 40 percent), 30 percent were in craft manufacturing and small commercial establishments, while 1.1 percent were in modern manufacturing, exemplified by the linen textile industry. The only hint of industrialization came from the 500 or so railway workers, all male, and from a small number of female professionals, primarily teachers.[21]

In Amiens, across the English Channel, work had begun on removing the city walls in 1809. The task was implemented only gradually, and several sections of the bastions remained standing into the twentieth century. In addition, the city hall was enlarged and renovated, squares were built and vistas cleared. By midcentury, Amiens was a stop on the railway line between Paris and the Belgian border, and also the junction for another line going to the Channel ferries at Bologne. Businessmen and boosters had succeeded in maintaining the city as a textile producing center. They organized a society which trained workers to operate the newly invented Jacquart looms, sponsored studies on workers' housing and savings banks, and "encouraged" enterprise in the city.[22]

Amiens nonetheless had a less important position as a manufacturing city in the 1850s than it had had in the pre-Revolutionary period. Competition from the British cotton industry was part of its problem. In addition, its organization of production had changed hardly at all. Armand Audiganne, who traveled about France reporting on French industry, could barely disguise his scorn in 1860:

> We must say that the "fabrique" [of Amiens] is surely one of the northern manufacturing centers where progress is less of a habit. One is struck by the contrast between an attractive city, with broad views, spacious boulevards, magnificent promenades on all sides, and a "fabrique" which by its very nature seems to be closed in on itself, fearful of seeking bold expansion or initiative. The manufacturers of Amiens have shown extreme slowness in deciding to use new machines. . . .[23]

The word *fabrique* refers to the putting out or domestic system of production. The *fabrique* was "a group of merchants who brought raw materials or semi-finished products . . . and distributed them to workers grouped in small shops or in their own rooms, in the city or in the countryside."[24] A few years later, another visitor reiterated Audiganne's conclusions. Reybaud also noted that in the woolen textile industry old practices prevailed. In family shops, parents and children took turns at looms, as they had done for generations past. In Amiens, Reybaud found "several dyeing and cloth finishing shops, generally working by the old method, and several fancy cloth shops, in which the manufacturer himself exercises personal supervision. The workers of these shops are the only ones who should be designated urban workers."[25] The situation in Amiens did not change much in the course of the century. In 1859, there were two cotton spinning mills employing ninety-seven workers, and by 1887 a single mill employed thirty-nine workers. Only a small linen mill prospered in these years.[26]

The majority of adult male workers were in manufacturing in 1851, but they labored at jobs that were neither mechanized nor concentrated in factories. The census summaries show more than 40 percent of the female population working in 1851. Most worked in the textile and garment industries. Many of these were organized still as domestic manufacturing as they had been during the eighteenth century. The other large employers of women were domestic service and food selling. As in York, the nineteenth century brought no major transformation of women's work in Amiens except for the relatively rare textile factory.[27]

TEXTILE CITIES: ROUBAIX, STOCKPORT, AND PRESTON

A new type of city developed in the process of industrialization. The most striking examples of industrial cities were the textile and mining towns. Roubaix, in the department of the Nord in France, was a city born in the nineteenth century. One of its poets called it a "city without a past in art, without beauty, without a history."[28] Indeed its major buildings, its church and city hall, were built during the nineteenth century. The city hall today is blackened with soot from the coal-burning factories which line the streets, row after row, beginning about two blocks away from the central square. These factories are the base upon which the city was built, the central core of its existence. In 1864 the city archivist hailed Roubaix as "the Manchester of France . . . there is no more dedicated industrial center, more progressive; the Roubaisien weaving industry creates, invents without relaxing; and what it doesn't invent, it perfects victoriously."[29] Reybaud declared with satisfaction that in no region of France "had the changes attendant on industrialization had more success."[30]

Factories developed on a large scale in Roubaix in the 1860s. Even before then, however, it was an important center of cloth production. Before the Revolution of 1789 the putting-out system had expanded. New spinning machines, imported from England, were introduced by 1815. In the 1820s steam engines were installed in spinning mills. The flexibility of Roubaix's economy was clearly illustrated in the 1830s when a slowdown in the cotton industry and competition from British and Alsatian mills led entrepreneurs to switch to wool production. At this time, however, weaving was still a domestic industry.[31]

In the 1860s wool weaving as well as spinning became a factory industry. In 1843 there had been some 30,000 persons employed by the *fabrique* of Roubaix, most of them living in cottages in the countryside. By 1861, when the total population of the city was 49,000, there were at least 10,000 textile workers living in the city. Opportunities in factories also attracted thousands of Belgian migrants, and by 1872, 56 percent of Roubaix's inhabitants were foreign-nationals. The textile workers crowded in rows of tenements known as *forts, cités,* or *courées.* The buildings, smudged with smoke, with a single tap for water at the entry and outhouses in the courtyards, housed thousands of workers in cramped quarters. In 1869 a report described one *courée* only 2.1 meters wide (2 ½ yards), which was twenty-two houses deep and sheltered 123 persons.[32]

Roubaix's occupational structure can be observed best in the 1872 census, which clearly listed most female occupations. Over 50 percent of the city's labor force worked in the textile industry in 1872. A little less than half of the textile workers were women. Women workers were 31 percent of the total labor force. Fifty-four percent of the married women who worked were textile operatives, but only about 17 percent of married women worked. (See Figure 4–7.) The rate of labor-force participation of young people under fifteen was high: 38.9 percent of girls aged ten to fourteen, and 36.5 percent of boys, worked.[33] In 1872 almost 50 percent of all women over fifteen worked, 55 percent of them in textiles. Most of these female textile workers were young and single. Some 82 percent of them were under thirty.

Like Roubaix, the English textile towns were dominated by a single industry. Engels noted in the 1840s that in the towns of Preston and Stockport,

> the workers form an even larger proportion of the total population than in Manchester. . . . Although nearly all these towns have between 30,000 and 90,000 inhabitants, they are practically no more than huge working class communities. The only parts of these towns not given over to housing the workers are the factory buildings, some main streets lined with shops, and a few semi-rural lanes where the factory owners have their villas and gardens. The towns themselves have been badly planned and badly built. They have dirty courts, lanes and back alleys. The pall of smoke which hangs over these towns has blackened the houses of red brick. . . .[34]

Of Stockport, which he surveyed from the train viaduct which passed over the Mersey River, Engels wrote, "Stockport is notoriously one of

ROUBAIX 1872

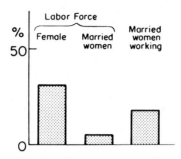

Figure 4.7   Levels of Female Employment

Source: See footnote 33, Chapter 4 (p. 241). (Unless otherwise noted all figures for cities are based on the data described in this note.)

the darkest and smokiest holes in the whole industrial area, and . . . [it] presents a truly revolting picture. But the cottages and cellar dwellings are even more unpleasant to look at." The *courées* and *forts* of Roubaix had their counterparts in industrial Lancashire, just as did the factories and machines.

In Stockport and Preston, cities born with industrialization, most of the labor force was in textile manufacture. In Preston, Michael Anderson found that "between a quarter and a third of [the] . . . adult male population [was] directly involved in factory industry."[35] But an ever greater portion of the population had experienced factory labor as children. In Manchester/Salford, the percentages of boys and girls working were very high. In 1852, for example, 76 percent of all fourteen-year-old girls and 61 percent of all boys of that age were employed in the mills.[36] In addition to children, young women formed the bulk of factory workers. In Stockport nearly half of all cotton workers (aged ten to sixty-nine) were female in 1851. Moreover, 40 percent of all workers under thirty were female, while females accounted for 20 percent of all those in their twenties.[37].

In contrast to the female workforce of York, there were barely any domestic servants in the textile towns. Only 3 percent of the population over age fifteen in Preston in 1851 were servants and apprentices. Young women in mill towns were most often mill girls. Older women not in factory work did ply the trades of their counterparts in Amiens and York, however. For there were large numbers of women in the petty trades and in unskilled casual labor of all types. For the most part, however, female workers in the textile towns earned wages in factories. In Roubaix, Stockport, and Preston, mechanization and the concentration of industry in factories created "modern" jobs for women.[38]

A MINING/METALWORKING TOWN: ANZIN

It would be a mistake to assume that all industrial cities resembled textile cities. Although tenements and factories might line their streets and smoke blacken their buildings, mining and metalworking centers created relatively few jobs for women. In Montluçon, Rive-de-Gier, Carmaux, and Anzin, the labor force was chiefly male, for the type of industrial employment available tended to exclude women as workers. Audiganne wrote in 1861 that Rive-de-Gier was a "paradise for women" since they did not have to work but could live on the earnings of a father or husband. If women did work, it was outside of heavy industry.[39]

The coal-mining and metalworking center of Anzin, France, is an example of a type of industrial city different from Roubaix or Preston. Located in the department of the Nord, some forty miles south of Roubaix, Anzin began to develop as a coal center in the eighteenth century. Anzin's real expansion began, however, after the 1850s as the demand for coal increased in France. Migrants poured into the area, and by 1866, only one-third of all males had been born in the city. By the 1860s the straight road through the valley of the Lescaut River, going from Anzin to Condé, was lined with small settlements of workers' houses, clustered around coal pits. Writing of his city, a poet echoed the thoughts of Roubaix's bard:

> Your name is black, Anzin, as black as your face.
> You have your heroes, but where is your history?[40]

The poet well described the appearance of the town. Its red brick buildings were sooty, its urban landscape was overshadowed by the nearby mines. High and black were the *terrils,* the slag heaps near each pit. Wooden pit frames, *chevalets,* housed the wheels, gears, and chains for the pumps and elevators. A large brick building served as the repair shop for the mining machinery. Nearby stood the *corons,* the row houses with small gardens which the company built for its workers. Some 37 percent of the miners employed by the Anzin company lived in this kind of housing.

The city of Anzin in 1866 consisted of 1,727 households, living in 1,422 houses: 7,283 persons. One-third of the male labor force worked in the mines. The mines employed 526 men and boys and 57 females, mostly girls.[41] There were many kinds of jobs available at the mines. Women, for the most part, worked on the surface, sorting and cleaning coal. In the pits, girls as well as boys pushed wagons and hauled coal, doing the exhausting work so excruciatingly described by Zola, as in the following passage, where Catherine is showing Etienne how to work as a hauler:

> She was obliged to show him how to straddle his legs and brace his feet against the planking on both sides of the gallery, in order to give himself a more solid fulcrum. The body had to be bent, the arms made stiff so as to push with all the muscles of the shoulders and hips. During the journey he followed her and watched her proceed with tense back, her fists so low that she seemed trotting on all fours, like one of those dwarf beasts that perform at circuses. She sweated, panted, her joints cracked, but without a complaint, with the indifference of custom, as if it were the common wretchedness of all to live thus bent double.[42]

After 1874, women and girls were restricted by law to surface work only.

The 1872 census for Anzin shows that coal mining employed a smaller portion of the labor force than it had in 1866. Even in 1866, in addition to the mines, a nail factory employed 291 men and boys. The pits near the city were being exhausted and new mines with miners' housing were located outside the city limits. The combined mining and metal/machine sectors, however, employed 49 percent of the labor force. A considerably smaller proportion of the labor force (23 percent) than in Roubaix was female. Married women, however, were a slightly larger proportion of the labor force than they were in Roubaix. (See Figure 4–8.) Over half of all female workers were in petty commerce and dressmaking. 14.4 percent of the women with listed occupations kept cabarets and cafés, 33.7 percent of them were dressmakers. Of the married women workers, 55 percent were to be found in these categories of work. Most married women who worked in Anzin, then, worked in household-related activities, which could be combined with domestic responsibilities. In Anzin, as in Roubaix, there were opportunities for children to work. But in Anzin employment existed primarily for boys.

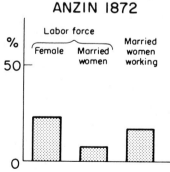

Figure 4.8   Levels of Female Employment

More than 50 percent of boys aged ten to fourteen in our sample were employed.

Table 4–4 contrasts the labor forces of York (1851) and Anzin (1866). The differences in male and female employment follow from the different economic structures of the two cities. In York, men and women were concentrated in craft manufacture and the retail trades. Twice as large a proportion of women were domestic servants in York, because the mixed economy had many more households which could afford to hire servants. In Anzin, households such as those of miners could little afford to hire a servant girl. Such households also had daughters and wives not otherwise employed to perform household tasks. Most interesting of all is the contrast between the sex ratios of the labor forces of the two cities. In York, the ratio was 219, that is, there were two times as many male as female workers. In Anzin, the ratio was 655. Anzin was a city of male workers.

TABLE 4–4.   Comparison of Labor Force: York and Anzin (in percent)

	York, 1851		Anzin, 1866	
	Male	Female	Male	Female
Modern manufacturing and				
extractive industries	8.9	1.1	74.0	35.8
(of which mines)			(35.2)	(23.0)
(of which textiles)				(2.1)
Agriculture	9.9	2.1	6.1	2.1
Building	11.9	0.1	4.8	0
Transport	7.6	0.5	1.8	0
General labor (unspecified)	6.1	1.6	—*	—*
Domestic Service	3.5	58.9	3.1	26.2
Public service and professions	9.4	5.8	1.8	4.0
Other manufacture (craft) and				
commerce	42.7	29.9	12.3	27.8
Total number in labor force	11,225	5,129	1,491	248

*No figures given.
SOURCES: Anzin Census of 1866, Summary Table, ADN M 473.27; Armstrong, *Stability and Change*, p. 45.

WOMEN WORKERS IN CITIES

Occupational opportunity varied greatly in different types of cities during the nineteenth century. Table 4–5 shows clearly that women's

TABLE 4–5. Female Labor Force in York, Roubaix and Anzin

	Women Workers as a Percentage of Females over 10	Percentage of the Female Labor Force in		
		Domestic Service	Craft and Shop	Manufacturing
York (1851)	33.4	58.9	29.9	1.1
Roubaix (1872)	34.5	14.8	15.1	54.5 (textile)
Anzin (1866)	7.8	26.2	27.8	35.8 (of which 23 percent in mining)

SOURCES: Armstrong, *Stability and Change*, p. 45; 1872 sample of nominative list for Roubaix; 1866 occupation summary of Anzin.

work-force participation varied with the availability of female jobs. Roubaix's textile industry recruited female employees. In York there was work for women in the more traditional sectors while in Anzin, the opportunities for work were overwhelmingly for men.

From this table and other information we also can discern similar patterns of women's employment in urban settings. First, the vast majority of female workers were young and single. Mill girls, domestic servants, and garment workers were all primarily single girls. In York, 58.9 percent of all women workers were servants, an occupation which required that a woman be single and, usually, young as well. In Stockport, as we have noted, most female operatives were under thirty years of age. Various studies of textile towns in Lancashire indicate that most women workers were between sixteen and twenty-one, and some 75 percent were single.[43] In Roubaix (1872) 69 percent of women workers over fifteen were single. Similarly in Anzin (1866), the occupations which had the largest percentages of working women were those in which young, single women worked: domestic service and mining. (By 1872, in Anzin, the pits were farther from the city proper. The proportionate importance of coal miners in the population had declined, and although the main industries of the town had predominantly male work forces, a commercial sector had developed which employed many more women as dressmakers or keepers of cafés than in 1866.)

Second, whatever the predominant employment of a city, most married women workers were clustered in areas of traditional employment. In York they were retailers and petty traders; in Anzin, too, they were small shopkeepers, dressmakers, and seamstresses. In Roubaix, however, most married women workers held factory jobs. In 1872, when occupations were recorded more precisely by the census, 17.5 percent of married women worked and more than half of them (54 percent) were in textiles. Similarly, in Preston, Anderson found that married women did work in factories. The demand for women workers was so great, the opportunities and wages for men so low, that in Roubaix, Preston, and Stockport, married women entered the mills.

In Preston, "23 percent of children under 10 who had a co-residing father had working mothers; almost exactly half of these mothers worked in factory occupations." The unique characteristic of women's work in textile cities was the fact that in these cities, with their high demand for female labor, married women worked in factories. Nevertheless, even in Preston, Anderson also found that many married women worked at home running a small provision shop or rooming house. Others were charwomen and day laborers. In the Preston sample for 1851, 26 percent of married women earned wages. And "well over a third of all working wives ... were employed in non-factory occupations." Anderson adds that many more were in "irregular" occupations which were not recorded in the census.[44]

The kinds of jobs women held depended to a large extent on the particular economic structure of a city. But, whatever the specific work, single women dominated the ranks of female wage earners. Married women workers were proportionately fewer, and they were usually found in areas of traditional employment, in irregular and casual labor, except in the textile cities.

5

Demographic Change

Long-term demographic changes accompanied structural shifts in the economies of Britain and France, and they helped shape the context within which women's work and family activities were performed. Demographers refer to these changes as a "demographic transition," a process as far-reaching and important for the history of populations as industrialization was for economic history. The demographic transition involved a change from the high mortality and high fertility characteristic of preindustrial societies to patterns of low mortality and low fertility. But the process of change took place in two steps. First, mortality declined while fertility remained high or even increased, thus accelerating population growth. Then, as mortality continued to drop and as first child and then infant mortality fell sharply, fertility began to decline as well, slowing rates of population growth.[1]

THE DEMOGRAPHIC TRANSITION IN ENGLAND AND FRANCE

As Figure 5–1 shows, the timing of the demographic transition differed in England and France. In both countries the rate of population growth had increased by 1780. From a rate of growth of about 0.22 percent per year from 1700 to 1755, France moved to an annual rate of 0.5 percent between 1775 and 1801. In England, population grew about 0.33 percent annually between 1700 and 1780; 1 percent a year between 1780 and 1801. But while England's population continued its expansion well into the nineteenth century, French population growth slowed down after 1820.

In both countries a drop in the death rate contributed to population growth. By 1750, in England and France, the epidemics of plague and

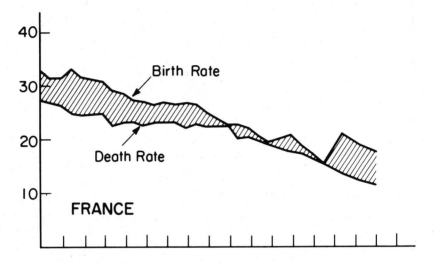

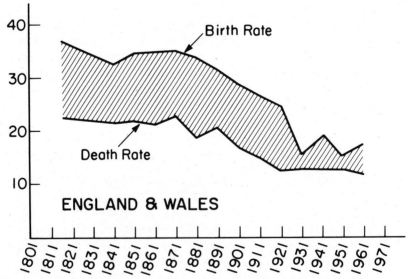

Figure 5.1   Crude Birth and Death Rates for Britain and France, 1750–1960

Source: B. Mitchell, *European Historical Statistics, 1750–1970*.

the widespread famines, which previously had decimated the populations of towns and villages, had disappeared. Local records, upon which eighteenth and early nineteenth century studies are based, show an end to the great peaks of mortality so typical of earlier periods. In France, crude death rates fell from 28.2 in 1801–10 to 19.4 by 1901–10. Similarly, in Great Britain, the rates dropped from 22.4 in 1838 to 18.2 by 1900. Age-specific death rates show that the life expectancy of younger people between ages five and nineteen improved most markedly in both countries. On the other hand, infant mortality remained high until the twentieth century.[2] Nonetheless, the decline in deaths of children and teenagers affected the figures on expectation of life at birth. While in the early eighteenth century, British life expectancy at birth had been about 30 years, by 1850 it was 40.3 years for males, 42.8 years for females. In France, the figure was 35.6 in 1801–1805; 49.1 in 1901–1915.[3]

Differences in the birth rates of each country account for the differences in rates of population growth. In England the birth rate remained high, reaching a peak in 1862–78 of 35 births per thousand. It began to decline after 1879, and, from 1896 on, the average birth rate was below 30 per thousand. In France, in contrast, the birth rate had fallen from a pre-Revolutionary high of 36–37 per thousand, to 33, by the first years of the nineteenth century. By the 1850s, as a result of the deliberate use of birth control, it had fallen to 26 per thousand.[4]

A consequence of the differences in the evolution of the birth rate in Britain and France was a different age distribution of the population of each country. The low birth rate in France meant that its population aged in the nineteenth century as compared with the British population. From the mid-nineteenth century on, in contrast to Britain, a smaller proportion of the French population was under twenty years of age and a much larger proportion was over forty, as table 5–1 shows. Smaller proportions of young persons in childbearing age groups, of course, contributed to continuing low birth rates. And both the low birth rates and the smaller numbers of employable young people probably kept French women working for longer periods of their lives. The age structure of the French population, and its low birthrate, in other words, may have contributed to the higher aggregate rates of women's employment in France as compared with Britain.

Marriage patterns changed, too, in the course of the demographic transition. The age at which couples married fell and the number of people who ever married increased. By the twentieth century, more people married, and married younger than had done so in the eighteenth century. This was true much earlier in France than in Britain. Between 1830 and 1885, the average age at first marriage fell in France

TABLE 5-1. Age Distribution per Thousand Females[*]

		1851	1871	1891	1911	1921
England/Wales	0-20	444	445	441	428	309
	20-40	313	309	308	328	327
	40-60	168	178	169	193	249
	60-80	70	71	72	79	118
France	0-20	353	348	346	342	290
	20-40	311	302	299	302	307
	40-60	326	228	224	231	251
	60-80	101	110	118	123	128

[*]Females only are used to reduce the effect on age structures of male war deaths.
SOURCE: Philippe Ariès, *Histoire des populations françaises* (Paris: Editions du Seuil, 1971), p. 203.

from 25.5 years to under 24. By 1901, some 42 percent of French women aged 20–24 were married, as compared to only 25 percent in Britain.[5] (Table 5–2) These differences clearly contributed to the higher participation rate of married women in the French labor force, since there were fewer single women in the pool of employable women.

During the nineteenth century, then, France's demographic development differed from Britain's. France had lower fertility, an older age structure, a lower age at first marriage and higher rates of nuptiality. In Britain similar patterns emerged only late in the nineteenth and during the twentieth centuries.[6] The demographic characteristics meant there were important aggregate differences in the reproductive lives of French and British women. French women married earlier than their British counterparts, but they also bore fewer children and ended childbearing at an earlier age. Hence reproductive activity involved less time, leaving more time for employment. In the aggregate, the occupational and demographic structures of France combined to em-

TABLE 5-2. Percentages of Women Never Married in Three Age Groups in 1901

| | Ages |||
	20-24	25-29	45-49
Britain	73	42	15
France	58	30	12

SOURCE: E. A. Wrigley, *Population and History*, p. 223.

ploy more women and more married women than were employed in Britain during the nineteenth century.

Patterns of fertility, mortality, and nuptiality varied considerably for different social and economic groups within each country. If we are to gain insight into the experiences of particular groups of people, we must probe beneath national aggregates and examine the evidence contained in scattered studies of specific cities, regions, and occupational groups. The generalizations we can make on the basis of these studies necessarily are limited. But we have used the studies to describe some aspects of the demographic history of rural and urban working-class families during the late eighteenth and early nineteenth centuries. This description will provide the context for our analysis of changes and continuities in working-class women's family roles during the early stages of industrialization.

MARRIAGE AND NUPTIALITY

Historical demographers differ in their assessment of the impact of industrialization on marriage patterns. Although the decline in the numbers of propertied peasants and craftsmen removed some economic constraints on marriage, there was no sudden or universal drop in the age at marriage of propertyless couples. The comparative experience of Britain and France also cautions against a simple correlation between proletarianization and early marriage, since it was France, the nation of small peasant proprietors and shopkeepers, that earlier experienced a drop in marriage age. Evidence from local studies, moreover, suggests that the ratio of men to women in a particular city strongly influenced age at marriage as well as nuptiality rates. And differences in religious beliefs and practices also affected matrimonial decisions.

Yet the local studies do show that expanded occupational opportunities, changes in the household organization of work, and permanent migration to cities did affect marriage practices. In some cases, the age of marriage fell. In other situations sex ratios kept the age at marriage high, but courtship and parental supervision of marriage changed. In yet other instances couples substituted "free unions" for legal marriage. On the other hand, older patterns persisted among children of craftsmen or peasants who had property to transmit.[7]

The practice of delaying marriage until a couple had access to resources continued most strongly in situations where parents had property which children waited to inherit. The folklorist Arnold Van Gennep, citing evidence from various regions in France, noted that peasants engaged in very long courtships. "The girls are not in a hurry, and, as long as they don't need a housekeeper to help run a farm, the boys take a long time in deciding. In matrimonial matters . . . peasants are slow to act."[8] In the Limousin region of France in the 1850s parents still negotiated their children's marriage contracts, and the age at marriage was high even though couples did not set up their own households, but lived with the parental family, usually the groom's. For men, the average age at first marriage was thirty-one in the department of Correze, for women, it was twenty-five.[9] Michael Anderson's evidence from Lancashire indicates that in rural areas with agriculture based on small farms, the age at marriage was higher than it was either for landless agricultural laborers or for industrial urban workers. Independence came late because "the age at which a farmer's son could marry was largely determined by the age at which he could persuade his father to allow him some share from the family plot."[10] (In these areas the age at marriage of the bride was relatively late, too, compared to the age of urban brides.) As late as the twentieth century, some French peasant families delayed or prevented their sons' marriages in order to maintain the family property undivided. Old peasants interviewed by Pierre Bourdieu in the 1960s recalled such experiences in their own lives.[11]

Some areas of mixed agriculture and industry also encouraged late marriage. Families kept children working at home as long as possible in the interests of acquiring some land to help support the group. Dowry requirements persisted in these semi-peasant families, and sons and daughters married late, when sufficient resources were accumulated to provide means of support for them. In Tarare, where the French doctor Villermé found "workers attached both to agriculture and manufacture . . . working at home *en famille* . . ." he calculated that the age at marriage in 1835 was thirty years for men, twenty-seven for women.[12]

Yet the availability of wage labor for both men and women could also alter patterns of courtship and marriage in some rural areas. The importance of economic foundations for a marriage continued, but when wages replaced inherited property, couples became more independent of familial constraint. In the late eighteenth century domestic industry diminished peasant restrictions on marriage in the Swiss highlands. Wrote one observer, "Thanks to the prospects which were opened to the farmer by his labor and that of his children, he no longer set early and anxious limits to the fecundity of his marriage. Previously fathers and sons avoided dividing fairly large and, even more, modest holdings, for they were concerned that each piece nourish its holder. This fear vanished entirely with the diffusion of manufacture and cottage industry."[13] Marriages became more numerous and earlier in these areas and they were contracted "without any thought to material considerations." Contemporaries referred to the marriages of couples "owning neither bed nor household utensils" as "beggar weddings."[14] Weavers in the French town of Vraiville behaved in a similar fashion. They tended to marry other weavers. (In the period 1823–52, in 57.5 percent of weaver marriages, both the bride and groom were weavers.) They also tended to marry at somewhat younger ages than other occupational groups. During the entire nineteenth century (1803–1902) the average age at marriage for males was twenty-five; for females, twenty-three. A girl's skill as a weaver, perhaps possession of a loom as well, substituted for a dowry. "Capital in land or movable property . . . was less important for the establishment of the couple than the ability to work possessed by both protagonists."[15]

In cities, examples of delayed marriage could be found during the nineteenth century. The skilled barrelmakers of Bordeaux in the period 1844–56 continued the practice of earlier generations of craftsmen, marrying only when they had established their mastery of the trade, in this case at age twenty-six. Corporate endogamy was very high as well. In some two-thirds of all weddings in which the groom was a barrelmaker, the father of one of the couple was also a barrelmaker. Brides were younger than their husbands, twenty-three years old on the average. But an important difference existed between girls born in Bordeaux and those who migrated there. The native women were, on the average, twenty-two years old at marriage, presumably because their fathers provided dowries for them. Migrant brides, on the other hand, had an average age of twenty-six, undoubtedly because they had to work and save a dowry of their own.[16] In Amiens, in 1851, there was a similar age difference between native and migrant brides.[17]

Among domestic servants, the practice of accumulating savings for marriage was widespread. Many of these rural girls acted according to older assumptions which required that a girl have a dowry. Le Play cited numerous examples of young women who had gone to the city to amass the required dowry, hoping in some cases to return home and marry someone who had inherited land. Sometimes a young man and woman together migrated to a city, he seeking work in a trade, she in domestic service. They married only after having saved money to set up a household.[18]

The age at marriage varied a great deal in different cities as a result of the availability of certain types of jobs for young people and, consequently of differing sex ratios. In the city of York, the sex ratio for people aged twenty to thirty-nine years was 1,191 women to 1,000 men in 1851. The age at marriage was relatively high. Among laborers in York,

the mean age at first marriage of men was 25.4 years, of women, 24.4
This was lower than the mean for white-collar workers and for "middling" working-class couples. Armstrong has concluded that there was
"prudence at all levels, but especially at the highest."[19] Yet in the textile
city of Preston, where women outnumbered men, the age at marriage
was also relatively high.[20] In the French textile city of Mulhouse, Villermé reported in 1830–35 that the average age at first marriage was
twenty-eight for men, twenty-six for women.[21] Another indicator of age
at first marriage is the proportion of women under twenty-five married.
In York (1861), this was 33.8 percent, in Preston 35.5, in Roubaix 34.4.
This low proportion married under age twenty-five confirms a relatively high age at first marriage. Nevertheless, the rate of eventual
marriage in midcentury textile cities was very high. In mining districts,
early marriage for women was more typical, and the proportions of
women ever married was higher as well.

The occupations available in cities affected not only the age at marriage, but the chances that a woman would ever marry. In industrial
cities rates of marriage were higher than in the artisanal/commercial
centers of Amiens and York. In Roubaix, in 1861, 12.4 percent of
women aged forty-five to fifty-four were single; in Preston, in 1851, the
figure was 10 percent; while in Anzin (1866) it was 11.8 percent. In
contrast, at Amiens in 1886, 24.3 percent of women aged forty-five to
fifty-four never married; at York the figure was 16 percent in 1851. The
higher percentages in Amiens and York stem in part from the fact that
jobs in those cities tended to draw single women who had to remain
single if they were to continue working.[22]

FREE UNION AND ILLEGITIMACY

Taken alone, the ages at and rates of marriage are not always good
indicators of changes in marriage practices since they were affected by
sex ratios in particular areas. Other kinds of evidence, however, indicate that parents with no property were unable to prevent a child's
marriage, since wage earning gave him or her a certain degree of
economic independence. Moreover, for migrants to cities at least, there
was greater autonomy in the choice of a spouse than had been possible
in village communities. And among some groups, couples did not marry
at all, living together in what contemporaries called "concubinage."
These free unions had existed in the past, but they seem to have increased in England and France during the nineteenth century. At Mulhouse, Villermé noted large numbers of free unions, or "marriages à la
parisienne." These unions, especially those between workers in the

same trade, might be "durable, often very happy," and the parents did not abandon their children.[23] At Reims in 1836, "a large number [of textile workers] live in concubinage . . . many remain attached [to one partner] for life."[24] The demographer Bertillon estimated in 1880 that the proportion of free unions to legal ones in Paris was as high as 1 in 10. He described the couples as functionally married. Their "durable associations" were probably "inferior to legalized marriage, but far superior to remaining single or engaging in debauchery."[25]

We have no systematic data on free unions. Observers of working-class life thought they increased during the nineteenth century, but their reports are unreliable. They rested on impressionistic accounts, not careful surveys of marriage records and household composition. In addition, the observers frequently underlined their calls for reform with appeals to the moral standards of the upper classes. The poverty of urban life, they argued, created economic and social instability and immorality as well. The stories of an increase in free unions thus served to illustrate the prevalence of immorality and to distinguish working-class morals from those of the upper classes. As such, they may have greatly exaggerated the extent of free unions among workers.

It is thus uncertain whether or not more couples lived together without marrying during the nineteenth century. The data exist, however, to show that illegitimacy rates definitely changed. Local studies show an increase in illegitimacy in cities particularly, but also in some rural areas starting about 1750. The rise in illegitimacy indicates an increase in stable and unstable unions among the lower classes. On the average, neither Britain nor France experienced the skyrocketing illegitimacy rates and ratios which were characteristic of German and central European countries, but there was nonetheless a clear increase. French cities had higher illegitimacy ratios (illegitimate births/100 total births) than did rural areas; in England, the opposite tended to be true, that is, rural illegitimacy ratios were higher than urban.[26]

In both countries, urban illegitimacy rates reflected the fact that lying-in and foundling hospitals were located in cities. These attracted rural women to a city to give birth to or to abandon their babies. In addition, the presence of large numbers of single women (particularly servants) away from the families and communities which customarily supervised marriage and courtship meant a greater incidence of seduction and abandonment (unstable unions) and hence illegitimacy. Stable unions, too, seem to have been more common in cities. These were unions of long duration which had not been legalized since no property was at stake, and since (in France at least) it cost money to get married. Obtaining a marriage license and procuring the necessary papers involved fees which workers could not or did not want to pay. A report to the French National Assembly, in preparation for the Law of 1850, which provided financial and administrative assistance to "indigents" wishing to marry, detailed the difficulties workers might face. They had to have four or five different kinds of documents. Until 1846, they had to pay to get each one. Moreover, migrants were required to write for the documents to local officials in their hometowns. Many, of course, even if they were literate, could not write that kind of letter. These people might legalize their relationships when, for example, charitable societies provided assistance. In France, from the 1820s, the Society of Saint-François-Régis and the Society of St. Vincent de Paul helped procure papers and paid required fees, in an effort to moralize working-class life. Many of those who married under the societies' auspices had lived in stable unions for as long as twenty years.[27] They had not married earlier because there was neither property to protect or transmit, nor any need to establish a son's blood right to enter a skilled trade.

High rural illegitimacy ratios in England, as compared to France, stemmed from the predominance in the agricultural work force of landless wage earners. The sexual relationships of such men and women were not governed by the rules of the peasant economy, which required that marriage had to wait for material possession of land and that courtship and marriage were subject to family and community surveillance and control rather than to individual whim or desire. While peasant families would see that their daughters married the man who made them pregnant (and it was unlikely that any daughter became pregnant by an unacceptable man), a landless family had little to say about its daughters' suitors and did not have the resources to force marriage. So, although there was increased illegitimacy in both France and England, the continued importance in France of the peasantry kept down rates in the countryside as compared with the cities.

This discussion is not meant to imply that free unions became a norm among wage earners; rather their existence and the fact that they seem to have increased between 1750 and 1850 is but one example of how the processes of migration and proletarianization could affect marriage practices. Among the increasing numbers of wage-earning families, most people continued to marry, but the rules of courtship and marriage were different from the rules of marriage under the family economy.

BIRTH AND FERTILITY

There is no agreement among demographic historians about whether fertility actually increased during the late eighteenth century. It is clear, however, that birth rates remained high in both Britain and France and that after 1820, the French birth rate began to fall. The fall in the French birth rate is attributed to the deliberate use of contraception, probably coitus interruptus, by French peasant families particularly.[28]

In the late eighteenth and early nineteenth centuries, as in earlier periods, couples began to have children soon after they married. Those who married at young ages, of course, bore more children than those who married later, but there was no universal pattern of early marriage in the first decades of the nineteenth century. Changes in adult mortality rates may have had the most important impact on fertility. If fewer marriages were broken by the death of a spouse, more children would be born.

Infant and child mortality also declined somewhat by the early nineteenth century. The greater number of children who survived to adulthood created the appearance of increased fertility, since their presence meant that the household was more crowded and that parents had more mouths to feed. Indeed, it seems to have been the survival of such children that led French peasants, anxious to keep the family property intact, to limit the size of their families.

Although infant mortality was lower than it had been in the past, rates remained high during the nineteenth century, particularly in crowded urban neighborhoods. High rates of infant mortality kept fertility high for the same reasons as in the past. The death of an infant meant that a nursing mother stopped nursing and hence ovulated earlier than if she had continued to nurse. The fact that families continued to lose significant numbers of children in infancy justified the continuation of strategies of high fertility.[29]

FERTILITY IN INDUSTRIAL CITIES

Within both England and France, industrial cities had high birth rates, higher than those either in commercial and administrative cities or in rural areas. Table 5–3 shows these differences clearly. The high birth rates of industrial cities led contemporaries to recall Malthus's fear that wage earners were "improvident," that they bred without considering the consequences of their actions, and that their large families impoverished them further.

An examination of occupational opportunity and demographic structure in these cities, however, leads to a different kind of explanation. Job opportunities in mines and textile mills attracted young worker migrants. The occupational structure of the industrial towns of Roubaix

TABLE 5–3.   Crude Birth Rates (Births per 1,000 Inhabitants); Selected Cities in France and England

Anzin	1851: 38.4	Preston	1851: 34.8
	1861: 37.9		
Roubaix	1861: 42.8	Stockport	1851: 36.5
	1866: 44.8		
Amiens	1851: 33.5	York	1841: 28.8
	1861: 26.2		1851: 31.4
France	1851: 27.1	England and Wales	1841: 32.2
	1861: 26.9		1851: 34.3
	1866: 26.4		

SOURCES: For Great Britain, Census of Great Britain, 1851, Vol. II, and E. Elderton, *Report on the English Birthrate*, p. 56; for France, B. Mitchell, *European Historical Statistics, 1750–1970*, p. 128; Anzin, registers of birth and death, 1851, 1961; Rapports du Maire, Roubaix, 1861, 1866; *Bulletin Municipale d' Amiens*, 1851, 1961 (Authors' calculations from raw data.)

and Anzin had different patterns of female employment. In both cities female workers were primarily single women. The major industrial employment in each town also had favorable opportunities for young male workers. Sixty-two percent of male mine workers in Anzin were under thirty. In Roubaix 81.6 percent of female textile workers and 49.3 percent of male textile workers were under thirty. Men and women had relatively short work lives in both the mining and textile industries where jobs were not only sex-typed, but age-specific. The age structure of occupations in both towns attracted young migrants who then married and had children. These children could begin to earn wages at a fairly young age. There was little reason, given these jobs for children, for families to limit births. (In Amiens, on the other hand, crude birthrates were lower because many women in childbearing age groups were unmarried, for they were servants.) High birth rates in the industrial cities thus reflected the composition of the population—many young couples with children—and not necessarily more children per couple. The concentration of these families in crowded tenements, crawling with children, undoubtedly led observers to believe that birth rates among workers had risen. Rather, young populations and job opportunities for young workers kept birth rates from falling.

The high fertility of the industrial cities is confirmed by other measures than crude birth rates. Table 5–4 gives fertility ratios for several of the cities under review. The fertility ratio compares children under

TABLE 5–4.   Fertility Ratios* (Number of Children under 5/Number of Women Ever Married, Ages 15–44)

Anzin	1861:	.827	Amiens	1851:	.619
	1872:	.913 (sample)		1886:	.279
Roubaix	1861: 1.1169		Stockport 1851:	.822	
	1872: 1.095				

* This measure counts only surviving children, so it underestimates true fertility.
SOURCES: Anzin, Roubaix census samples; Stockport 1851, Amiens 1851, Chudacoff and Litchfield, "Towns of Order and Towns of Movement"; Amiens 1886, *Bulletin Municipale d'Amiens*.

five to the number of women who ever married, aged fifteen to forty-four, at one point in time. This measure underestimates true fertility, since it counts only children surviving, not children ever born. This table confirms the comparative crude birth rates in table 5–3. The new industrial cities have much higher rates than the older city of Amiens. In both tables, Roubaix has the highest fertility. Why, although both were industrial cities, was fertility higher in Roubaix than in Anzin?

First, when we compare the two cities we find that in Roubaix a larger proportion of the female population was of childbearing age. In 1861, 33.6 percent of Anzin's female population was aged twenty to forty-four, as compared to 38.9 percent in Roubaix. Crude birth rates were higher in Roubaix than in Anzin partly because of the age structure of the female population.

Second, the proportion of textile workers' families in Roubaix's population was greater than the proportion of mining families in Anzin's population. Opportunities for children to work in textiles undoubtedly drew large families to Roubaix. And such jobs, if not an incentive to reproduction, at least did not discourage high fertility. Mining and textile families tended to be large. The presence of proportionately more industrial families in Roubaix probably contributed to its higher fertility ratios.

A third factor stemmed from different mortality rates in each city. Infant mortality rates were far higher in Roubaix than in Anzin. High infant mortality leads to higher fertility for reasons we have discussed in Chapter one. Rates like these meant that parents' expectations in nineteenth-century industrial cities that many of their children would die were completely realistic. Although older children were surviving to a greater degree than they had in the past, wage-earning families did not limit fertility. Anticipation of death continued to influence family planning. Moreover, among such families in Anzin and Roubaix, surviving children represented future family wage earners.

DEATH AND MORTALITY

Despite the increase in life expectancy, mortality patterns varied considerably for different economic and social groups. Upper-class families in both countries were healthier and longer-lived than were the rural and urban poor. But among working-class families, too, there were important variations. Certain occupations lowered adult life expectancy. Conditions of life in the urban slums of industrial textile cities led to appallingly low life expectancies and high rates of infant death. In Roubaix, in 1873–76, infant mortality was 239 deaths per 1,000 live births, far exceeding the French national average of 201/1,000 in 1870.[30] (Table 5–5)

Although plagues and epidemics no longer wiped out whole families and towns, premature death was still a frequent occurrence in the households of the lower classes, particularly in cities, but in many rural areas as well. One estimate, based on the life expectancies cited above

TABLE 5–5. Infant Mortality Rates (Deaths of Infants under One per 1,000 Live Births)

Year	France	England/Wales United Kingdom	Year	Roubaix	Anzin
1840	162	154			
1850	146	162	1856–60	—[†]	119
			1861–65	213	161
1860	150[*]	148	1866–71	239	137
			1872–75	239	136
1870	201[*]	160	1876–80	234	119
			1881–85	207	114
1880	179	153			
1890	174	151	1891–95	212	123
1900	160	154	1896–90	213	129
			1902–05	188	109
1910	111	105			
1920	123	80			
1930	84	60			

[*] Figures for France in these years undergo territorial changes.

[†] Figures not available for Roubaix.

SOURCES: B. R. Mitchell, *European Historical Statistics, 1750–1970* (New York: Columbia University Press, 1975), pp. 127–133; R. Felhoen, *Etude statistique sur la mortalité infantile à Roubaix et dans ses cantons* (Paris: Vigot, 1906), p. 12. Rates for Anzin calculated from Etat civil birth and death registers.

for 1850, suggests that only half of all infants born would survive to age fifteen without either dying themselves or experiencing the death of a parent. Fewer than 10 percent of these infants would survive to age fifteen with both parents and all siblings alive.[31] Not until the development and diffusion of health measures in the twentieth century did the death toll of working-class families decline.

These, then, were the demographic conditions which helped shape women's patterns of work during the first half of the nineteenth century. The frequency of early death was somewhat diminished. Fertility remained high for most groups, and illegitimate birth rates increased. This increase, and high fertility in industrial cities can both be traced to increasing proportions in the population of landless, wage-earning workers.

6

Women in the Family Wage Economy

Early industrialization did not create dramatic changes in the types of jobs women did. Yet the changes associated with economic and urban growth did alter the location of work and increased the numbers of women working for wages. Most significant, in fact, was the spread of wage labor which accompanied industrialization. The decline of the household mode of production meant that women more often worked away from their homes. The concentration of certain jobs in specific regions or cities, moreover, drew young rural women farther from home than their predecessors had gone to find employment. For increasing numbers of women, as well, the essence of work was earning a wage. Since they were members of family wage economies, their work was defined not by household labor needs, but by the household's need for money to pay for food and to meet other expenses, such as rent. In the family wage economy the interdependence of family members and their sense of obligation to the family unit remained strong. The importance of family membership and family ties continued. As in the past, daughters and wives worked in the family interest. The old rules of the family economy continued to operate in new contexts. But changing conditions, and particularly the spread of wage labor, began to change the relationships of daughters to their families as well as the allocation of married women's time among their productive and household activities.

We do not mean to suggest that all lower-class families were family wage economies. The household mode of production continued among

French peasants and among some English and French craftsmen. In 1860, the French reporter Audiganne described weavers' cottages in the countryside outside Rouen:

> Here, the life of the family is rooted in custom: father, mother, sons and daughters spend all day around looms, producing together, each according to his strength. . . . The fruits of their labor and daily expenditures are shared by all.[1]

Agricole Perdiguier, recalling his early-nineteenth-century childhood on a farm in France, wrote that his father made everyone work, even the girls and "especially the two oldest . . . Madeleine and Babet worked with us, like men."[2] The French sociologist Frédéric LePlay collected numerous case histories from the 1850s through the 1870s which document the continuation of the family economy among English and French workers' families.[3] Nonetheless this mode of production and family organization was on the decline in both countries.

The family wage economy was an increasingly prevalent form of family organization. The wages of family members formed a common fund which paid for expenses and supported the group. A twentieth-century observer described the family wage economy among the poor of London in 1908. She called it a "joint family."

> Joint households are perhaps the most distinguishing feature of domestic life among the poor; there are few homes in which no trace of the system is to be found. . . . The joint household is only tolerable so long as it maintains an accepted head, and each member pays the mother a sum to cover all expenses and shares in the common meals.[4]

The composition of the household no longer was dictated by a need for household laborers, as in the family economy, but by a need for cash. The balance among wage earners and consumers in the household determined family fortunes. Reybaud, the French commentator on the work and family life of the popular classes, first described what Seebohm Rowntree was later to call the "poverty cycle." Family prosperity or poverty, wrote Reybaud, was closely tied to family composition. When a couple first married, they prospered, for both worked for wages. But after the babies came,

> the household was full of young children who needed supervision, cost money, and brought none in. Pregnancy and lactation diminished the resources the wife could contribute. The man carried the common burden practically alone. As the children grew, this situation improved; between

8 and 15 years of age, they stopped being a burden and became a resource; now all hands were occupied, and as small as their wages might be, they added a supplement to the budget that could not be disdained.[5]

When the children moved out to set up their own households, the parents were again on their own. The parents' wage-earning ability declined, sickness and other crises overtook them, and misery often ensued again. The need to balance wage-earners and consumers in the household underlay many of the decisions about women's work and domestic responsibilities in the family wage economy.

DAUGHTERS IN THE FAMILY WAGE ECONOMY

In the family wage economy a daughter's work continued to be defined by the needs of her family. Young children worked as soon as they were able to, and they were socialized to the notion that the family interest required their participation. As daughters grew older, family circumstances and the existence of job opportunities initially determined the type and location of their work.

In both countries there were legal requirements for the education of children by the 1840s, but they were ineffective for the most part. After the English Factory Act of 1844 the numbers of factory children attending school did increase because the law forced manufacturers to educate their child employees for several hours a day. One report indicated that between 1843 and 1846, the number of children under twelve in factory schools rose from 9,316 to 15,781. Yet there were inadequate public facilities for education in cities like Manchester. One study estimated that the majority of children in Manchester "picked up some schooling between 3 and 12 years of age at irregular intervals. . . ."[6] But, for the most part, they remained uneducated. In addition to the lack of facilities, however, were family pressures on children to earn money. If their labor was not needed, children might go to school, but when jobs were available or money was short, children were sent to work. As late as the 1880s, a rural schoolteacher's log book reflected family priorities for children: "Pretty good school on Monday," he wrote, "but many girls away in the afternoon for a report was spread that some gleaning was to be had. . . ." And in Manchester, children out of school might be "idling in the streets," or more likely, "selling matches; running errands; working in tobacco shops. . . ."[7]

In France, statistical surveys show an increase in the number of children receiving primary education after the Guizot Law of 1833. In addition, a law of 1841 required factory owners to school their young employees. Girls and boys took advantage of expanding public facilities, and their schooling was reflected in a marked aggregate decline in illiteracy (as reflected in records on military conscripts and in a bride's or groom's ability to sign his or her marriage act).[8] Yet, among rural and urban working families, literacy levels remained low because children were sent to work instead of to school. From the 1840s on, school inspectors found their efforts frustrated by parental indifference or opposition to school. In the woolen textile center of Reims in 1867, an official reported that children's education was sacrificed for "the material interest of the family." An anguished schoolteacher in the industrial Nord reported in 1861 that "at ten, sometimes at nine or eight, even the weakest children are stolen from us to be sent to ruin their bodies and lose their souls in the dust and disorder of workshops for a few sous a day." In the 1870s factory children in the Nord who attended classes for workers did not learn to read or write but only to memorize the catechism. One estimate suggested that half the workers in the city of Roubaix "know nothing, or almost nothing."[9] School inspectors' reports for rural and urban districts in the department of the Somme in 1870 show that about 600 children aged seven to thirteen received no instruction whatsoever. Twenty-six percent of the children aged twelve to sixteen were totally illiterate.[10] The inspectors consistently blamed the children's parents, and called for measures to educate them to the necessity of sending their children to school. "Guilty of the most criminal indifference, parents, who themselves have no education . . . think that their children will be satisfied if they have only as much as they do. . . ."[11] A more sympathetic inspector reported that "one of the principal causes of school non-attendance stems not exactly from the indifference of parents for instruction, but from poverty, from the need above all to satisfy those material interests which affect [their] very existence."[12]

Whether or not family circumstances permitted a daughter to take advantage of increasing educational opportunities, it is clear that the family's economic needs had first priority and that these shaped her future. The Parisian father of two daughters hoped that "their work, soon to be paid, will come to aid in the expenses of the household." A girl, about to leave school and become a seamstress, explained her action this way: "I would like to have continued my studies, in the end to become a teacher. But I am not the only child in my family and it is necessary that I work."[13] Juliette Sauget, born to an agricultural laborer in 1866 in a rural hamlet in the Somme, went to work when she was very young. She became a servant on a neighboring farm, she recalled, to help "ease the burden on my poor parents."[14]

Like Sauget, daughters of propertyless families in rural areas of England and France typically became domestic servants. Two-thirds of all domestic servants in England in 1851 were the daughters of rural laborers.[15] We have no comparable national figures for France, but local studies reveal a similar pattern. Close to three-fifths of servants in Versailles in the period 1825–53 came from the countryside. So did more than half of Bordeaux's female servants. In Marseille, "virtually all of the city's domestic servants were immigrants." Of all domestic servants married in Marseille in 1864–71, 57 percent were migrants from rural areas. Similarly, in Melun in 1872, 54 percent of domestics were either migrants from rural areas or foreigners.[16] The Sauget family is again illustrative. After several years as a farm servant, Juliette Sauget moved with her sister to Amiens, where they both found positions as servants. Another sister entered service in Paris. The Sauget family had four daughters, three of whom became servants. On the other hand, four of its five sons remained in the country.[17]

Parents sent their daughters into service because such jobs were plentiful. The expanding middle-class populations of cities created more demand for household servants. No special skills were required of young girls. They performed a variety of household tasks, ranging from cleaning and caring for children to general assistance in family shops or businesses. The fifteen-year-old servant living in the household of a Parisian launderer in 1852, for example, helped in the laundry as well as with household chores.[18] In addition, service offered a relatively secure form of migration for a girl. Having a place to live and food and clothing eased the adjustment of a rural girl to city life.[19]

Indeed, when employers in other trades sought to attract rural girls, they often offered living conditions similar to those available to servants. In the garment trades, boardinghouses lodged young seamstresses. Enterprising women with some capital employed and housed such girls in such large metropolitan centers as London, Paris, and Toulouse, where the garment industry concentrated.[20] The setup facilitated migration to a city, for it solved the problem of housing and food for a newly arrived girl. And, of course, it permitted employers to supervise closely the work of their employees. Forty-five women lived in one boardinghouse in Toulouse according to the census of 1872. Thirty of them were seamstresses. Of these, twenty were girls between the ages of nine and fifteen. Most of the others were under twenty. Only four of the women came from Toulouse itself. Fourteen came from rural communities in the Haute-Garonne (the department in which Toulouse is located). The remainder came from rural areas in other departments.[21]

Factory owners, too, attempted to recruit young rural girls by providing dormitories and supervision for them. They convinced parents that their establishments were safer than those which provided no living arrangements and they argued that the conditions in their factories resembled the best aspects of domestic service. "A working girl admitted to La Seauve," wrote one observer of a factory-dormitory, "finds a family rather than a factory," and he compared her existence there favorably with her rural home.[22] Some French employers, such as M. Bonnet of Lyons, hired nuns to supervise the moral conduct of his employees. The Protestant Emile Koechlin hired "an honest family to supervise them. . . ." Bonnet even went as far as arranging marriages for his girls. Their wages, which he saved for them, constituted a dowry. Another French *patron* provided a dowry of 100 francs for any working girl in his employ for five years.[23] Paternalism of this sort enforced factory discipline, but clearly also it was aimed at recruiting country girls by offering conditions of protected migration similar to those associated with domestic service. This is not to say, of course, that all rural girls migrated to "protected" jobs. Nor were most employers paternalistic. Instead, the existence of such opportunities spoke to what was probably a widespread parental concern about helping a daughter find a secure and safe situation.

Parents' interest in their daughters' jobs came not only from concern for their safety, but from economic motives as well. In the context of rural impoverishment, of tiny holdings inadequate for the support even of a couple, or of landlessness, children became increasingly vital resources. A daughter's departure served not only to relieve the family of the burden of supporting her, but it might help support the family as well. A daughter working as a servant, seamstress, or factory operative became an arm of the family economy, and arrangements were made to ensure her contribution even though she did not live at home. Sometimes emotional ties were sufficiently strong for girls to maintain contact with home. They visited their families, they brought other family members to live with them in the city, and they sent money home. The heroine of Samuel Richardson's novel *Pamela* may have amused many a real servant with her impossible devotion to purity and virtue. But they would have recognized the motives that led her to send money to her parents: "so that you may pay some odd debt with part and keep the other part to comfort you both."[24] Marie R., daughter of a blacksmith in the French department of the Meurthe, entered domestic service in 1836, first in a large town near home, then in Paris. Her goal was to save some money in preparation for marriage. LePlay tells us that she managed to acquire savings and a small trousseau during seven years of work, always, however, "sending a part of her earnings to her mother."[25]

Marie R. was undoubtedly exceptional. Most girls like her probably sent home only an occasional sum. The need to save a dowry, the instability of jobs in domestic service and the garment industry, and the low wages and periodic slumps of the latter particularly, made it unlikely that a girl would have money to spare. It may be, too, that distant daughters more conscientiously maintained ties with their parents when they hoped to receive a share of the family property. Landless parents, on the other hand, had little material hold on their daughters. Yet even when they left home, some daughters seem to have continued or tried to continue to contribute to the family. They remained active members of the family wage economy even though they did not directly draw on the family fund.

In some cases parents formalized a working daughter's responsibility to the family wage economy by arranging to receive her wages from her employer. The familiar option of sending a daughter into service thus was transformed into a family-wage-earning activity. The servant girls working at the Flahaut farm in France during the period 1811–77 are an example of this practice. M. Flahaut did not pay them directly. Instead he sent food or clothing or coal to their parents. Sometimes he paid the rent on their farms. Hubscher tells us that for certain farmers who rented their lands, daughters' contributions were "indispensable, without them it would have been impossible to cultivate the fields they rented." He adds that the "financial support" of the daughters for their parents "seemed absolutely normal" to both parties. It represented a "strong family solidarity which required a mature and economically independent child to contribute to the support of its relatives."[26] Similar arrangements for parents to receive a daughter's wages were made with factory owners, especially those with paternalistic living accommodations. Writing of what he considered "an excellent practice," Villermé described such arrangements in Sedan in 1840:

> Young people under 20 are not admitted to these *pensions* without the consent of their parents, to whom they always give all their wages until they reach 15 and sometimes even 20; they are allowed to keep their overtime pay, however, and spend it as they wish.[27]

Parents might even pay a small sum for a daughter's "apprenticeship" and then receive her wages when she began to earn them. Such control was difficult to maintain, of course. Many a rural girl obviously did lose contact with home. Long-distance migration made it inevitable that a departing daughter might eventually be lost to the family wage economy. What is surprising is that ties of family and the sense of obligation to one's parents long persisted among working girls.

WAGES OF WORKING DAUGHTERS

When working daughters lived at home their wages were unquestionably a part of the family fund. The mechanization of agriculture in England created demand for agricultural laborers in some areas and whole families hired themselves out in "gangs." The growth of domestic industry, too, during the eighteenth century, and of textile factories during the nineteenth, often permitted families to keep daughters at home who might otherwise have gone into domestic service. Domestic industry involved all family members and spinners were in particular demand. William Radcliffe recalled how in the 1760s his family moved from agriculture to textile production as their land holdings diminished:

> The principal estates being gone from the family, my father resorted to the common but never failing resource for subsistence at that period, viz, the loom for men and the cards and hand-wheel for women and boys. He married a spinster ... and my mother taught me (while too young to weave) to earn my bread by carding and spinning cotton, winding linen or cotton weft for my father and elder brothers at the loom, until I became of sufficient age and strength for my father to put me into a loom.[28]

Daughters in these families spun, and their work was highly valued.

Rudolf Braun's masterly study of the coming of domestic industry to the mountain highlands of Switzerland analyzes the process in close detail. Even though it is geographically outside the limits of this book, it is the best available illustration of a process that occurred in England and France as well. Many families, Braun says, found their small property enough to sustain them only when they combined farming with cottage industry. Moreover, weaving enabled landless families to live and even to buy some land. Daughters especially were desired, for they were useful as spinners and family production needed more spinners than weavers. "Only wait until your daughter grows up," a neighbor told a young girl's father, "then you can put some money aside." The sister of this girl "wove at home until her fortieth year, putting all her earnings into the common pot."[29] At that age, with no savings for a dowry, she had no hope of finding a husband. Her occupational title and marital status were synonymous. Although the term *spinster* designated both a woman who spun and an unmarried woman as early as the seventeenth century in England, the term gained currency as scores of young women performed that task and as examples like that of the Swiss daughter became increasingly apparent during the late eighteenth century.

Spinning and weaving also provided additional revenue for the children of farmers who hired themselves out when farm work slackened. These children, says Braun, lived at home and paid their parents a weekly or monthly allowance from their earnings. Parents were assumed to be entitled to a child's contribution. Notions about the responsibility of all members of the family economy coexisted with the actual or potential economic independence of wage-earning children.

These practices existed too among early factory families. The reorganization of textile production into factories often drew many families to new mill towns. Instead of single daughters migrating, whole families often moved to take advantage of manufacturers' appeals for "families chiefly consisting of girls," or "healthy strong girls."[30] Wrote one witness to the migrations in 1834:

> Families had to come in from different places and learn to spin . . . and whole families together were sent for by the masters. . . . People left other occupations and came to spinning for the sake of the high wages.[31]

Men or widowed mothers brought their families to Manchester, to Preston, and later to Roubaix, sometimes hiring themselves out in family units. The family labor unit was simply transferred from the farm or from cottage industry to the factory. In some cases, the father made an agreement with a mill owner to receive all the wages for the work of himself and his children. Sometimes the family actually worked as a group; in other cases members were dispersed throughout the factory. Either way they were considered and apparently considered themselves members of a team, earning a family wage. The following two examples illustrate the practice.[32] In John Howlett's agreement at the Greg and Sons mill in the 1830s, the employers agreed to pay Howlett 24s a week the first year; 27s the next. The 24s which represented his work and that of his four children was itemized this way:

	Age	S D
John Howlett	38	12 0
Mary Ann	16	4 6
Ann	14	3 6
Celia	12	2 6
Timothy	10	1 6
		24

John Stevens made a similar arrangement for himself and his four children:

	Age	S	D
John Stevens	38	12	
Elizabeth	18	6	
Rebeckah	14	3	6
James	12	3	
Mary	10	1	6
		26	

Studies of factory account books in this period repeat listings like these again and again. Workers were grouped in families. The wages, though itemized individually, were paid to the parent of the employed child. In each of these cases daughters were working in the factory at the age girls usually went into service. Moreover, they were not independent workers, but family wage earners whose parents had hired them out.

Factory-based textile production came later in France, but there, too, the practice of parents hiring out their children prevailed. Daughters became piecers, reelers, spinners, and weavers. In Tourcoing in 1853, fathers and children worked in teams at the factory. The Métigy family, for example, together earned 46 francs 50 a week. This money was earned by the father, Joseph, forty-three years old, a wool spinner, by his three sons, aged sixteen, fourteen, and thirteen, and by his twenty-one-year-old daughter Elisa.[33] (The children were all piecers.) In Amiens, records from the 1840s show that children began work as early as six or seven. Most child workers were aged ten to fourteen. Parents obtained working papers for their children at the age they ordinarily might have begun to assist at home or have entered apprenticeship or domestic service in the past.[34] The difference was that the children entered a factory instead of a household and that they earned wages which went directly to their families. Children became, in the words of a commentator writing in 1863, "a resource." "The little they earn is added to the modest income on which the family lives."[35]

The need for a child's earnings and the expectation that the child worked for the family could make parents harsh taskmasters. Jeanne Bouvier remembered that when she was eleven her mother found her a job in a silk factory outside of Lyons. When her pay was not raised after several weeks of work, her mother beat her, assuming she was at fault. Parents clearly had no small part in introducing their children to the work discipline of early factories. The pressures inside the factories were compounded by parental demands. In 1865, the Prefect of the

Cantal described family discipline at the factory. Children began work at twelve years of age. "They work under the direction of and on account for their parents. . . . As a result, they are not directed by the employer and his agents in matters which concern the maintenance of order and discipline. Their fathers and mothers are their masters . . . during working hours."[36]

Daughters were a particularly important resource for families in mill towns, for they predominated in the labor forces of such cities. The availability of the work and the certainty that daughters' wages would augment the family budget led parents to send their daughters to the mills instead of into domestic service. Indeed, middle-class families complained because of a scarcity of domestic servants in mill-town areas. In Stockport, for example, 53 percent of all single women were factory operatives in 1851, while only 7.8 percent were servants.[37] In Roubaix, where 81 percent of single women over fifteen worked, over half of them were textile workers and 10 percent servants.

These working daughters contributed to the family fund even when they were hired as individuals (rather than as a member of a team headed by a parent). Indeed, a commentator noted in Lancashire that "the children that frequent factories make almost the purse of the family. . . ."[38] In mill towns most working children with parents residing in the city lived at home. Young boarders were usually migrants and orphans. When daughters (and sons) lived at home, they turned over all or some of their wages to their parents. This was true not only in textile towns, but also among urban and rural families whose children entered other trades.

Daughters of craftsmen in old cities such as Paris and London, York and Toulouse, who did not help with production at home frequently had entered trades in the seventeenth and eighteenth centuries, but apprenticeship usually involved living in another household. The decline of many artisan industries in the nineteenth century deprived daughters of a role in household-based family production and sent them into the labor market. For some, training still did involve living in another household. Thus the daughter of a Sheffield knifemaker moved to her grandmother's house, when she was ten, to learn to sew. "She is no longer a cost to her family, but she is not paid for her work."[39] Increasingly, however, the organization into small workshops of the garment trades and of such other trades as artificial-flower making, bookbinding, food production and canning, matchmaking, and metal polishing made it necessary for wage-earning daughters to continue to live at home. Even highly skilled workers such as Parisian dressmakers, who received three years of training before beginning to earn wages as high as 100 francs a month, lived at home, and paid their parents board.[40] Lacemakers in small towns like Le Puy lived at home paying board to their parents as soon as they began to earn money.[41] In Roubaix, young people gave their parents "almost all of their wages."[42] Young seamstresses paid some or all of their wages to their parents depending upon family need and particular practices. Le Play described an Englishwoman who began sewing at age fourteen in 1826. "Her parents permitted her to keep some of her earnings and when she married eight years later, she had accumulated a small dowry." On the other hand, the daughter of a locksmith, born in 1822, became a tailor to assist her family. "Since they took all of her earnings, she possessed no savings when she married." The sum she turned over might vary, but a daughter's work often helped round out the family wage. The fourteen-year-old daughter of a Parisian dockworker gave to her parents all of the money she earned ironing. In 1856, this amounted to one-fifth of the family's total annual income.[43]

Not only did parents expect contributions from their daughters, but daughters expected to contribute to the family fund. We have cited evidence already that indicates the daughter's sense of responsibility to her family. The analysis by John Schaffer of a questionnaire given in 1877 to thirteen-year-old girls about to graduate from Parisian primary schools documents this conclusion. Schaffer found that 71 percent of the 2,000 girls replying said they intended to become manual laborers. Of these, 62 percent planned to become seamstresses. Their occupational plans reflected the city's occupational structure, for in 1872, the garment industry was the second largest employer of Parisian women. Many of the girls indicated they had chosen their jobs because their families needed money. Many also indicated that their parents, and particularly their mothers, had chosen their jobs for them. Schaffer has concluded that "family-oriented responses were most highly associated with those girls from working-class families who chose manual work." Wrote one girl, "Seamstress is the profession that *maman* has chosen for me, and I know that she only wants that which can be most useful for us." Another girl explained her reasons for working this way:

What happiness, when I will have earned my first money to place it in my mother's hands and say to her, "Yours *Maman*. It isn't much, but it will help you."[44]

The tone of this response may have been exceptional, but its substance was not. Most rural and urban girls were sent to work in the family interest. Indeed, in some cases, family strategies developed which relied heavily on the continuing financial contributions of daughters. And, as in the past, daughters expected that this would be the case. Close family ties and the emphasis on the primary importance of the family unit continued in the family wage economy, even when there was no property to bind children to their parents.

CHANGING FAMILY TIES

Yet once a girl embarked on her work, family ties changed. Daughters could become more independent of family controls than in the past. The location of work away from home, and the fact that they earned individual wages and lived in cities instead of small village communities, increased the autonomy of working-class daughters. Even if a working girl lived at home, her relationship to her family might change. As a wage earner she learned about money and what it could buy. She could contribute her wages and her knowledge to family decisions and she might claim some measure of influence over the allocation of family resources since her wages were part of those resources. The other side of independence, however, was vulnerability. Working girls earned low wages and their employment was often unstable. The loss of protections once provided by family, village community, and church increased a girl's economic and sexual vulnerability.

Gradually, despite the continuity of family values among rural and urban working families, changes in the organization of production and in the structure of occupational opportunity for women altered the relationships between parents and daughters during the nineteenth century. The results were both more choice and more risk for young women.

The availability in cities of jobs for women meant that girls were not restricted to domestic service. Often service was only the first step, a means of entry into the city. When a girl lost one job, she pursued others. Many a young woman moved back and forth between domestic service and the numerous unskilled trades in a city. Many of the garment trades were seasonal, too, forcing girls to seek other kinds of work in slack periods. When Charles Benoist reported on women's work in the Parisian garment industry, he wrote:

> Yes, indeed, her budget balances. But with winter comes cold, with unemployment hunger and with sickness death. Irresistably, the question arises, How do these women who number in the thousands in Paris, how do they live? Live! Ask rather how they keep from dying.[45]

One grim alternative in Paris, London, and many other cities was prostitution. In 1836, Parent-Duchâtelet found that the majority of prostitutes in Paris were recent migrants. Almost one-third were household servants and many initially had been seduced by promises of marriage and then abandoned, pregnant or with an infant. He also remarked on the instability of women's employment which drove them to prostitution when they could not find work.[46] Prostitution, in other words, was a form of employment for women when all else failed. Prostitutes in London told Henry Mayhew in the 1850s that unemployment had driven them to their "shame." One, the mother of an illegitimate boy, explained that she could not find work as a seamstress, and so to keep herself and her son from starving she was "forced to resort to prostitution." Another described the "glorious dinner" her solicitations had brought. And a woman explained her prostitution to the anonymous author of *My Secret Life* as her way of enabling the rest of the family to eat: "Well, what do you let men fuck you for? Sausage rolls?" "Yes, and meat-pies and pastry, too."[47]

Prostitution, of course, was a desperate measure. In good times, cities offered women a range of opportunities. Many left a first job in domestic service and found other kinds of employment. Indeed, for some women, the possibilities for earning money in the city, if not actually unlimited, must have seemed extensive to young girls from the country. And these jobs presented an alternative to returning to rural towns and villages where work was scarce and did not pay as well.

The existence of alternatives also meant that girls could reject the physically more demanding work of a farm, for example, and remain in the city, an option which earlier had not been available on the scale it was in the nineteenth century. Le Play's account of the experiences of the daughter of a small propertied peasant in the countryside of Champagne captures the process as it affected one family in 1856.

> For the past two years, the oldest daughter has been sent to Châlons for part of each year, as an apprentice in a *maison de lingerie.* She is not paid, but receives her food free. After her apprenticeship is finished, she will be a domestic in a house in some nearby city. When she is at home, she helps her mother with her needlework and replaces her in caring for the household. [The mother was a seamstress and her earnings were "one of the principal resources of the family."] . . . but since she began going to the city, she does certain farm chores only with great repugnance. Despite her resistance, however, she is forced to thresh and to collect manure along the road.[48]

One cannot but conclude that, for this daughter, permanent departure was only a matter of time.

Another aspect of women's occupations, of course, was that, except in textile factories, wages were low and employment was unstable.

Accumulating enough money to send home must have been impossible for many girls. Their consequent inability to help their families undoubtedly diminished contacts and ties with their former homes.

Whether or not they maintained contact, rural girls increasingly did not return home. The migration of the domestic servant, which in the past was often temporary, increasingly tended to become permanent. Even when a girl did keep in touch with her parents, the fact that she did not intend to return home loosened family ties. Rural girls no longer used their work as a means of gaining resources which would enable them to become farm wives. Instead they became permanent urban residents.

The life of Jeanne Bouvier, born in the department of Isère in 1865, provides an interesting example of this urban migration. Bouvier entered the gamut of female occupations, ultimately settling in Paris as a seamstress. As a child, she lived on a farm, which her father had inherited from his parents. He was both a farmer and a barrelmaker. Jeanne helped her mother in the fields, but her particular job was to watch the cows. Since that chore left her hands idle, her mother made her knit as well. When she was ten, her parents sent her to a convent for ten months to learn her catechism. She also learned to read and sew there. When she was eleven, in 1876, her father's trade was ruined. Phylloxera, the disease of grapevines, devastated wine production in southern France and hence the barrel trade. M. Bouvier could not support his family with the farm alone. All family members now had to earn wages, so Jeanne's mother found her a job in a silk-spinning factory, where she worked thirteen hours a day spinning the silk threads that supplied the Lyons silk-weaving industry.

After a time, she was sent back to the country to live with her maternal grandfather, then to another silk factory. The work made her ill, so a cousin in Vienne found her a job with some truck farmers. There she was a maid of all work, caring for their children, their cows, and the vegetable gardens. During a visit to her godmother, Jeanne complained of her unhappiness, and the godmother told her not to go back to the farm. The next day she helped the fourteen-year-old Jeanne find a job in a silk factory. This one housed its employees, so Jeanne had a place to live as well. From her wages she bought her own food. (She does not say whether she sent money to her mother, or whether she was expected to do this.) Then her mother wrote and told Jeanne that she had to come with her to Paris. The girl resisted, but her godfather reminded her of her obligation to obey (though her mother had no means of enforcing the demand). "If your mother wants to take you to Paris," he told her, "you must go with her. If you had no parents, you would not have to go."

Jeanne's mother had found jobs for them both with a brush manufacturer in Paris. (Small businesses of this kind proliferated in cities.)
Jeanne was an apprentice, her mother a maid of all work. After eight
days, both mother and daughter were fired and received no pay. Some
cousins helped get them jobs, first as domestic servants. Then they
found Jeanne a position as a hatmaker. Family auspices of this type were
important for Jeanne during the early stages of her working life. Without the network of kin and godparents, she would have had great
difficulty finding work.

Jeanne lived with her cousins for a while, paying fifteen francs a week
for room and board. She felt they spent too much on food, so she saved
some money, bought a bed, and rented a room. From this point on,
Jeanne Bouvier was on her own. She had fewer contacts with her family
and rarely saw her mother. She made friends with some other girls her
age who rented rooms in the same building, and she basked in the
warmth of the friendships they established. When the hat trade
foundered, she sought another job. She took on piecework and sewed
garments in her room, but found that paid too little. So she entered a
shop as a seamstress, gradually working her way up to the highest levels
of skill. By this time Jeanne Bouvier had become a Parisian.[49]

Permanent migration of this kind was encouraged not only by expanded opportunities for women to work in cities, but also by changes
in families themselves. When families became wage-earning instead of
producing units, family members no longer shared a common interest
in the property which guaranteed their livelihood. Of course, daughters
often had left home in the past and so had not always worked on the
land or in the shop. But the resources owned by their parents had had
an important influence on their futures in the form of dowries or marriage settlements. When parents had no resources but their own and
their children's labor power, they had few long-term material holds on
the loyalties of their children. Of course, material considerations were
not the only basis of parent-child relationships. The values of the family
could and did transcend the conditions which gave rise to them. (Jeanne
Bouvier accompanied her mother to Paris simply because she was her
mother.) Membership in a family also provided many nonmaterial benefits. Again, Bouvier's experiences are illustrative. Family ties helped
her find jobs and negotiate difficulties whenever she moved. But the
absence of property often meant there was no reason to return home;
indeed, it precluded such a return even if a child desired it.

Even when daughters remained at home, as happened more often in
urban families, or when whole families migrated to textile towns, the
fact that they earned wages had important effects on family relationships. Family members were no longer bound inseparably to a family

enterprise. Instead, the goal became earning enough money to support the minimal needs of the group. The family wage was the sum total of individual members' contributions. Inevitably, in this situation, contributions became individualized. One might work with other family members, but this was not necessary. Children earned wages in textile factories, whether or not they worked alongside their parents. Spinners could hire children who were not their own as reelers and piecers. Ultimately, the wage (however low or unfair) represented remuneration for an individual's labor.

The family now required a financial contribution from each member instead of simply his or her work for the household. Although evidence indicates that children followed the rules of the older family economy, parents had no ultimate means of forcing them to do so. Of course, social and emotional pressures existed, and many a mother must have embarrassed her delinquent child in the manner of the young French barrelmaker's mother who demanded in 1866 that the union punish his employer for underpaying her son. An investigation revealed that the boy had not given his mother all his wages, and he was surely ridiculed, if not condemned for his action, by his peers as well as by neighbors and relatives.[50] In addition, parents could order their children out of the house, thereby depriving them of some of the services, as well as the food and shelter, for which their contributions paid only in part. (There were great advantages to living at home. Mothers, particularly, performed important services for family members that would have cost more if provided by strangers.) But the need of parents for their children's wages made this a risky course. Indeed, parents seem to have tried to keep wage-earning children at home as long as possible, even if this sometimes meant caring for a daughter's illegitimate child (until the costs of its care outweighed the advantages of her contributions).[51]

A teen-aged child's ability to earn wages and, particularly in textiles, the importance of those wages for the family meant that children were no longer as dependent as they once had been on their parents. In fact, the roles might sometimes reverse, with parents depending increasingly on their children. In textile towns, for example, where work was most plentiful and most remunerative for young people in their late teens and early twenties, according to Michael Anderson "children's high wages allowed them to enter into relational bargains with their parents on terms of more or less precise equality."[52] "The children that frequent the factories make almost the purse of the family," observed a contemporary, "and by making the purse of the family, they share in the ruling of it. . . ."[53] In France, an observer at a later period bemoaned the decline of apprenticeship training and the easy availability of wage labor for children. As their wages increased and sometimes surpassed their parents', he wrote, children assumed they had the right to a say in family matters. "When the father earns more than his children, he still has the right to his authority; from the day they earn as much as he does, they no longer recognize his right to command."[54] Furthermore, by earning wages a child established a measure of potential independence. She could move elsewhere and still earn her keep. Hence, while the ability to earn wages increased the importance to a family of a daughter's labor, it also created the potential for a daughter to leave home at an early age.

COURTSHIP AND MARRIAGE

Young girls were sent to work in the family interest. Their expectations about marriage, as well as the examples of courtship practices set for them were shaped in a context in which family influence and family control were important. Changes in a family's wealth or property holding and in the type and location of jobs for girls diminished a family's ability to control and to protect a daughter's future.

Migrants to cities were in the most vulnerable situation, for they were outside the context of family, property, local community, and church. Even for city girls, however, suitors were often unfamiliar. A boy's character and family were often unknown. In a small town or within a network of craftsmen in a city, a young man's credentials and character were known. Strangers were suspect. Indeed, when a girl became pregnant before marriage in many communities she was condemned only if the father was a stranger, since local boys could be counted on or compelled to legalize the situation. As suitors were more often strangers to the family, courtship became more autonomous, but also more risky for young girls.

In the city, alliances with men began for many girls as they might have at home, the girls seeking potential husbands, hoping to establish families of their own. They had been socialized to this expectation; indeed many had been sent off to accumulate the requisite resources. The availability of steady wages in textile towns might substitute for savings. Girls in the garment trades, on the other hand, often found their wages barely sufficient for their own support. Indeed employers justified the fact that they paid women half of what they paid men by saying that women's wages were only part of a family wage. In the households these girls came from, subsistence depended on multiple contributions. So, many looked for husbands with whom to establish a family wage economy. "If there is one opinion that is widespread among the popular classes," wrote one commentator, "it is that a single woman cannot earn a living in Paris. . . . A good half of young workers, if not the majority, find themselves with this alternative: to live in privation or to marry."[55]

For some, cohabitation was a prelude to marriage and actually involved an adaptation of behavior customary in many rural villages. Engaged couples had often slept together before the formal wedding ceremony. The promise to marry, since it was not broken lightly in a village context, legitimized premarital sexual intercourse. A reporter for the London *Morning Chronicle* noted even in 1850 that in rural areas the "practice of cohabitation before marriage is almost universal." When the girl became pregnant, the man made "an honest woman of her."[56] In the city a young couple might live together until the girl accumulated a dowry, or some savings. The couple cohabited while trying to save because their joint wages went farther when they shared housing and food costs. A couple might not always share a common dwelling, however, for if the girl was a servant, she would have to live in her employer's household. The requirement that a servant be single also postponed legal marriage for some couples.[57]

Whether on their own or in urban wage-earning families, girls were more autonomous in their choice of husbands than daughters had been in the past. Servants might meet their future husbands on their own in local retail shops. Even when occupational endogamy remained high among couples, as it did in textile towns, parental sponsorship of marriage declined. A bride and groom were more likely to meet at work, apart from any familial influence. And the couple, rather than their parents, set the economic standards and requirements for marriage. Servants, for example, married late and often had substantial savings. The highest-paid factory operatives, on the other hand, married early, presumably so they could launch a family when they were at the height of their earning power.

The absence of the constraints of family, property, local community, and local church increased autonomy, but they also led to the disappointment of some marital expectations. Vulnerability was the other side of autonomy, particularly for migrants. Men did not fulfill their promises because of lack of money, a lost job, the opportunity for work in a distant city, or simply lack of interest. And the women's families were nowhere at hand to enforce the promises. Late-eighteenth-century evidence for Lille, based on women's declarations during childbirth, shows that most unmarried mothers had come to the city as textile workers or servants. Fully 70 percent of these women came from families broken by the death of at least one parent. The men involved were in professions marked by unstable tenure, such as servants, traveling workers, or soldiers. The women were vulnerable: ". . . seducers

could pursue their ends more easily, because they did not fear an aveng-
ing father, often violent, ready to make them pay for the dishonor."[58]
In Nantes, in the late eighteenth century, information drawn from
declarations to midwives at childbirth shows that mothers of illegitimate children were, for the most part, servants and working women.
These women testified that promises of work and of marriage usually
preceded intercourse with the fathers of their bastards.[59] In Aix in
1750–88, and in Lyons in the Years II and III of the Revolution, the
déclarations de grossesse show that illegitimate pregnacies often were
preceded by promises of marriage. One young girl, a hatmaker in Lyons, testified that the hatmaker who visited her "made promises of
marriage which she believed easily because there was no difference in
their professions or their ages."[60] The similarities in their ages and their
jobs became for her a substitute for personal familiarity with the man.
A London needleworker explained her plight in 1851: "He told me if
I came to live with him he'd care I should not want, and both mother
and me had been very bad off before. He said he'd make me his lawful
wife. . . ."[61]

Of course, not all girls found themselves abandoned by their suitors.
Contrary to the impression created by reformers who talked only of the
immorality and licentiousness of industrial cities, most young girls who
became servants or seamstresses or textile workers did eventually
marry. Some married after an initial disappointment. Juliette Sauget,
for example, had an illegitimate child before she married an artisan.[62]
A recent historical study of domestic service suggests, furthermore, that
as many as one-third of all domestic servants not only married, but
managed to attract husbands of somewhat higher status than themselves.[63] But whether they improved or only maintained their economic position by marriage, most working girls did marry. After
marriage they rarely remained full-time workers. Increasingly, full-
time employment was characteristic only for single women. Whether
they worked to help support their families or only to feed themselves,
single women spent most of their time earning wages. When they
married, whatever autonomy they had enjoyed ended. As wives and
mothers, they worked for their new families and much of their time was
spent at home.

MARRIED WOMEN IN THE FAMILY WAGE ECONOMY

Under the family wage economy married women performed several
roles for their families. They often contributed wages to the family

fund, they managed the household, and they bore and cared for children. With industrialization, however, the demands of wage labor increasingly conflicted with women's domestic activities. The terms of labor and the price paid for it were a function of employers' interest, which took little account of household needs under most circumstances. Industrial jobs required specialization and a full-time commitment to work, usually in a specific location away from home. While under the domestic mode of production women combined market-oriented activities and domestic work, the industrial mode of production precluded an easy reconciliation of married women's activities. The resolution of the conflict was for married women not to work unless family finances urgently required it, and then to try to find that work which conflicted least with their domestic responsibilities.

Figures on married women's employment from England and France reflect this clearly. Married women working in factories represented only a small proportion of all female factory operatives and an even smaller proportion of all married women in the labor forces of England and France. At its height, in the 1870s, over one-third of the British textile industry's women employees were married or widowed; but the inclusion of widows overstates the case, since, as we shall see, the position of a widow—the sole support of herself and her children—was not comparable to that of the married woman living with her husband. Moreover, even in the early factory towns, married women tended to become cotton pickers. Cleaning and beating the cotton with sticks was done by hand, not machine, and the pickers worked near but not in the mills. The work was performed intermittently and was not subject to factory discipline. "It appears to have been the custom to allow them to come and go as they pleased. . . . This degree of liberty attracted . . . women whose domestic duties prevented them from leaving their homes for twelve hours a day."[64]

In general, married women tended to be found in largest numbers in the least industrialized sectors of the labor force, in those areas where the least separation existed between home and workplace and where women could control the rhythm of their work. "I like it better than the factory, though we can't earn so much," an English lace-runner told an investigator in 1843. "We have our liberty at home and get our meals comfortable, such as they are." Home work was a typical resource for those who also "have their children to attend to and the meals to prepare. . . ."[65]

In France in the 1860s, where home and workplace were one in the many small-family farms and family-run businesses, some 40 percent of all married women worked. In industrial England, in contrast, in 1851, only 25 percent of married women had "an extraneous occupation."[66]

In France demographic and economic factors combined to bring married women into the labor force. In England there was a larger supply of single women, and the large-scale organization of the economy favored their employment and excluded married women.

The sectors in both countries which tended to employ similar proportions of married women were those created by the expansion of the nonmechanized garment trades and by urban growth, which increased the demand for unskilled, casual service workers. In the needle trades piecework could be done at home and so attracted married women. Census data give us no precise indication of the overall numbers of married women in the unskilled, temporary jobs increasingly available as urban populations expanded. Some women who worked at these jobs did not consider themselves formally employed, while others feared that reporting a job to the census taker would bring a visit from the tax collector. Yet it is clear from our analysis of the censuses of Amiens, Roubaix, and Anzin, and from studies of York, Preston, and Stockport, as well as from accounts by contemporaries that married women in both countries earned wages as carters, laundresses, charwomen, peddlers of food, and keepers of cafés and inns. The Sheffield knifemaker's wife described by Le Play in the 1850s prepared "a fermented drink called 'pop' which she bottled and sold in the summer to inhabitants of the city."[67] She undoubtedly told the census taker that she had no occupation.

Similarly, the numerous women who took in boarders were invisible as a wage-earning group. Local studies only recently have begun to document the prevalence of this practice in many urban areas. Indeed, one study has revealed a striking example of this practice among Irish families in nineteenth-century London. There, a dramatic increase in boarders occurred in households with very young children. This coincided with the mother's withdrawal from the labor force.[68] A formal occupation was replaced by an informal one, and women were able both to bring in wages and to care for their children. Whatever their specific occupation these women earned money and were part of the floating population of temporary or casual laborers which formed the "secondary labor force," the informal job market which escaped official statistics, in nineteenth-century cities. On the national scale there were undoubtedly more married women in these occupations than in textile factories, for example, and therefore more married women in wage- or cash-earning activity than can be derived from national or local censuses. An investigator of women's work in London in the 1890s summed up the experience of a century when she noted that "wherever there is irregular employment, married women will be found amongst the employed."[69]

Patterns of married women's employment reflected employer preferences for workers with no other demands on their time. Single women were more likely to work steadily, for longer periods of time, and without interruptions. Married women were likely to become pregnant and miss work, or their family responsibilities could keep them home. Married women were thus clustered in those jobs which were temporary and episodic, which corresponded to their less certain commitment to wage earning. These jobs were also low-paying, exploiting the usually desperate need that drove a married woman to seek employment and the fact that she had neither the skill nor the organizational support which might command higher wages.

Patterns of married women's employment also reflected household preferences. Men, who could command higher and more regular wages, were the family's primary wage earners. If more money were needed, children would be sent to work. Since the household benefited from the mother's management of domestic affairs and children, she only went to work when need was great, when her husband was unemployed or ill, and when there were no children at home who could work. Figure 6–1 is a schematic diagram of women's work-force participation over the course of the life/family cycle. It smoothes out the big differences between Britain and France in its illustration of the impact of industrialization and urbanization, and of the separation of home and workplace, on women's employment. Full-time work was confined to the years before marriage and, perhaps, to the first year or two of marriage, before children were born. After children were born, women's work followed a more episodic course. Many simply withdrew from wage-earning activity. Others moved in and out of it, depending on family need. This was most often a consequence of what Michael Anderson calls "critical life situations"—crises caused by illness, unemployment, or death of the husband.[70] The arrival of several children could also seriously strain family resources. At this point, too, women sought means of earning some money. Some took jobs outside the home, particularly in textile towns where those were the best-paying opportunities available. Others took on piecework to complete at home. Women workers in the London garment trades followed this pattern into the twentieth century: "Before marriage they go to the shops, and after marriage, if obliged to earn money, take the work home."[71] More often, however, married women with young children improvised cash-producing activities to substitute for full-scale labor participation. As in the past, selling food, doing laundry, and taking in boarders were the resort of urban working-class women. "Mrs. Jennings had been in service as cook in a gentleman's family. [When she married] In order to improve their scanty income, she took in a little washing, and she also washed for myself and fellow lodger."[72] The English straw plaiter Lucy Luck

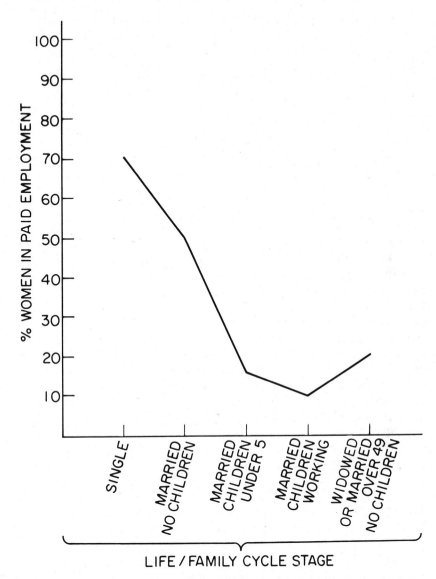

Figure 6.1   Schematic Diagram of Women in paid employment by
Life/Family Cycle stages. France and Britain, about 1850

"was in the workroom part of the time and had [her] work at home the
other part." In the slow season, at one stage of her life she had to find
other ways of earning money. "During that time I have been out charring or washing, and I have looked after a gentleman's house a few
times, and I have taken in needlework. This was before any of my
children were old enough to work. . . ."[73]

As children grew older and found employment, the pressure on their mothers eased. This tended to be the period of lowest wage-earning activity by married women. Old age once again pushed them into the job market. Most crises of illness and unemployment for husbands came at this point, when children had left home and no longer contributed to the family fund. The wife then was the only substitute available for an ailing husband. When he died, she had to become self-supporting. Older women returning to work after long absences took whatever jobs they could find. Their low levels of skill and sporadic employment experience restricted them to unskilled, irregular, and low-paying jobs. Typically, even in textile centers, these were not in factories.

> The unskilled workwoman at the bottom of the social scale . . . is generally elderly, if not aged, infirm, penniless and a widow, she never expected to have to work for a living, and when obliged to do so has recourse to the only work she ever learned to do [sewing]. She is nervous and timid and takes work at whatever price it may be offered her. . . .[74]

Younger widows, with children to support, were in a similar, desperate situation.

Yet despite the fact that their work was irregular, married women were still expected to be family wage earners. The economist Nassau Senior routinely included in his calculations of family income, the wages "of the married labourer, those of his wife and unemancipated children."[75] The French reformer Jules Simon, while decrying factory labor for women, nonetheless admitted in 1861 that "women's work is needed by the family."[76] Le Play found that women's activities were "a significant supplement to the earnings of the husband."[77] His and other calculations indicated that women's earnings accounted for from 10 to 50 percent of a family's income. It is clear, too, that women saw themselves as economically productive. A parish report described the rural woman in England, wife of a laborer, who could find no work because of an economic crisis:

> In a kind of general despondency she sits down, unable to contribute anything to the general fund of the family and conscious of rendering no other service to her husband except that of the mere care of his family.[78]

This sense of an obligation to contribute economically continued among urban women of the working classes. In a factory town, women who did not take jobs were "looked upon as lazy."[79] There was a work ethic held by women in working-class families that may not have been present among their middle-class counterparts. More exploration is needed of the reality or myth of the "idle middle-class woman" of the nineteenth century. But whether they were idle, as the standard accounts contend, or whether they worked hard, as Particia Branca has argued, most seem to have remained at home.[80] Some evidence indicates, for example, that middle-class husbands took on two jobs before permitting their wives to seek work. The cultural values of the middle classes may have prevented married women especially from leaving home to work. No such prohibition existed among the working classes, and though married women may have preferred to remain at home when family finances permitted it, they were expected to earn wages if necessary.

Yet increasingly, the contributions from married women were expected only if the wages of other working members were insufficient for household subsistence requirements. Their productive activity, in other words, became a kind of reserve, a last resort. That it was often used does not contradict the point. It only tells us how precarious were the lives of working families, how unstable or poorly paid men's jobs were, and how vulnerable to illness or death, and therefore to poverty, were even financially comfortable households.

In addition, of course, to internal crises, wage-earning families were subject to the vagaries of the economy. Variations in the price of bread could, as in the past, push a working family over the poverty line. So could cyclical depressions in industry. In Rouen, for example, in 1830, according to one calculation, expenditures on bread reached 130 percent of the earnings of a linen weaver. Two years later, the figure was 200 percent of a cotton weaver's wages in Cernay.[81] A wife who may not have worked in prosperous times sought wages in these difficult years. This imaginary dialogue between some working women and a "Lady," published in *La Politique des femmes* in 1848, captures the contingent quality of a married woman's work:

> *The working woman:* Women's wages have declined everywhere. Our misery is their profit.
> *The Lady:* My dear friend, women's earnings are insignificant. The man is the head of the family and when his wages are good, the woman is happy.
> *Another working woman:* And when the man is sick or irresponsible?
> *Another:* And when women become widows?[82]

DETERMINANTS OF MARRIED WOMEN'S WAGE LABOR

A family's financial need was a function of business cycles but also of the family cycle. In addition to crises which occurred within most working families with unfailing regularity, financial need depended upon a husband's opportunities and his level of wages, the number of dependent children in the household, and the number of family members available to work. These factors, in combination with the occupational structure of the city, produced a number of variations on the pattern of married women's work-force participation.

In Anzin in 1860, before the coal boom which increased wages, the average miner earned 3 francs 25 per work day. The miner was often the only wage earner, at least until his sons followed him to the mine. The fact that miners' families had to survive on those wages alone undoubtedly led the companies to offer a number of fringe benefits to their workers. Free coal was available to all, and low-cost housing was available for at least some workers. The Anzin company's paternalism extended, in certain years of high prices, to buying grain in quantity and then reselling flour to its workers at prices below market levels. Even then, the family budget was strained by the arrival of children. At this point, some wives went out to work, or took on wage work done in the home. Matters improved when "the oldest child goes to work [and] the others soon follow."[83] The kind of work which married women could find—cleaning, or sorting coal on the surface of the mines—paid very little: an average daily wage of 1 franc 55 in 1882. Going out to earn these wages detracted from a wife's ability to fulfill the domestic responsibilities on which her husband depended, and which furthered his ability to earn a wage.[84] Food had to be prepared according to shift schedules; the miner's blackened clothing had to be laundered. The autobiographies of miners' children from England and France recalled how "home life was a burden to womenfolk." "The miner's wife and perhaps the eldest daughter . . . [had] no end of trouble in fetching in the water and heating it on the fire and in cleaning up after the men had their baths and their clothes had been dried." The table was "never cleared" and the fire had to be kept "constantly burning."[85] The vegetable garden and animals a wife raised constituted an important contribution to family subsistence. Hence, unless she "lost her breadwinners," a miner's wife did not usually leave home to earn a wage. Other women in Anzin, those whose husbands worked in the metal industry or were artisans and shopkeepers, were much more likely to work. This group of wives was more similar in its behavior to the wives of Amiens than to coal miners' wives in their own community.

In a city like Amiens, the situation for wage-earning families was not as clear-cut. Men's wages, in artisanal trades, ranged from 2 to 3 francs 5 daily in 1862, but there were no fringe benefits involved. Housing costs were high compared to those in Anzin. In the few textile mills there, men earned a maximum of 2 francs 50 a day. (Only silk spinners earned a daily average of 3 francs.)[86] The availability of domestic house-keeping or laundry work and of a variety of other unskilled jobs made it possible for women whose families needed money to earn it. They tended in the 1850s and 1860s to be wives of the lowest-paid and least permanent male employees. Over the rest of the nineteenth century, the long, slow decline of artisanal trades increased the numbers of families whose wives had to work. Here, as in Paris and London, the garment industry remained a domestic industry in part because of the profitability of large supplies of cheap female labor.[87]

In the textile towns of Roubaix, Stockport, and Preston, demand for women workers was great, and relatively large numbers of married women were drawn into the mills. Jobs for adult males, on the other hand, were scarce; only a few became well-paid spinners. Most of the rest took what unskilled work they could find, and their wives or children supported the family. Ellen Barlee reported from Lancashire in 1862 that

> The temptation [for wives to work] is great; for, so large is the demand for female labour, that fifty women can find employment where the man fails. . . . Thus, it is quite true that many women do keep their husbands and families; the men merely doing such jobbing work as they can pick up.[88]

Married women who worked were most often wives of men in casual or low-paying employment. Engels reported in 1844 that in factories in Manchester only half of the married working women had husbands also in the factories. Moreover, wives of spinners did not work, while those of less-well-paid piecers and weavers did.[89] In the 1890s, Royal Commission on Labour investigators revealed the reasons for married women's work:

> Only about half of the married women cotton operatives were . . . wives of men also employed in the mills. The remainder were married to men in less well-paid and more uncertain jobs, as in Oldham, for example, where it was found they were wives of "outdoor workmen, such as masons, navvies, bricklayers, labourers and such like persons who were unable to find work for more than thirty weeks in the year; thus the women had to go out."[90]

As late as the early twentieth century insufficiency of the husband's wage (combined with the availability of jobs for women) continued to be a primary motive for married women's work in textile factories. In France, as in England, reformers concluded that if owners of mills paid men high enough wages, their wives would no longer have to work.

Jean Jaurès, socialist deputy and member of the investigating commission of 1904, urged employers to alleviate the condition of working-class families by permitting women to remain at home. New machinery could increase the output of individual workers, he observed, but "the wages of the working man, of the head of the family, must be increased, so that what is now a family wage [can be earned by him.]"[91]

Conditions in textile towns were replicated in other centers which had high levels of female employment and only low-paying opportunities for men. In the Staffordshire potteries, for example, an inspector found that "only in 18 percent of cases . . . was there no financial necessity for the wife to work." Indeed "a woman is looked upon as lazy unless she takes her share in contributing to the family income."

> The men and boys appear to be willing to do their part in the domestic work of the home, and it is no uncommon sight to find a man cleaning and sweeping, caring for the children and even putting them to bed in the evening, when the women were engaged in the family washing. . . .[92]

Yet despite the cooperation of other family members, a mother's long absences each day took their toll, particularly on infants. Households with working mothers had relatives living with them who presumably took care of young children. In Stockport, Roubaix, and Preston the incidence of such households was higher than in Amiens or Anzin.[93] Elderly relatives particularly assumed child-care responsibilities. Families with no kin available entrusted infants to older siblings. Some young children were sent to the homes of older women who watched over large numbers of babies for a fee. In France, after the 1840s especially, *crèches* were established usually by city initiative or by religious orders, but they cared for only a fraction of the children who needed care.[94] In any case, babies in these circumstances had to be bottle-fed with animal milk or soups. Because sterilization was unknown, the incidence of digestive disease and death was very high. Infant mortality rates were appreciably higher in areas where mothers worked for long hours away from home. In fact, in Lancashire, where Preston was located, infant death rates declined during the cotton famine created by the American Civil War. Unemployment forced mothers to remain at home. More babies were nursed for longer periods and fewer of them died.[95]

An alternative to bottle feeding, practiced on a large scale in France, was to turn an infant over to a wet nurse. (The reasons for the differences in the scale of this practice in England and France need further exploration. They are surely related first to the larger proportion of married women working in France and also to the availability of a

larger rural population which could serve as wet nurses. Even in
France, however, the custom of wet-nursing was restricted largely to
older urban settings. It was not widespread in the new manufacturing
cities of the North. This may have been a carryover of established ways
in the old cities. New cities did not have the requisite network of
connections with underemployed rural women.) Wet-nursing was
widespread in cities where married women were employed. In Paris,
working women—seamstresses and garment makers for the most part
—hired wet nurses to care for their babies. Villermé described a similar
situation in Lyons and in Sedan during the 1830s and 1840s.[96] If an
infant survived the trip to the wet nurse, often a long distance over
rough roads, if furthermore the nurse had sufficient milk to nourish it
and the other children she took in, and if it survived the other hazards
of infancy under the care of an often indifferent parent-substitute, then
the child was returned to its parents at an age when it could care for
itself. The point, of course, is that many infants never returned. Usually
they died. The cost of procuring a substitute for a working mother was
high in two respects: a portion of a hard-earned wage went to the
caretaker or wet nurse; and the chances of any infant surviving were
worsened. Yet the survival of the family unit took priority over an infant
life. And when need was great and jobs available for them, married
women worked even at the point in the family cycle when they were
most needed at home. As one factory operative explained her return to
work shortly after the birth of a child: "Well, we must live!"[97]

Husbands' wages, however, did not entirely account for married
women's work. The insufficiency of a husband's wage for the support
of the family meant that supplementary earnings were necessary. But
when other family members—children—could earn wages, wives
tended not to work. The availability of children, but also the opportunity for them to find employment, was another influence on married
women's work-force participation.

In Anzin, Roubaix, and Stockport, jobs for children of ten years and
over were virtually guaranteed. Indeed, children were described as
family resources. In the mining town, sons' and daughters' wages were
a supplement that improved a family's financial situation. In Stockport
and Roubaix, children of both sexes were employable, and when they
went to work their mother left the factory and stayed at home. In textile
towns, as we shall see, children substituted for their mothers as family
wage earners. English officials recognized this, and in 1833 legislators
opposing a child labor law argued that "the restriction of the hours of
infant labour could compel the mothers of families to work in mills; a
consequence which is much deprecated as extremely mischievous."[98]
Inspectors seeking enforcement of the 1841 child labor law in France

reported over and over again that families needed the wages of their children. The more callous of them spoke of parental cupidity and ignorance, the more sympathetic described the "imperious necessities of domestic life."[99] Some officials even urged that the law remain unenforced in times of economic depression. Workers, too, complained of the ill effects on the family brought about by the restriction on their children's work hours and on the ages at which they could begin to work. In 1853, a year of high prices and food shortages in France, a teacher wrote a petition to the Prefect of the Aisne for a group of weavers, whose signatures reveal they were barely literate. They asked that children be permitted to work with their fathers at age eight, "temporarily, during these hard years."[100] In hard times, mothers and children both sought work. But whenever possible, and in more stable economic periods, children were preferred to their mothers as family wage earners. Hence the alternating patterns of women's and children's labor-force participation in cities such as Roubaix and Stockport.

Figure 6–2 shows two variations on the pattern of a married woman's work life. The patterns vary according to the economic structure of the city and the possibility of children's work. These graphs show the percentage of families in which wives worked in Anzin and Roubaix in 1872 (solid line) by the age of their youngest child. The dotted line represents the percentage of families with working children (of any age) living in the household. In both Roubaix and Anzin, wives worked most commonly in families where there were no children at home at all. Roubaix, with its excellent opportunities for female employment in textiles, had more childless wives employed than Anzin. In neither Anzin nor Roubaix did wives' work fade away when children under five were in the household. This period, when children were very young, was the time of greatest need for the household. Children were then consumers of food, but seldom contributed wages. The graph suggests that the imperative of need kept many wives working in both cities when they had small children but few wage-earning children. In these industrial cities the priorities of the family wage economy made many wives put productive activity before child nurture.

As the curve of the percentage of families with working children climbed, with the age of the children, the behavior of married women in the two cities diverged somewhat. In Roubaix, the mother's labor force participation dropped rather sharply. It is clear that children and mother were trading off paid work roles. The mother withdrew from market work as the children began to contribute wages to the family. In Anzin, the decline of the labor-force participation of wives is not so steep or definitive. The different forms of wives' employment are important here. In Anzin, the majority of working wives' labor took place in household situations. Women were storekeepers and dressmakers,

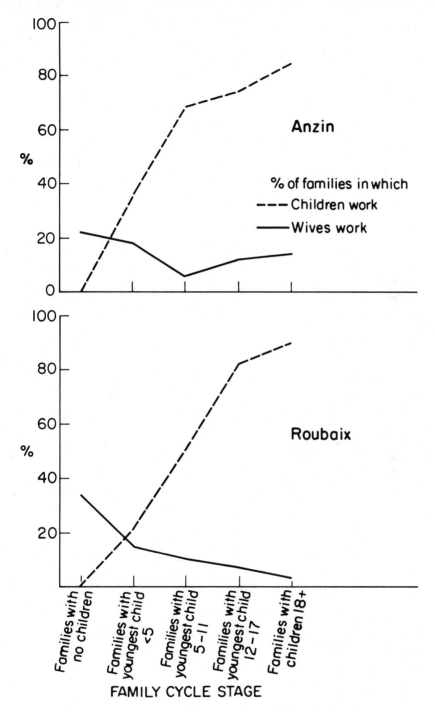

Figure 6.2   Family Patterns of Wives' and Children's Employment: Anzin and Roubaix, 1906

for example. These jobs were not as restricted to the young as jobs in the textile industry tended to be. They also did not require a woman to leave home to do her work. In Anzin, the continuation of home-based work for women made it possible, and indeed likely, for wives to work even if their children were earning wages which contributed to the family fund.

Financial need and family circumstances created different patterns of married women's work in different cities. Particularly where jobs were only available away from home, a married woman's productive role was no longer the complement of her domestic responsibilities, performed continuously throughout her lifetime. Instead, productive activity became a supplementary function, performed sporadically at times of family need and performed more or less intensively depending upon the extent of that need. As in the past, married women's labor power was a family resource. But increasingly, among urban wage-earning families it was considered a reserve resource, to be called upon only in times of financial need. That it was held in reserve did not diminish the importance of married women's wage-earning capacity, for it often meant the difference between survival and destitution for family members. For married women, wage-earning activity away from home became harder to reconcile with household activity. Most women resolved the conflict between home and work by withdrawing from permanent employment, becoming temporary workers when their families' need for their wages outweighed the advantages of their remaining at home and fulfilling economically important, but unpaid, domestic responsibilities.

MARRIED WOMEN: DOMESTIC ACTIVITY

The fact that a family was a wage-earning rather than a productive unit in no way diminished the wife's domestic responsibilities. The family division of labor continued to assign her the management of household matters. Shopping and cooking; making, cleaning, and repairing clothing; and caring for children all took a great deal of time. A woman's expertise in these matters also saved a family money. Men in specialized occupations such as mining had to have meals prepared at odd hours. And their clothing required constant washing and drying. Miners' wives produced meals and services for home consumption and bore many children. The domestic burdens of their lives were particularly time-consuming. When father and children worked in the mines, their schedules were frequently quite different. The miners had to leave the house at 4:00 A.M. They were home by 2:00 P.M. for their dinners. Children and young people who worked the "day" shift, started work at eight and finished at six. The wife and mother of such a family had to cook meals on two different schedules. She also did the wash for the various workers, all involved in the dirtiest imaginable work. The miner-poet son of such a woman wrote that when he was a boy *hercheur* (hauler) in the 1880s, he was often covered with cuts as from the "blows of a razor."

> My poor mother sobbed like the Magdalen
> As she washed my back with black soap.[101]

In a wage-earning family, a married woman provided clothing and a variety of services, including laundry and nursing the sick, but her most important task still concerned the provision of food. When reformers discussed improving the lot of the working-class family, they invariably addressed themselves to the wife. Those urging the formation of cooperative associations for buying food in Amiens in 1879, for example, insisted that their institution could teach the working class wife to economize "because she is in charge of buying and preparing the food for the whole family."[102]

Food remained the major item in a working-class family budget. There is much dispute about whether the diet of the working class improved or deteriorated early in the nineteenth century. It is part of a larger debate about the early effects of industrialization on the standard of living of the working class. But optimists and pessimists agree that most of a family's wages were spent on food. Michel Morineau's calculations for five different types of French working families from 1823 to 1835 reveal a wide range of expenditures. His estimates are only of expenditures on cereals (grain or bread) as a proportion of the earnings of the head of the household. The (often substantial) contributions of women and children to the family budget are excluded, so his figures are inflated. Nonetheless, they give a good idea of where a family's money was spent, and they illustrate the effect of fluctuations in prices on a family's financial situation.[103]

For all five family types there was a drop in the proportion of the man's wages spent on grains over the twelve-year period. Agricultural laborers spent 67 percent in 1823, 55 percent in 1835. Lyonnais silk weavers spent 48 percent in 1823, 39 percent in 1835. Yet the proportions fluctuated from year to year, reaching as high as 90 percent for a Rouennais spinner in 1829. The lowest for any family was 34 percent in 1835. The average for all families during the twelve years was around 55 percent. These figures refer only to grains. When vegetables, perhaps some meat, and beverages are added, close to three-quarters of a man's wages might be spent on the family's food. Rent, fuel, and some clothing took up most of the rest. Budgets from English working families are similar. A Northumberland miner with three sons also working in the mines had a family income of some £5 every two weeks. The family spent £3 on food alone and most of that went for flour. In another family in Suffolk in 1843, some 69 percent of the family earnings were spent on food and rent. Family budgets from the 1840s show that even well-paid skilled workers spent most of their earnings on food, and that many such families were heavily in debt when the price of bread rose.[104] The wife's role as a consumer was thus central to the family's economic well-being. Since almost all money was spent on food and since buying food was her responsibility, she controlled family financial resources.

In these families, as in artisanal and farming households, everyone seems to have acknowledged the mother's managerial role. Her daily efforts provided meals for the household, no quick or simple task in those days. (Families with mothers working away from home lived on soup and bread, or bought cooked food from itinerant street merchants until Sunday, when there was enough time to prepare a proper meal.)[105] One reason, surely, for the married woman's preference for remaining at home was so she could have time to manage the feeding of her family.

In times of crisis, the importance of her role was magnified, her decisions and demands unquestioned. Writing of the problems of unemployment in mid-nineteenth-century England, one contemporary noted:

> I have sometimes thought that a family undergoing such a trial is like a crew at sea, short of provisions, with a limited allowance meted out day by day. Here it is the wife that is captain, she is provider and distributor. The husband under such circumstances commonly leaves all to her, and right nobly does she discharge her part.[106]

Often the "captain" deprived herself of food, so that her husband and children might eat:

> An observation made by medical men, that the parents have lost their health, much more generally than the children, and particularly the mothers who most of all starve themselves, have got pale and emaciated.[107]

Here the continuities with the past are obvious. The centrality of food in the family budget and the mother's responsibility for providing food were still dominant features of working class-family life. The married woman's control over family resources and her self-sacrifice for her family were two sides of the coin of her domestic role.

Even in normal times, there seems to have been little question that the wife should manage household expenditures. Women bought food and clothing, paid the rent, and dealt with the pawnbroker. Recognizing their wives' control over the household, husbands could complain that the women lacked skill and did not know "how to economize." Reformers noted that one detrimental effect of married women's work away from home was to diminish their own domestic abilities (and hence their control over household resources) and worse, to deprive their daughters of the "education" a housewife required.[108]

Management of household finances could take a variety of forms and extend beyond simply spending money. In households where men worked at home, on account for a manufacturer or merchant who supplied raw materials and then sold the finished goods, wives negotiated the amount paid for their husbands' work. At Lyons and Saint-Etienne, in the silk-weaving trades, wives transported raw materials and finished products back and forth. They often carried heavy loads long distances, but they were not simply beasts of burden. They served as "intermediaries between their husbands and the *fabricant.*"[109] When disputes about payment arose "the wives often testified at hearings before the Conseils de Prudhommes; they knew better than their husbands the arrangements agreed upon with the fabricants."[110] Wives of English knifemakers performed similar functions. Indeed, the practice was so common in some trades that when factories replaced the home as the craftsman's location of work, employers continued to pay directly "to the wives the wages earned by their husbands."[111] In other families the wife received all the earnings of her working husband and children, doling out to her husband a small allowance for food eaten away from home and perhaps for wine or beer and tobacco. Describing a Parisian carpenter's wife, Le Play remarked that "to her alone . . . in conformity with the custom prevailing among French workers, are confined the administration of the interior of the home and the entire disposition of family resources."[112]

In still other cases, the husband gave his wife a household allowance and decided how much to keep for himself. (Working children paid an agreed-upon amount, retaining the rest for themselves.) This practice could become a source of dispute between husband and wife in many families, particularly when earnings were high enough to create a small surplus after household expenses had been paid. The writer Denis Poulot captured the tension of pay day for these families in his book *Le Sublime,* written in 1872. The working man feels esteem and fear for his wife, who is "a harsh policeman." "On Saturday, the wages are put on the table, she figures for two minutes and sees that everything isn't there. 'Joseph, 10 francs are missing; you haven't lost any time, I need them.' " At issue was not the wife's right to spend the family wages, but her right to determine how much she needed, her right to decide how much, indeed whether, her husband could spend some money on "his pleasure," which usually meant drink.[113]

Historians have a great deal to learn about the importance of "drink" in working-class life. They have disagreed about whether it was a sign, as Zola portrayed it, of the degradation of working-class life, or whether, as others have suggested, it was a sign of an improved standard of living.[114] More important for our discussion is what the debate over spending meant about relationships and values within a working-class household. Here, too, there are conflicting interpretations and no definitive studies. On the one hand, the drama of payday, as Poulot depicted it, could represent a conflict between the needs of the family, as represented by the wife, and the rights of the individual primary wage earner, in this case the husband. The fact that his wages constituted more than half of the family income in most cases, and that wages were a measurable contribution, may have established a basis for a husband to claim his right to spend what he wished. Drinking in a bar or café was, moreover, a form of sociability for working men. Artisans had long mingled work and leisure. Their bars were occupationally homogeneous, serving as hiring halls and centers of craft information, political organization, and social intercourse. For craftsmen in declining trades, these centers continued in importance as the locus of union organizing and of resistance to changes in their work. For these men, then, money for drinking was an occupational necessity, and, for them, this aspect of trade identification might conflict with family needs. [115]

Among factory workers and unskilled urban laborers, cafés were neighborhood rather than trade-associated institutions. Nonetheless, they might also serve as local centers of social and political contact. Here, too, the conflict between husband and wife might represent a conflict between different kinds of social identification, rather than between individualistic and familial values. Whatever the accurate interpretation, it is clear that when payday disputes arose, they involved issues that were unresolved within the family and not the domination of a wife by her husband. Moreover, as in Poulot's depiction, the husband recognized the validity of his wife's claim and her managerial role. Keeping back some money thus constituted defiance, or an attempt at modification, but not denial of the wife's power of the purse.

In the family division of labor, then, the wife continued to manage domestic responsibilities. Changes in the organization of production during industrialization and the increasing monetization of exchange, however, increased those responsibilities and the demands they made on a woman's time. Most important, perhaps, was the tendency in increasing numbers of urban families for children to remain at home for longer periods of time than in the past, frequently until they married and moved into households of their own. The precise configuration of this pattern varied, of course, but in general it meant that more family members lived in the household, thereby increasing the time required of a mother for domestic chores.

In the past, children of both sexes had often left home between ages seven and ten to enter domestic service or some form of apprenticeship. Among propertied peasants, an heir might remain at home; skilled craftsmen, too, would prepare a son to inherit the trade. Now, among the increasing numbers of wage-earning families there was no need to favor only one child. All children were equally valued as potential workers and as additional sources of family income. Of course, opportunities for children to work differed. In many areas, domestic service was still the only option for a daughter. So, as in the past, daughters departed for service when they came of age. For sons, however, the decline in skilled trades and in apprenticeship training meant that their jobs did not provide a place to live. Rural boys who migrated alone to cities had to board with relatives or in boardinghouses. But when whole families migrated, or within established urban families, the entry of a son or daughter into the labor market no longer coincided with his or her departure from home. In textile towns the demand for child labor meant that children of both sexes became family wage earners at young ages and that boys and girls continued, well into young adulthood, to live with their parents.[116]

Households in the past had taken on extra members to balance family labor needs when children were very young or after they had left home. But the wage-earning family's situation was different. While under the domestic mode of production, household labor needs were finite, there was no limit to the number of wage earners a wage-earning family could use, and therefore no limit to the numbers of children who could live at home. (In part, the overcrowded households of the working classes which so appalled contemporary observers may have been a function not of a vast increase in the birth rate, but of this tendency to keep working children at home.)[117]

Of course, children did not become family resources until they were old enough to work. There is little evidence to indicate that these families bore more children so that they could eventually become family wage earners. High fertility continued, as in the past, to be a function of high infant mortality rates, which, if anything, worsened in the crowded, unsanitary housing conditions of urban working-class neighborhoods. Among those groups marrying at somewhat earlier ages, marital fertility also increased. But bearing children and caring for infants did not change appreciably in this period. Infancy still seems to have been regarded as the "biologically necessary prelude to . . . adulthood," or at least to the age at which a child could begin to work. Mothers still expected their children to do household chores at an early age; indeed many memoirs stress the fact that mothers would not permit their children to "play." The time spent on infants and the nature of the care they received had not changed. Mothers incorporated them as much as possible into household routines. High mortality rates still led to a certain fatalism: "The mothers discuss the number they have buried with a callousness amounting at times almost to pride in the vastness of their maternal experience."[118]

When children became wage earners, however, the situation was different from what it had been in the past. In those families where they remained at home their presence helped family finances and sometimes also relieved the mother from having to work. It also expanded her domestic jobs. There was more food to prepare, more laundry to do —she was, in effect, supporting the family labor force which continued to grow as each child went out to work.

The longer period spent by children at home increased the family standard of living. This in turn enabled children to remain at home longer. It also strengthened their ties to the family and particularly to their mothers. Within the family, in fact, the mother's relationship to her children seems to have helped create the loyalty and sense of obligation to the unit which marked working-class family life. Families with neither skill nor property to transmit had no material hold on their working children, but mothers seem to have established strong emotional claims on them nonetheless. These were reinforced by a set of socially sanctioned values, which insisted that children owed their parents, and particularly their mothers, devotion and loyalty. Earlier in this chapter we referred to Jeanne Bouvier's sense of obligation to follow her mother to Paris, simply because she was "her mother." It was Bouvier's mother, too, who got her her first job, who introduced her to the world of work. Again, this was typical of the experience of many working-class children. While in the past, among craftsmen at least (and still among those skilled workers who controlled access to their trades), fathers were the ones who initiated their sons into an occupation, in wage-earning families it was more usually the mother who socialized her children (male and female) to hard work at an early age and who then found them employment when they were ready to go out to work. The schoolgirls answering the questionnaire in Paris in 1877 said again and again that *maman* had decided what job they would enter. Many, moreover, intended to enter the same occupation their mothers held.[119]

Anderson offers considerable evidence which suggests that in Preston "bonds of affection were particularly strong between mothers and their children, which seems to reflect both the greater role of the mother in the life of the child and also the fact that it was she above all who made sacrifices for her children and she who protected them from their father. She, in turn, therefore, seems to have received from them affection and gratitude. . . ."[120] Memoirs by workers substantiate this point. One Englishwoman attributed her life-long behavior to the influence of an image of her mother: "I have had many temptations during my life, but my mother's face ["her poor tired face"] always seemed to stand between me and temptation."[121] "Should the mother die," one observer noted, ". . . her little ones weep, indeed, as their only friend is gone."[122]

These bonds of affection or obligation were based on the mother's role in the household. She organized family life, fed family members and managed the budget. "My mother was a big strong Woman, and not cast down with a little thing, but struggled through with a family of seven Sons and two daughters, with a man that did not seem to take very little interest in home Matters," wrote Emanual Lovekin. "We were all under the controle of the Mother who held a Masterly hand."[123] The bond which developed between mothers and children served to keep working children contributing to the family fund, sometimes even after they left home. It was a bond that often survived the child's marriage, bringing some financial assistance and perhaps a place to live during a parent's widowhood or old age.

In addition to her management of household affairs, the mother performed other services for her family. Most important, she served as the family's link to a network of kin which was of increasing importance for urban working-class families. Michael Anderson has detailed the increased importance of kinship relationships in industrial Preston during crises of unemployment, illness, and death, and in the more routine events of childbirth and migration. In the absence of the small communities of the past on the one hand, and the as-yet-undeveloped state-supported social services on the other, family members had to depend on one another for assistance. Membership in Friendly and Burial Societies gave a form of insurance for certain families, but it was usually insufficient. Neighbors also seem to have been helpful, but relatives were more reliable and could be called upon despite the fact that they lived some distance away, or had not been seen in years. As Anderson describes it, a kind of reciprocity developed within a kinship system. People did things for relatives and expected a return, not necessarily from the individuals helped, but from others in the system. Married women seem to have been the organizers and perpetuators of this system. They were the ones who nursed the sick, who visited one another and cared for the young children of relatives. They also prepared the dead for burial and the food for festive occasions. They visited family members and invited them to Sunday dinner or to tea. They shared the family's food with other relatives and agreed to take in a cousin or nephew or sister-in-law newly arrived in the city. These actions secured for the women and their families guarantees of similar help when it was needed.[124]

In her relationships with her children and with kin, the wife in effect controlled some important family resources in addition to money. Her "masterly hand" secured the ties upon which were based the family wage economy and the kinship system of wage-earning families.

The working-class wife and mother managed the family economy and supervised the family labor force. She created the affective community which bound family members to one another. Among wage-earning families the domestic responsibilities of the married woman increased as new kinds of family ties developed among family members. Married women continued to perform a variety of tasks in wage-earning families, but changing conditions of work and the changing organization of production altered their ability to easily reconcile these activities. The tasks of wife, mother, provider of food, and organizer of household affairs and of children's wage-earning activities consumed most of her time. Although she became a wage earner herself when necessary, direct involvement with production took far less of her time than had production for home consumption or for the market in the past.

Overall, the separation of home and work had some important effects on married women's activity. They were eliminated from participating in most of the more productive, better-paying jobs by employer and household preferences for single women as full-time workers. Nonetheless, they were not barred from becoming wage earners in the family interest. Many improvised work which could be reconciled with household responsibilities. Others took temporary low-paying unskilled jobs. Married women's patterns of work-force participation generally were irregular and episodic. Among urban families particularly, married women's time was important at home. They cared for larger households, were involved in buying and preparing food for their families, and organized the wage-earning activities of their children. Indeed, in these families the mother's domestic activity seems to have become increasingly important and valuable to the family.

Women no longer worked continuously throughout their lives, balancing their time between productive and domestic responsibilities as they had under the household mode of production. Instead they alternated different activities over the course of their lives. As daughters and young wives they spent most time earning wages. After children were born, home and family took more and more time, wage earning took less. The arrival of children interrupted employment often for long periods of time, since wage earning seriously disrupted a woman's ability to care for her children. Under the industrial mode of production women had increasing difficulty combining their productive and reproductive activities.

PART III

Toward the Family Consumer Economy

Most women say frankly they want a higher standard of living and are prepared to work to obtain it. Examples of the aims of these women are to buy a car, to have holidays away from York, to buy a radiogram and to buy an electric washing machine for washing clothes or dishes.

B. S. Rowntree and G. R. Lavers, *Poverty and the Welfare State*, p. 56

7

Occupational and Demographic Change

By the early twentieth century, changes in the economies of England and France resulted in changed occupational opportunities for women. In both countries the textile industry declined in importance while other manufacturing enterprises grew. Heavy industry, which included mining, metallurgy, and engineering, became more prominent, as did the electrical and chemical industries. Larger factories, organized to produce goods for a mass market, replaced the older and smaller textile mills as the predominant form of industrial organization. The manufacture of machines to supply the new factories was an increasingly large endeavor. Entrepreneurs invested their capital less in textiles and more and more in the production of machines and machine parts, of rubber and chemicals, of bicycles and eventually automobiles. The transition from textiles to heavy industry meant fewer jobs in the manufacturing sector for women. For while textile production had recruited women and children, heavy industry offered employment at relatively high wages primarily for men. Early increases in the scale of production had drawn women into factories. Further increases in scale and the manufacture of new kinds of products pushed women out of the manufacturing sector. Of course, textile factories had not accounted in the past for the majority of female workers. They had been employed in more "traditional" forms of employment such as domestic service, garment making, and, in France, agriculture. These areas, too, declined in importance in the French and British economies.

A concomitant development, however, provided new types of jobs for women. As the scale of organization of the economy grew, bureaucratic and administrative organization expanded. Clerks, typists, and secretaries were needed in increasing numbers to staff company offices and to fill government positions. Mass production was accompanied by mass distribution. Large stores replaced small family businesses, and they employed large numbers of salesclerks. Compulsory education meant that more teachers were needed, while government involvement in health and social services demanded workers in these areas as well. These service, administrative, and professional jobs were part of what economists call the tertiary sector. They needed a cheap and plentiful labor supply. High wages in industrial employment drew male workers, as did jobs as supervisors and administrators. Confronted with a shortage of men and a large demand for white-collar workers, employers began to recruit women. As a result the twentieth century saw a "migration" of women from industrial and domestic production into "modern" white-collar employment.

THE FEMALE LABOR FORCE IN THE EARLY TWENTIETH CENTURY

The appearance of women in white-collar jobs at the end of the nineteenth and beginning of the twentieth centuries seemed to contemporaries to herald a new increase in the numbers of working women. Proponents of women's rights suggested that the entry of women into formerly male fields meant the dawn of a new era. One of the characters in Gissing's novel *The Odd Women* reflects this view when she talks of the potential the typewriter represents for the emancipation of women:

> Because I myself have had an education in clerkship, and have most capacity for such employment, I look about for girls of like mind, and do my best to prepare them for work in offices. And . . . I am *glad* to have entered on this course. I am *glad* that I can show girls the way to a career which my opponents call unwomanly. . . . I want to do away with that common confusion of the words womanly and womanish, and I see very clearly that this can only be effected by an armed movement, an invasion by women of the spheres which men have always forbidden us to enter.[1]

Some of the women who entered white-collar jobs came from the middle classes. For them work for wages was a new development, a departure from the enforced leisure of middle-class daughters and wives. Commentators tended to equate the experience of these middle-class women with the experience of all women. Hence they concluded

that jobs for women increased absolutely in this period and even suggested that the existence of these jobs reflected new attitudes about
women's position and abilities. Some historians since have concluded
that expanded occupational opportunities for women in this period led
to changed attitudes about women and eventually, in England, to their
political enfranchisement. Before we can examine or evaluate such
conclusions, we must ask some questions about white-collar jobs and
about changes in other female occupations as well. Were there more
women in the labor forces of Britain and France by the early twentieth
century?

When we examine figures for the two countries, we find little change
in female labor-force participation. In France there was a small but
steady increase in the proportions of women working and in the percentage of women in the labor force. Some of this increase came from
a redefinition by census takers of the meaning of labor-force participation. Women who had always been working were counted as such for
the first time in 1906. In Britain the proportions of working women
barely changed at all. (See Figures 4–3 and 4–4.) The major development in the female labor forces of both countries involved a redistribu-
tion of women workers from the industrial to the tertiary sector of the
economy. The increase in white-collar employment, then, did not mean
an increase in women workers. It simply represented a shift of women
workers from one type of job to another. Although single middle-class
women were drawn into these jobs for the first time, they represented
a minority of the female work force. The vast majority of working
women—in white-collar as in manufacturing jobs—came from the
working class.

THE DECLINE OF TEXTILES AND "TRADITIONAL"
EMPLOYMENT

By the early twentieth century, France was still less industrialized
than Britain. While manufacturing dominated the British economy,
small-scale agriculture remained important in France. In 1906, 46 percent of the French labor force was employed in agriculture, only 29
percent in manufacturing. In contrast, only 9 percent of the British
labor force was employed in agriculture in 1911, 51 percent in manufacturing. Yet in both countries the sectors outside of agriculture which
had employed the largest numbers of women began to decline.[2] The
share of the labor force employed in textiles decreased in Britain from
13.8 percent in 1851 to 8.2 percent in 1911; in France comparative
figures were 6.9 percent in 1856 and 4.8 percent in 1906. The percent-

age of the female labor force in textiles in Britain dropped from 22 percent in 1851 to 16 percent in 1911. Similarly, in France 10 percent of all working women were textile workers in 1861, 7 percent in 1906. (Figure 7–1)

Somewhat later and more gradually than in textiles, the numbers of workers employed in the garment industry fell. In Britain, the downturn began after 1901. In France, employment in the garment trades reached a high point in 1906 and then began to fall. In some cities pockets of home production in the needle trades continued to employ

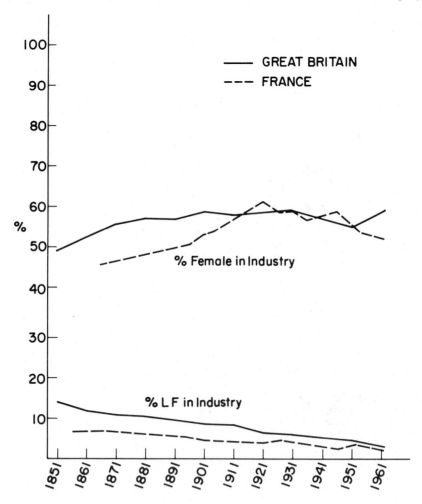

Figure 7.1   Textile labor force in Great Britain and France, 1906 and 1936

large numbers of married women. Indeed, the sewing machine made possible the continuation of home manufacture well into the twentieth century. In France, especially, manufacturers faced with labor shortages sought to tap the labor of potential workers who could not work in factories. And the small, relatively cheap sewing machine allowed them to hire married women who could work at home. Nevertheless, home work was on the wane by the second decade of the twentieth century. One contemporary described it as a marginal industry:

> [T]he sweating system is, after all, but a kind of guerilla warfare carried on upon the flanks of the main engagement. You find it at its height in certain exceptional communities like London, where the cost of rent is so heavy as to make it more economical for the employer to let the workers pay the rent instead of himself. Again, the accumulation of human beings in a great center like London is so vast that the purchaser of labour is in a position to compete with machinery without standing to lose. This is why the human pressure becomes so intolerable.[3]

Domestic service, too, began to decline in importance as an employer of women. The nineteenth-century national differences between the two countries in the proportions of women who were servants continued, but in both cases there was a decline. The percentage of nonagricultural working women in France who were servants fell from 19 percent in 1896 to 16.4 percent by 1936. In Britain the drop was far steeper—from 42 percent in 1901, when over two million women were employed as servants, to 30 percent in 1931 (still a remarkably high figure).

The decline in servants was a consequence of several factors. First, service customarily had been the recourse of rural girls, a means of migrating to the city. In both countries by the twentieth century, there were more choices of jobs in the urban setting. Poor immigrant girls continued to furnish the bulk of servants in the twentieth century. The girl from Brittany in the nineteenth century and later from rural Italy, Spain, or (most recently) Portugal was the typical French servant. Her counterpart in England was from Ireland, Scotland, or improverished northern regions. Many rural girls also went directly into jobs in factories and shops. Second, the supply of girls under fourteen was curtailed by school and labor legislation. Schooling moreover made a fourteen-year-old fit for better employment than household drudgery. Those who were servants now included a higher proportion of older women than in the past. In England, for example, between 1881 and 1901, while the number of servant girls under fifteen fell by 34 percent, the number of those between twenty-five and forty-four increased by 33 percent and those over forty-four increased 20 percent.[4]

The change in the age structure of the servant population meant that many married women were performing work that had been almost exclusively the province of single girls. This was possible not only because the supply of girls for domestic service decreased, but also because of changes in the demand for servants. By 1914, economic pressures on middle-class households had reduced the demand for live-in help. In Paris, for example, rents rose dramatically after 1905, as a result of inflation and an acute housing shortage. The sixth-floor garret rooms, ordinarily reserved for servants of families living on the lower floors, were often rented to working-class families.[5] The staff of servants in English households was also curtailed, and middling families preferred to have a woman come in each day, thereby economizing on her room and board. In addition, of course, the availability of such labor-saving technology as the vacuum cleaner and of neighborhood laundries made it increasingly possible for the middle-class housewife to do housework with fewer servants, or with none at all.[6]

In general, increases in the cost of living forced many families to reduce the numbers of their servants, to do without them entirely, or to substitute less expensive charwomen for girls who lived in the household. Indeed in France, while the numbers of domestic servants declined between 1921 and 1951, the number of charwomen (*femmes de ménage*) rose. In 1921 there was 1 *femme de ménage* for every 11 domestics; by 1951 the ratio was 1 to 4. This meant, of course, that older women, married or not, were as suitable as any others for employment. New settings for this kind of employment also opened by the turn of the century. Growing numbers of hotels, restaurants, and large office buildings required unskilled laborers to dust and clean, change beds, wash dishes, and set tables. Here again, living in was not required, nor were any skills or experience. The work was not restricted to the young or single. In France, while the number of live-in female domestics declined from 688,000 in 1906 to 422,000 by 1936, the number of *femmes de ménage* increased from 96,000 to 153,000. Figure 7–2 offers another perspective. It graphically demonstrates the aging of the population of domestic servants between 1906 and 1936. By the later date there was a pronounced increase in all women over thirty years old, particularly among those between thirty and fifty-nine years old. As the numbers of domestic servants declined, the age structure of the occupation changed as well.[7]

As the older sectors of women's employment contracted, new sectors of production opened. In both countries heavy industry—metallurgy, mining, and engineering—employed more people by the early twentieth century. Although in France the numbers of women employed in the metal trades increased dramatically after 1906, most new jobs de-

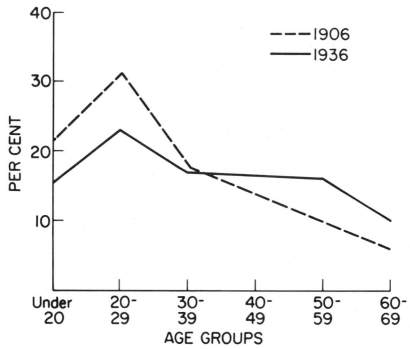

Figure 7.2   Age Distribution of Female Servants in France, 1906 and 1936

Source: Jean Daric, *L'activité professionnelle des femmes en France*.

veloped outside of heavy industry. Women moved into jobs resulting from the growth of the chemical industry, the expansion of food processing and canning, and the proliferation of paper and cardboard box manufacture.

Technological improvements in older trades such as printing also provided jobs for women. Indeed, in France, by the early twentieth century there appeared to be great diversity in the industrial jobs available for women. The proportion of females in many industries had increased. (See Table 7–1.) More than one economist worried about the impact on men's jobs and wages of the employment of women in previously male occupations.[8] From the 1880s onward, French trade unions, too, became more and more outspoken. The debates and resolutions of various national federations clearly reflect the increasing employment of women in new areas, as well as the confusion of syndicalists and socialists about how to resolve the problems posed by competition from women.[9]

Yet despite some increases in the proportions of women in the metal, chemical, and printing trades, there was still a far greater proportion

TABLE 7-1.   Proportion of Females in Various Branches of Manufacturing in France, 1866–1954 (in percent)

Industry	1866	1906	1954
Clothing	78	89	81
Textile	45	56	56
Metallurgy	8	4	15
Food and other agricultural products	11	18	31
Chemicals and rubber	14	29	32
Leather and hides	19	15	37
Printing	18	21	32

SOURCE: Henri Nolleau, "Les femmes dans la population active de 1856 à 1954," *Economie et politique* (1960), p. 14.

of females in the garment and textile industries. Furthermore, there was an overall decline in the percentage of working women employed in manufacturing. In Britain, the percentage of the female labor force in manufacturing fell from 45 percent to 37 percent between 1911 and 1931. In France, the percentages of working women (outside of agriculture) employed in manufacturing dropped from 47 percent to 39 percent between 1906 and 1936.[10]

INCREASES IN WOMEN'S WHITE-COLLAR EMPLOYMENT

The decline of female employment in the manufacturing sector was offset in both countries by an increase of women working in "modern" services, that is, in sales, clerical, administrative, and professional jobs. The expansion of the production of manufactured goods and of the food industry brought with it an enlarged system of distribution. This, and the concomitant growth of urban populations, led to an increase in both the number and size of wholesale and retail stores. In England, for example, between 1875 and 1907, the number of shops increased by 56 percent.[11] The department store, founded first in Paris as early as 1824, had proliferated in some large cities by the end of the nineteenth century. There were twenty *grands bazars* in France by 1882.[12] In addition, the multiplication of specialty shops and the formation of cooperative consumer societies created a demand for a large sales force, and women sought this kind of employment. In France, the proportion of nonagricultural female workers employed in commerce climbed steadily from nearly 18 percent in 1906 to 27 percent by 1946. The

Parisian department store Le Magasin du Louvre reported in the 1890s that there were 100 applicants for a single position as a salesgirl. In England, the census of 1911 counted some 500,000 shop assistants.[13] This form of employment accounted for the largest number of female white-collar workers, nearly three times as many as teaching, the next highest category.

The transformation of clerical work and the expansion of low-skill white-collar jobs that accompanied the growth of commercial and administrative bureaucracies such as banks, insurance companies, and postal agencies, also provided numerous opportunities for young women. Indeed, during the twentieth century, the profession of clerk became a female one. Dickens's Bob Cratchit or Stendhal's Julien Sorel represented a now extinct breed—the educated aspiring young man, more than a servant, not quite an equal, the right arm of a wealthy gentleman. By the twentieth century the job of clerk involved little of the opportunity for advancement it had in the past. Office work was now organized according to narrow specialties: some workers filed, others typed, still others folded letters or ran errands. A number of clerks replaced the lone figure of the past. The low skill required and the numbers of positions to fill made women good recruits. Some argued that the typewriter, in use after 1882, was eminently suited to female abilities since typing was like playing the piano. The first typists in England were referred to as "female typewriters." It was not the typewriter, however, but the structure of occupational opportunity that led to the rapid replacement of men by women in offices during the twentieth century. In England, fewer than 1 percent of clerks were women in 1851. By 1914, women represented 25 percent of all commercial clerks. While the number of male clerks increased fivefold between 1861 and 1911, the number of female clerks increased 400 times. (By 1951, women represented nearly 60 percent of all clerical office workers, and office work employed over 1.25 million women, the largest number of any occupation.) In France the more gradual transformation of family businesses into large corporations created fewer opportunities in private enterprise. But there, too, office work was feminized. These jobs paid better, on the average, than did either factory work or domestic service. The Bank of France reported late in the 1890s that it had as many as 1,000 inquiries for twenty-five jobs. In Paris, in banks and insurance companies there were seven times as many female employees in 1921 as there had been in 1911. By 1956, 54 percent of all clerical office employees were women.[14] (See Figure 7–3)

As national and local governments provided increasing numbers of services to the public, the size of administrative agencies grew. The city of Paris, for example, employed 20,000 women in administrative ser-

vice in 1911, 30,000 ten years later.[15] The expansion of the post office
in both England and France by the end of the nineteenth century and
the growth of telephone and telegraphic services were particularly
important influences on women's employment. In fewer than ten years,
between 1888 and 1895, the volume of letters carried by the French
Post Office more than doubled, and the service could not find enough
male workers to fill jobs as postal clerks.[16] Women had held these jobs
in the past, but usually only in provincial offices and then only if they
inherited their position from a deceased father or husband. In 1892,
however, desperate to find people to sell stamps, weigh letters, and sort
mail (especially in Paris), the post office began to hire women on a large
scale. (The position of *facteur*, the letter carrier delivering mail on foot,
is to this day a male job.) The supply of eligible employees (depending
on the rank of the job, either a woman who had completed primary
school or one somewhat older who could pass a qualifying examination)
far exceeded the post office's needs. In 1892 only 205 men had applied
for 1,151 positions. In contrast, after 1892, the Postal Administration
reported as many as 5,000 female applicants for some 200 positions.[17]
The situation in England was similar. There the post office doubled its

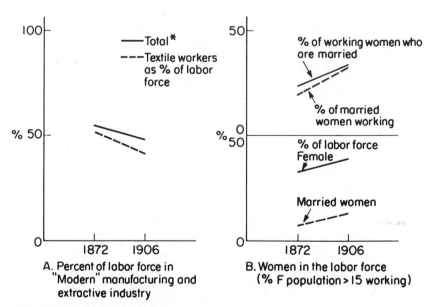

A. Percent of labor force in
"Modern" manufacturing and
extractive industry

B. Women in the labor force
(% F population > 15 working)

*Total excludes 12% unspecified in 1872, 13%
in 1906

Figure 7.3 a & b   Labor Force Characteristics: Roubaix, 1872 and
1906

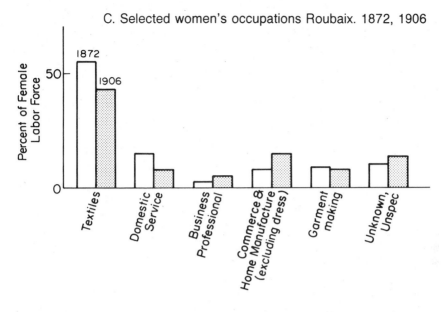

C. Selected women's occupations Roubaix. 1872, 1906

Figure 7.3 c

work force between 1891 and 1914 and by the latter date became "the largest single employer . . . in the country of female white collar workers."[18]

Unlike the post office, telephone and telegraphic services (under the postal administration in both countries by 1914) employed women from the outset. Chosen by competitive examination, the operators were given several months of training in the use of the machinery. No study of the social origins of these female employees yet exists. It may be that minimum age and examination requirements excluded daughters of the poorest families. On the other hand, the numbers of applicants and the low level of wages paid indicated that telephone operators, like postal clerks and their aides, also came from the working class.[19]

The two other important areas of female white-collar employment were teaching and nursing. The late-nineteenth-century education acts in England and France not only provided elementary training for young women, but also created potential employment for them. By 1914 in England, the number of women far exceeded that of men in primary school teaching. Women accounted for nearly 75 percent of all elementary school teachers, as compared with about 55 percent in 1875. The rate of increase of women in elementary teaching was four times as great as it was for men. (In secondary education, on the other hand, the proportionate numbers of men and women remained stable from the 1860s to 1914.)[20] In France, the tradition of separate schools for boys and girls meant that there were equal proportions of male to female teachers. The replacement of nuns by secular teachers and the creation of more schools for girls after the Ferry Law of 1882 meant that new opportunities were created for young women. The proliferation of Ecoles Maternelles, preprimary schools for very young children, which were staffed exclusively by women, also increased their representation in the profession.[21] In both countries women held an increasing share of primary school positions as the century advanced. Their presence led male teachers to expressions of opposition and hostility. Men were harder to recruit, however, and so were replaced by women, thereby feminizing at least the primary level of the teaching profession.

In France the Ferry Law authorized Normal Schools in each department with three-year courses to train teachers. Although a teacher could also be certified without formal preparation, the Normal Schools, which provided scholarships, tended to draw students from peasant and working-class families as well as from families of professional and white-collar employees. The few studies that exist indicate that during the twentieth century, the numbers of primary school teachers from working-class families steadily increased.[22] In England, until 1907, a few training colleges existed for teachers, but most aspirants to the profession simply served as paid pupil-teachers for five years after completing their own primary education. After 1907, scholarships were granted for secondary education to prospective teachers. Many still entered the profession, however, simply by passing a certifying examination. The demand for teachers after the passage of the Education Act led to the hiring of large numbers of teachers with neither training nor certification. While in 1875, 57 percent of women teachers were certified to teach, in 1914, only 32 percent had received any formal training. Most had passed a qualifying examination of some kind. Others "had merely received approval from the school inspector."[23] In 1914, the majority of elementary school teachers "were probably ... recruited from among girls of the working classes."[24] Increasing numbers of middle-class women also entered the field as it became a more respectable one, but teaching remained, even after 1914, a means of social improvement for the daughters of peasants, artisans, and factory workers. Despite the expansion of the field, teachers represented a small fraction of the entire female work force. In England about 180,000 women were employed as teachers in 1911, representing some 3 percent of all working women. In France, teachers also accounted for about 3 percent of the female labor force.[25]

Nurses represented an even smaller percentage of working women. But this field, too, increased its recruitment substantially, particularly in England, as governments took an interest and role in the improvement of health services. The story of Florence Nightingale's impact on the nursing profession in England has been told many times. She sought to professionalize a field which had long been the province of religious orders or of charwomen. Nightingale established training schools, rules for behavior, standards of character, and moral codes. She succeeded in making nursing respectable for girls of her own class. The expansion of hospital care for the ill and of government medical services in the army, under the Poor Law, and in urban districts created a larger demand. Nightingale's reforms and government health measures opened nursing as a field of employment for women of all classes. "Nurses are recruited from all classes . . .," wrote one hospital director, "in the hospitals a housemaid may be found sitting next to a baronet's daughter, and all the gradations of rank between these two may be found at the same table."[26] In fact, administrative roles were filled by the small minority of upper-class women and the vast majority of nursing jobs (some 77,000 in 1911) were taken by aspiring lower-class girls.[27] In nominally Catholic France, religious orders continued to dominate the nursing field, hence this line of work was a far less important alternative form of lay female employment.

Changes in women's occupations in the twentieth century led to greatly increased proportions of women in the tertiary sector. These changes can be observed in statistics of women's employment outside of agriculture in France between 1906 and 1936. In that period, the percentage of women in tertiary occupations increased from 44 to 56 percent; those employed in industry declined from 57.1 to 42.3 percent. There had been a similar shift in women's employment in Britain several decades earlier. Between 1881 and 1911, the percentage of women working in the tertiary sector nearly doubled, while the percentage of those in various branches of industry declined.[28]

These shifts in women's employment signaled some important developments. First, women were increasingly employed away from home and apart from a household context. (The most important exception was the French family farm.) By 1900, the separation between home and work which had begun a century before was virtually complete. Women now earned wages in factories and offices, in the company of others like themselves. Second, an increasing number of women were employed in jobs which required at least the rudiments of an education. Sales, clerical, and professional jobs demanded levels of literacy that had not characterized women's work in the past.

Yet, despite this, women's white-collar work was not well paid, nor did it call for extraordinary skills of any kind. Women's wages in "commerce," for example, were a third to a half of male wages; these women rarely held supervisory or administrative positions. Most women remained at low-paying jobs for the duration of their employment; opportunities for promotion were few. Third, despite the fear expressed by male workers, women were never integrated into the male labor force. As older sectors of female employment declined, new "female" jobs emerged. And as women entered occupations such as clerking, sales and, primary education, they replaced male employees in these fields. Rapidly, new kinds of "feminized" employment emerged, in the tertiary sector particularly.

As compared with the 1850s, women's work in England and France took new forms. The changes that occurred were associated less directly with the growth of technology and industry than they were the product of the expansion of commerical and administrative organizations. Though new jobs were available for women, these jobs tended to be segregated. As in the nineteenth century, certain occupations were female, others male. A minority of white-collar occupations in the professions offered working-class women improved status and the possibility of a lifelong career. But most jobs for women in the twentieth century—the new and the old—required few skills and offered relatively low pay.

WOMEN'S WORK IN CITIES

During the nineteenth century, different cities had different patterns of women's work. This continued to be the case during the twentieth century, when the large-scale changes we have discussed affected cities with different economies in different ways.

York and Amiens most clearly reflected the decline in domestic service and the rise of jobs in light industry and commerce. In York in 1899, Rowntree found "no predominating industry carried on under conditions that are peculiar to York."[29] Men worked for the North Eastern Railway Company either on the railway itself or in allied trades as bricklayers, painters, masons, and laborers. In addition there were a number of small factories. The largest, the cocoa and confectionery works, employed between two and three thousand people, most of them young, many of them women. (By 1936, the confectionary works was the largest single employer in York, with some 10,000 employees, two-thirds of whom were women and girls.)[30] Rowntree noted in his first visit that the demand for young persons was large. As a result, "practically every capable boy and girl can find employment in the factories."[31] Women's employment in York had changed by the turn of the century. Far fewer women were domestic servants, many more were factory employees, shop girls, and clerks. In 1911, 32.3 percent of the female population was in employment, distributed as follows: 36.1 percent in manufacturing, 19.5 percent in professional sales and clerical jobs, 37.2 percent in domestic service. (Others in poorly defined occupations such as general labor, and hotel and restaurant work totaled 7.1 percent.) Less than 10 percent of the female labor force was married; 7.3 percent of married women worked.[32]

By the early twentieth century, the textile industry of Amiens was mechanized. Some 2,000 looms located in textile factories produced linen, wool, and cotton. The industry was in serious difficulty in 1900, however, having been hurt by tariff laws, by overproduction, and by its continuing inability to compete with larger textile centers in the North and East. Some new industry had developed in Amiens. Male inhabitants could find work at sugar refineries and copper foundries, as well as at the shoe and boot factory which had opened in 1865. Although the cutting and preparation of shoe leather took place in large workshops, the shoes were assembled by home workers. Some 3,000 men and women were involved in various aspects of this industry in 1900.[33]

The shoe trade was only one aspect of the expansion of home work that took place in Amiens at the end of the nineteenth century. Between 1880 and 1900, the number of *maisons de confection* (businesses involved in contracting out home work) grew from thirteen to twenty-seven.[34] An investigation in 1903 revealed that some 72 percent of home workers were married women, wives of white-collar employees or of skilled and unskilled workers. These women earned from 10 to 30 percent of annual household revenues.[35]

In 1906, the Amiens labor force was more predominantly male than it had been in 1851. (The sex ratio was 151, as compared to 141 in 1851.) Domestic service was still an important component of the female labor force. Dressmaking accounted for about the same proportion of female workers in 1906 as it had in 1851. Textile work, however, was a much less common employment for women in 1906. There were new opportunities for single women in commerce, business, and professional employment (mostly teaching). Thirty-two percent of the female labor force was married. A large plurality of the married women who worked (35.8 percent) in 1906 were employed in the garment industry. The dress, shoe, and textile industries together accounted for 54 percent of married women workers. The labor force was growing in the sectors of modern business, commerce, and the professions. Single women benefited from these growing areas of employment. Married women continued to work in the garment and textile industries; they took little part in the growth of the tertiary sector.[36]

Stockport and Roubaix remained textile towns. Their populations were still engaged primarily in factory work. Nonetheless, by the end of the nineteenth century, changes in the organization of production in the mills and a slump in the textile industry had reduced the percentage of the total labor force engaged in textiles. As the size of the textile labor force in Britain and France diminished, however, women represented a larger proportion of textile workers (Figure 7–1). By 1911, women in the British textile industry accounted for 57 percent of all employees, compared with 49 percent in 1851. In France, women were 45 percent of the textile labor force in 1866, 61 percent in 1911. Local figures reveal the same development. In Lancashire, women were 50 percent of all cotton workers in 1851, 63 percent in 1901. In the Yorkshire woolen industry, too, the proportion of employees who were female rose from 40 to 50 percent in the same fifty-year period.[37] In Stockport women represented 61.9 percent of all cotton textile workers in 1911 (as compared with 52.6 percent in 1851). In Roubaix, females accounted for 35.6 percent of textile operatives in 1906 (as compared with 32.6 percent in 1872). (Woolen manufacture, such as that in Roubaix, employed fewer females than the cotton industry.)[38]

A contemporary statistician who was an expert on women's employment noted, at the end of the nineteenth century, that as the British textile industry declined, the characteristics of its work force changed. Proportionately more married women were employed per mill:

> Given a marked decline in the branch of trade under consideration, and before long the influx of girls and young women will cease; mills will be closed and new ones will not be opened, and it will be the older and more necessitous women who will seek employment in the mills still running. What is really an abandonment of the trade by the younger women, has the appearance inside the mill of an increased employment of married women.[39]

She noted also that the appearance of women taking over a trade was misleading. In fact, there was no net increase of female employment. "A better paying trade withdraws the men from the trade in which they are competing with women, and the women are left to run it; but at the same time the higher wages earned by the men in the other trade enable them to support their wives at home, to keep their children longer in school. . . ."[40]

Changes of this sort were evident in Roubaix and Stockport. Figure 7–4 illustrates the case of Roubaix. The drop in textiles as an employer of from 52 to 43 percent of the labor force was accompanied by a decrease in the proportion of the female labor force in the manufacturing sector. There was a small increase in the ratio of women to men in textile work. Although a plurality (42.3 percent) of working women was still in the mills in 1906, there was in increase in the proportions employed in other light industry, retail trades, and business.

Changes in Roubaix's industrial position had modified the pattern of women's participation in the labor force in other ways also. More of the city's married women and widows worked in 1906. Almost one-third of the labor force consisted of married women. Among textile workers, there was a higher proportion of married women than there had been in 1872: 37 percent as compared with 21 percent. Female textile workers were also older than their counterparts thirty-five years earlier: now only 65 percent of them were under thirty; only 4 percent of them were under fifteen.

By 1906, Anzin had a much more diverse economy than it had in 1872. Only 26 percent of the labor force was in manufacturing and extractive industries, 7 percent of them in mining. (See Figure 7–4.) Important new coal fields had been discovered and exploited in the adjacent department of Pas-de-Calais. This had greatly affected the older mine fields in the Nord. Anzin had actually de-industrialized in

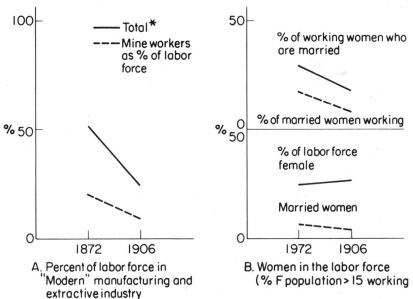

A. Percent of labor force in "Modern" manufacturing and extractive industry

B. Women in the labor force (% F population > 15 working

* Total excludes 25% unspecified in 1872, 29% in 1906

Figure 7.4 a & b   Labor Force Characteristics, Anzin, 1872 and 1906

C. Selected women's occupations Anzin. 1872, 1906

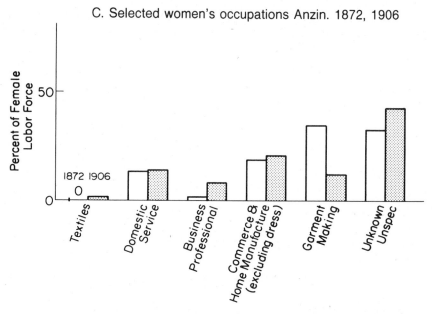

Figure 7.4 c

some ways. It was no longer an industrial city of miners and metal workers. Retail business had increased, as had the number and proportion of administrative employees of the mine company and other businesses. The proportions of women in the labor force had decreased markedly. A much smaller percentage of married women were in the labor force, and fewer married women worked. Gone were the numerous café keepers and dressmakers. (It is quite possible that the census count is an underestimate of married women's work, because so much of it was episodic and irregular. The change is striking enough however to be illustrative of the trend.) Single women constituted a larger share than in the past of the contracting female labor force.

The female employment situation in York was close to that of the aggregate experience of Britain. Roubaix represented a special case—the textile city—of which there were many British examples, like Stockport. Amiens was more typical of the French aggregate experience. Anzin had rather lower female employment than did France as a whole.

In all the twentieth-century cities, women tended to be concentrated in a narrow range of occupations. As in the nineteenth century, young, single women dominated the ranks of female workers. But they were less often in domestic service and more often in manufacturing and "commerce." Married women worked in largest numbers in textile towns, where female labor was still in demand. In all cases except

Roubaix, with its strongly sex-typed industry, married women were less prominent in urban labor forces than had been the case fifty years earlier.

THE FERTILITY DECLINE

The most striking demographic changes among the working classes during the early twentieth century had to do with declines in fertility and in infant mortality. Life expectancy at birth increased because fewer babies died during the first year of life. And family size diminished as couples deliberately controlled conception.

By the end of the nineteenth century the birth rate among French and British working class families declined dramatically. In France, as a whole, the fertility decline had begun early in the nineteenth century. By the end of the century, however, it was evident in regions and cities and among groups which had previously had high fertility. In Britain, the birth rate began to drop overall in the late 1870s. In France, the crude birth rate declined from 25.0 (children born per 1,000 population) in 1851–55 to 20.7 in 1901–5. In Britain, the crude birth rate fell from 34.1 in the decade 1851–60 to 21.8 in 1911–20. The number of legitimate live births per 1,000 married women aged fifteen to forty-four was 281 in 1851–60. By 1911–20 it had fallen to 174. Aggregate birth rates, of course, do not reveal class differences in fertility. British studies at the turn of the century showed that birth rates were falling more rapidly among the upper classes than among workers. Within the working class a decline in marital fertility was most apparent among textile workers, least among miners and agricultural laborers. Nonetheless, as compared with earlier figures, a decline in working-class fertility was evident. The average number of children ever born to British manual wage earners was 4.9 per couple married in the decade 1890–99; for those married in 1915, the figure was 2.9. Among unskilled laborers, the fall was also evident, if less rapid: from 5.1 for the 1890–99 marriage cohort to 3.5 for that of 1915.[41]

Similarly, fertility fell in industrial centers like Roubaix, Lille, and Anzin. Table 7–2, which gives crude birth rates for the cities, dramatically illustrates the drop in fertility in Anzin and Roubaix between 1861 and 1906. Figure 7–5 illustrates the decline graphically: it shows the ratio of children under five living in the families by five-year age groups of married women. There were many fewer children under five for married women of all ages in 1906. Clearly, by 1906 families were deliberately curbing births.

TABLE 7–2. Crude Birth Rates for Roubaix and Anzin,
1861–1906, per Thousand Population*

Year	Anzin	Roubaix
1861	37.2	42.8
1866	32.8	44.8
1872	33.0	42.4
1876	33.0	42.4
1881	28.7	39.0
1891	26.9	36.4
1896	22.9	32.5
1901	27.5	29.9
1906	26.5	27.0

* Births averaged for three years centering on census year.
SOURCES: *Rapport du Maire* for Roubaix yearly from 1863; for
Anzin, births counted from yearly registers of the Etat Civil.

The population of Roubaix was aging, as was the population of
France, as a consequence of declining fertility. In 1872, 66 percent of
Roubaix's population was over fifteen; in 1906, the figure was 74 percent. Only 7 percent of the population was under five in 1906, as
compared to 13 percent in 1872. As early as 1895, a Roubaix statistician
had noted that the fertility decline was well under way. He wrote:
"France is losing population! Thus cry the statisticians: it is unfortu-
nately all too true, and one can see it clearly when one compares the
births and deaths of recent years."[42] A similar set of changes had occurred in Anzin. The population did not increase between 1901 and
1906. Anzin's population had also aged as fertility declined. In 1872, 67
percent was over fifteen; in 1901, 73 percent.

The drop in fertility stemmed not from compositional changes such
as sex ratios, nor from changes in the age and rate of marriage. Rather,
fertility fell because, as the secretary of the National Federation of
French textile workers put it in 1904, "the workers practice continence
and seek to limit the number of their children." Birth control, he continued, was practiced on a "vast scale."[43]

Methods of family limitation were crude and simple in this period.
Abortion was probably at least as common as contraception, perhaps
even more so. Early in the twentieth century Ethel Elderton's corre-
spondents in the industrial areas of Britain reported that local newspapers carried advertisements for abortifacients more often than for
"Malthusian appliances."[44] One historian has suggested that working-
class women believed that self-induced abortion was not a sin or crime
if done before the fetus had quickened. He notes, too, that abortion was
a method of fertility control which did not require a husband's cooper-

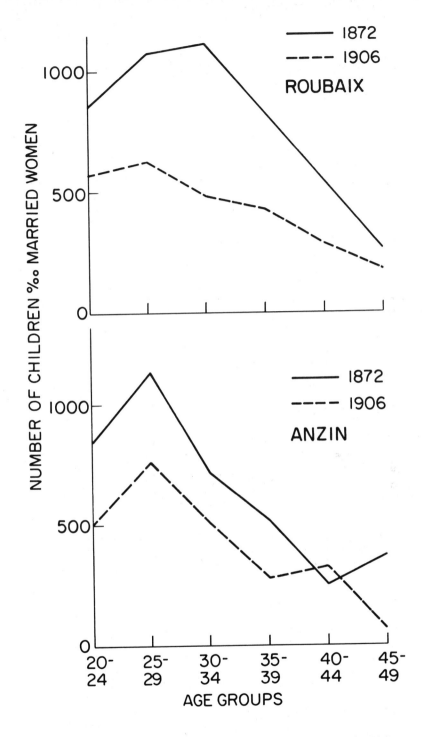

Figure 7.5   Fertility Ratios: Roubaix and Anzin, 1872 and 1906

ation.[45] Advocates of birth control, however, did not approve of abortion. The neo-Malthusians in England and France insisted that other female methods were preferable to abortion. The methods they suggested did not involve any new technology. These included sponges designed to block the cervix, and spermicidal liquids. Norman Himes's evidence indicates that sponges soaked in acid solutions of vinegar or brandy had long been used as contraceptives by women. The invention of the diaphragm by a Dutch physician in 1882 does not seem to have caused the fertility decline. Indeed, there is little evidence that even the organized "birth-controllers" advocated its use.[46]

Clearly the dissemination of contraceptive information by neo-Malthusians contributed to public knowledge and to public discussion of the issue of family limitation. The activities of the British Malthusians and the publicity surrounding the trial of Charles Bradlaugh and Annie Besant, who had published and distributed birth control information, probably alerted some families to the possibilities of using birth control.[47] A similar, though much smaller, movement in France, also urged workers to limit the size of their families. Some socialists joined the neo-Malthusians and urged French workers not to produce children who would become cannon fodder for capitalist wars. Members of the French Regeneration League toured industrial cities like Roubaix, urging workers to restrict the size of their families. (After 1920, these activities were outlawed because the state sought to encourage population growth. A large population, it was felt, would replenish the losses suffered during the First World War and would improve France's military position vis-à-vis Germany.)[48]

Despite their activity, however, the decline in the birth rate did not stem from the neo-Malthusians. These groups provided information to working-class families already convinced of the need to limit fertility. The receptivity of the families came, in turn, from a number of economic, social, and political changes which occurred during the last decades of the nineteenth century. The first of these, and the one often suggested by contemporaries, was a change in the working-class standard of living. Rising real wages among certain groups of workers created "an increased love of ease, of pleasure and of luxury with which children interfere. . . ."[49] "The better class of workman soon recognized that unless his family were curtailed, he would have to succumb to a lower standard of living."[50] Ease and luxury hardly describe the situation of working-class families. It is probably more accurate to say that a desire for a better standard of living and the sense that they could attain it by their own action led these families to limit births.[51]

A second influence came from what economists refer to as a change in the "economic value of children."[52] Investigators of the falling English birth rate pointed repeatedly to the importance of this factor. Changes in the organization of work and in technology made child labor increasingly superfluous. It became harder and harder for parents to find work for young children. In addition, child labor legislation (in 1878 in Britain and in 1874 in France) and compulsory education laws (1876 in Britain and 1882 in France) at once increased the period of a child's economic dependence on her parents and created new possibilities for better employment when she completed school. "The child, owing to factory and educational legislation, had become more and more a protracted source of expenditure; the moral leaders of the people had taught that the parents had 'no right' to children unless they could support them, and this theory had replaced the old evangelical doctrine that: 'it is God who sends children and He will in due course provide for them.' "[53]

In Roubaix and Anzin, economic and legal factors combined to restrict the employment of children. In both cities, the economic exuberance of the 1860s and 1870s was past. The textile industry of the Nord had suffered a recession from 1897 to 1903. The number of spinning mills in Roubaix dropped from thirty-one in 1890 to twenty-four in 1900; two combing mills (10 percent of the plants) had disappeared. Ten out of forty-seven spinning mills had closed down.[54] There had been a slow recovery starting in 1903, but Roubaix continued to lose population. In the city, laws on child labor and compulsory education were implemented. Seventy-eight percent of children under fifteen were in school. Many fewer children worked in 1906 than in 1872; 15 percent of boys aged ten to fourteen, 10 percent of girls. Similarly in Anzin, jobs for children declined. In 1906, only 16.6 percent of boys aged ten to fourteen worked, as opposed to some 50 percent in 1872. The conditions of the declining textile industry in Roubaix and the virtual disappearance of coal mining from Anzin offered no encouragement for families to have large numbers of children.

The other side of the loss of jobs for young children, of course, was that the "cost of children" increased. Children were financially dependent on parents for longer periods of their lives. In addition, sending them to school and preparing them for jobs as adults involved new costs. A large number of children in a family would make the full support of any individual child more difficult.

A fourth factor, suggested by some demographers, was the falling rate of child and infant mortality. It may be that declining death rates (visible after 1861 in both countries) for children between the ages of one and fifteen also influenced family fertility strategies. The survival of additional children to adulthood created financial burdens for working-class families. As more children survived, families began to employ birth control. (The influence of infant mortality is less clear, since the dramatic fall in infant deaths seems to have followed the decline in the birth rate. While the fertility decline was evident in France in the first half of the century and in Britain in the last quarter, infant death rates fell only in the first decades of the twentieth century. The fertility decline seems to have preceded the infant mortality decline rather than to have been caused by it.)[55]

All of these factors somehow combined to influence working-class fertility strategies at the end of the nineteenth century. An increasing number of families seem to have adopted a more calculating attitude about childbearing and about their own as well as their children's futures. Perhaps, as a result, parents also invested more heavily in individual children. As they restricted the numbers of their children, they spent more time and money on those children they did have.

DECLINING INFANT MORTALITY

Despite the falls in fertility, infant mortality remained high among French and English working men's families until the twentieth century. When Rowntree visited York in 1899, he found the infant mortality rate of 176 deaths per 1,000 births higher than the overall rate for England and Wales (160/1,000). In the department of the Nord in France, infant mortality was at its height during the period 1893–1900. The poorest families had the highest death rates, and in areas where married women worked away from home, infant death rates soared. The cause of death was most often due to gastroenteritis, the result of unsanitary conditions connected with bottle feeding.[56]

Nineteenth-century infant and child mortality rates meant that parents could count on no more than nine out of ten (and often only eight out of ten) children surviving their first year of life and not many more than six out of ten surviving to age twenty. Child mortality rates of those aged one to four began to fall after 1865. The drop in rates for children five to fourteen years old was more striking. Infant mortality, however, improved relatively little before 1900. Table 5–5 illustrates the continuing high rates of infant death in both Britain and France from the 1860s to 1901.

Deliberate attempts to save infant lives began in both Britain and France in the 1870s. In France, after an extensive investigation, the government enacted the Roussel Law in 1874, which regulated the practice of wet-nursing. Wet nurses were required to register with government bureaus, and parents had to report to a government agency the fact that they were putting a child out to nurse. In the same period the British required compulsory registration of all births and deaths, regulation of lying-in houses, and registration of child minders and nurses. Both governments hoped that regulation would reduce the careless treatment of infants by nurses or child minders, which was thought to be responsible for many deaths. Additional legislation was aimed at keeping mothers home, at least immediately after childbirth, and at reducing the hours of their employment. In France, the law of 1892 limited women's work to eleven hours a day and outlawed night work by women. The British Factory and Workshop Act of 1895 restricted the early return of women to work after childbirth. There were many reasons for the passage of this legislation, but at least one of them had to do with the impact of women's work on "child life."[57] Doctors testified that if mothers could be induced to nurse their babies for several months and longer, then infant deaths would diminish. A report in Britain in 1908 reflected the thinking behind much of this legislation. It emphasized the importance of a mother's care to the survival of her child and the responsibility of governments to ensure that maternal care was provided for children. (Table 7–3)

The law, as it stands, prohibits the employment of mothers in factories and workshops during the first month after childbirth. It is so worded that it is hard to enforce, but, at best, it is a law for the mother and not for the child. If the child is to be saved, we must extend the present period of prohibition until gradually this system of employment dies. Gradually, then, the proper balance would be restored; the mother would serve her children and her husband by her presence in the home, not by her presence in the factory. In that way she best serves the State; and while she passes from her place in the factory to her place in the home, the State should, directly or indirectly, protect her, should see that she suffers no loss. The employer who withdraws her from the service of her home for his own service should insure her against the loss of those wages he has taught her to lean upon—sometimes forced her to lean upon. And the State should take charge: the children of the State are the business of the State; if it neglect that business there is nothing that will atone.[58]

In accordance with this outlook, the French government enacted a law in 1902 which compelled parents to vaccinate their children.[59]

In addition to these laws, some voluntary efforts were made to provide reliable, sanitary institutional care for infants of working mothers. *Crèches* had existed in France, at least since the 1840s. There is evidence that day-care centers were established in French towns throughout the 1850s, 1860s, and 1870s. These centers, however, could provide care for only a minority of the children who needed it, and they often foundered because of a lack of funds.[60] In 1876, as a companion to the

TABLE 7–3.   Children Surviving to Selected Ages, France, per thousand

Year		1	5	10	15	20
1861	Male	818	699	670	654	632
	Female	846	725	693	673	642
1881	Male	816	727	702	688	668
	Female	845	753	727	710	687
1901	Male	841	784	766	754	736
	Female	868	811	792	778	758

SOURCE: E. A. Wrigley, *Industrial Growth and Population Change* (Cambridge: At the University Press, 1961), p. 107.

Roussel Law, a group of doctors founded the Société d'Allaitement Maternel, to encourage mothers to breast-feed their babies. In the 1890s well-baby clinics were established in a number of French cities. In addition, and perhaps most important of all, Depots de Gouttes de Lait, centers for the distribution of sterilized milk, were also set up. The first of these was founded in Nancy in 1880.[61] In Roubaix, a private charity for the protection of children opened in 1894. It not only taught parents how to sterilize bottles and milk, but helped poor women buy items they otherwise could not afford. A private legacy sponsored a Goutte de Lait center in 1903. In the waiting room of this center (which also housed a clinic) a large sign reminded mothers that "The first duty of a mother is to nurse her baby herself."[62] In Anzin, a clean-milk center (Goutte de Lait) opened in 1905. Similar organizations, modeled on the French, were set up in Britain after 1900.[63] Visiting nurses and volunteer assistants made the rounds in working-class neighborhoods in both countries, teaching mothers the fundaments of infant care.

The result of these efforts, probably particularly of medical care for babies and of the availability of sterilized milk, was a dramatic decline in infant deaths among the working classes after 1901. In the French

TABLE 7–4.   Britain: Survival of Infants to Age 1, per thousand

1856–60	849
1881–85	862
1901	849

SOURCE: G. F. McLeary, *Infantile Mortality and Infants' Milk Depots* (London: P. S. King and Son, 1905).

department of the Nord, for example, infant death rates fell from 194/1,000 in 1900 to 128/1,000 in 1914 to 116/1,000 in 1921.[64] In York, when Rowntree returned in 1936, infant mortality had dropped to 56.6 per 1,000 births.[65] The decline in infant death rates, the earlier decline in fertility and changes in the economy created a new context within which women's wage-earning and family activities were defined.

8

Women in the Family Consumer Economy

During the early twentieth century working-class families remained family wage economies. The household's need for wages continued to define the work of family members. Membership in a household still meant sharing in the economic support of the family unit as well as "eating from one pot." The family was an economic unit and a unit for purposes of consumption. Among increasing numbers of families, however, the standards of consumption were rising. The goal of working families in the mid-nineteenth century had been to earn enough to subsist. As many family members worked as were necessary to earn a "target income" which would maintain a minimum level of subsistence. By the early twentieth century the higher wages of men particularly and the availability of cheap consumer goods raised the target income of working-class families. Necessities now included not only food and clothing, but also other items that once had been considered luxuries. What we have termed the family consumer economy, then, was a wage-earning unit which increasingly emphasized family consumption needs.

The organization of the family consumer economy was not dramatically different from that of the family wage economy. The management of money and of family affairs in an increasingly complex urban environment did, however, require additional time and a certain expertise. As a result, the household division of labor tended to distinguish even more sharply than in the past between the roles of husband and wife, and of daughters and wives. Husbands and unmarried children were family wage earners, while wives devoted most of their time to child care and household management. Wives continued, however, to work sporadically in order to earn wages to help raise the family's level of consumption.

SINGLE WOMEN'S WORK

Writing of an organization founded in France in 1902 to improve the technical training and therefore the economic position of working-class girls, an author noted that parental opposition created serious difficulties for the group. Families were reluctant, he wrote, to extend a daughter's education beyond the age required by law:

> Parents who are waiting to "place" a daughter when she leaves school and who are counting on her wages to help the family budget often hesitate when new sacrifices are asked of them. . . .[1]

For historians interested in women's work, the description is a familiar one. It conveys the fact that in the twentieth century a daughter's work continued to be shaped by her family's needs. Although in both France and England the structure of educational and occupational opportunity for working-class girls changed in important ways, family considerations still influenced their work and their lives. This is not to say that families remained unchanged. Within the working class household, relationships between parents and children were altered by the impact of declining mortality and fertility, as well as by economic changes. The family was still a central institution for all its members, but families increasingly were organized as family consumer economies. As in the past, new developments within the family and among family members represented not a dramatic departure, but an adaptation of older practices to new or changing circumstances.

Working-class parents continued to expect that their children—male and female—would work and contribute to the family once they had finished school. During the last decades of the nineteenth century compulsory education laws enacted in both France and England required that all children receive some primary education, and child labor laws regulated the age at which they could begin work. In England the Education Act of 1876 made school attendance compulsory for children from ages five to fourteen, but ten-year-olds were permitted to quit school and hold jobs. In 1899, the minimum age for employment was raised to twelve and by 1918, to fourteen years.[2] Under the French Ferry Law of 1882, free primary education was provided for all children from six to thirteen years. In 1892, a law set thirteen as the minimum working age for children.[3]

The enlargement of educational facilities and the attempt to extend schooling to lower-class children coincided with a decline in the demand for child labor, particularly in industrial establishments. Technological improvements in textile factories, for example, made the employment of young children increasingly uneconomical as early as the 1860s in England and by the 1880s in France.[4] The outcry of reformers and government attempts to police establishments which employed young children further discouraged their employment. An investigator in Manchester in 1865 reported that more children between ages three and twelve were on the streets than were either at work or in school.[5] Charles Booth found that after 1881, the numbers of children under fifteen in the labor force of England and Wales had declined sharply.[6] Similarly, in France, the Ferry Law accelerated a process already under way. By 1876–77 some 57 percent of all children were attending schools free of charge, exempted by the economic situation of their parents from tuition charges.[7]

Officials could complain bitterly of the difficulties of enforcing the law: "The principle of compulsory education is an abstraction," wrote one French inspector in 1903. "Almost everywhere young girls leave school at eleven or twelve and even earlier. In the Bourbonnais; the Allier, Lorraine, the proportion is 30 percent and even 50 and 68 percent; in the West, more than 50 percent."[8] English truant officers, too, reported difficulty in enforcing the law; but in London attendance rates were raised from 76.7 percent in 1872 to 88.2 percent in 1906.[9] In France, too, by 1890, most of the school-age population attended school for at least part of the year.[10] The overall effect of the laws, as well as of the decline in child employment, was to institutionalize school attendance as a stage in the lives of increasing numbers of working-class children and thus to prolong the period of a child's dependency on his or her parents. Though attendance might be irregular, interrupted by family demands on a child's time, the early years of childhood—usually until age thirteen or fourteen—were now spent in school. During these years sons and daughters lived at home and, though they might earn a bit at after-school jobs, they were supported essentially by their parents. Indeed the work of children under the legal working age was fit in around time spent at school. In London, for example, matchbox making was "the first occupation of little girls expected to make themselves useful between school hours."[11]

The ability of parents to support school-age children depended, of course, on a family's economic situation. The poorest kept their children at home to work in the fields, to mind younger children while a mother went out to earn wages, or to assist their mothers in domestic industry. In the years immediately following passage of the acts, parents sometimes protested and more often violated the education laws by falsifying birth certificates and school diplomas or by simply hiding their children when the truant officer called. Until 1881, English parents could obtain special orders from a magistrate to exempt their children from the laws, and many did. Half-time attendance at school was permitted until 1901 in England for working children between ten and fourteen years of age. Children of the poorest families usually constituted the bulk of "half-timers."[12] "The importance attached to the earnings of the children in the families of the poor," wrote Rowntree in 1899, "reminds us how great must be the temptation to take children away from school at the earliest possible moment, in order that they may begin to earn."[13] He found in York that children between the ages of five and fifteen constituted the highest proportion of those living below the poverty line. Rowntree used the notion of a poverty line to distinguish among different types of workers and their families. There were two types of poverty. The first characterized "families whose total earnings are insufficient to obtain the minimum necessaries for the maintenance of merely physical efficiency." This Rowntree called "primary poverty." The second type of poverty, "secondary poverty," described "families whose total earnings would be sufficient for the maintenance of merely physical efficiency were it not that some portion of it is absorbed by other expenditure, either useful or wasteful." Rowntree found that families moved in and out of poverty over the course of their lifetimes, depending on the size of the family and on the crises that befell it. His findings further indicated that close to 40 percent of all workers would be living in poverty at some point during their lives.[14]

Increasingly even the poorest families complied with the law whenever possible, and younger children often benefited most in these families. Declining fertility in these families meant fewer mouths to feed. And once several older children were at work, it became possible to maintain a nonworking child for a longer period of his or her life. The youngest daughter of a Parisian working-class couple was the only one of her siblings to continue her studies. Even with two sons working, the family still could not afford to finance her *baccalauréat*, but she obtained a commercial degree. "That permitted her to have a skill," her father recalled, "to manage for herself."[15] A similar example comes from East London. A mother describing the influence of sibling position on a child's education noted, "It was always that way with the oldest. With big families we were waiting for them to go to work. The younger ones were better off in every way. They got the best of the education and they got the advantage of better jobs too."[16]

By the twentieth century, school attendance was compulsory and literacy was an increasingly important requirement for employment. Parents accepted these facts and not only complied with the law, but urged their children to learn to read. Illiterate or semiliterate parents and grandparents took some pride in their children's accomplishment and they were often "the first to get angry with . . . grandchildren who, all preoccupied with playing . . , sulked about going to school."[17] Some accounts relate the emphasis parents placed on the intelligence of their children, calling upon them to count or recite or read for relatives or friends. Parents often expressed the hope as well that by pursuing their education, children might "exchange the blue shirt of their fathers for the white-collar of the bourgeoisie."[18] A sense of long-term investment in children's futures developed among some working parents.

Yet the new emphasis did not extend beyond the primary level, nor did it conflict with parental expectations that children would become family wage earners. Few people were willing to prolong a child's economic dependency by investing in apprenticeship or in additional technical training. Some families—the more prosperous artisans and shopkeepers—might send a daughter to a commercial college so she could become a secretary or high-level white-collar worker. Others sent girls to Normal Schools or to be trained as nurses. A small elite of working-class families in France sent their children to technical schools to become foremen, supervisors, and perhaps engineers. But before 1914, these were a tiny minority, "a drop of water in the sea of employment."[19] Rowntree reiterated the point made by the French author cited above when he wrote:

> The temptation is also great to put them to some labouring work where they can soon earn from five to eight shillings weekly rather than to apprentice them to a trade in which they will receive but low wages until they have served their time.[20]

The desire to place children in employment as soon as possible reflected the importance of their earnings to family finances at all levels of the working class. Indeed, the difference in York between families at the top and the bottom of the economic scale was largely a function of the proportion contributed by children's wages. Those families at the top received 25 percent of their income from children, those at the bottom only 7 to 10 percent. The high point of a family's financial situation usually came when children began to contribute to the household fund.[21]

Thus education served to postpone, but not to deter, the pressure on children to work. Moreover, in many cases the pressure on teen-agers seems to have intensified. Rowntree's story from York may be apocry-phal, but it well illustrates the sense of urgency families felt about getting children jobs: A boy asked his teacher the time. "Half past ten my lad, but what's the matter?" "Please sir, then may I go, sir: My mother said I should be 14 at half past 10 this morning and I could leave school when I was 14, sir."[22] Another author remembers that in Salford at the turn of the century children "left school in droves at the very first hour the law would allow and sought any job at all in factory, mill and shop."[23] Matters had not changed in York (nor elsewhere in England) when Rowntree returned in 1936. "Working class children usually leave school at 14 and go to work, most of them in factories."[24]

When a working-class daughter finished school she was prepared for a low-skill, low-paying job as a factory operative, a domestic servant, or a white-collar worker. Occupational opportunities for girls had changed in several ways by the first decades of the twentieth century. Factory employment, though gradually declining, had diversified. A number of new industries now hired women, taking up the slack left by the con-tracting textile sector and creating additional jobs in cities and towns which did not have heavy concentrations of any single industry. At the same time, unskilled positions as salesgirls and clerks were readily and increasingly available for girls who might otherwise have entered do-mestic service or factory employment. These kinds of jobs were seen as equivalent to factory positions and were usually lumped together in the range of options available to working-class girls. A small but impor-tant minority, those whose families could afford to support them or do without their wages while they received additional training, went on to become teachers and nurses. Parents, and particularly mothers, often helped their daughters find employment. But daughters also seem to have exercised a good deal of initiative in finding their own jobs.

Changes in the structure of domestic service meant that service was no longer the characteristic employment for young girls. Women who became servants while young were forced to do so by circumstances or by lack of alternatives, and they now stayed in the occupation for life. Thus Lilian Westall (born 1893) became a laundress at fourteen—de-spite her family's poverty she was allowed to finish school—but did the job poorly and was let go. She soon found work as a housemaid, minding children, sweeping, and scrubbing for a variety of employers, many of whom fed her badly and exploited her inexperience. During World War I she entered a munitions factory, but after the war such jobs became scarce and she found that living at home was impossible, so she went back into service. After her marriage she worked for an uphol-sterer, but left to have her first child. Then she returned to domestic work, in a hotel, then cleaning in a store, then as a housemaid. Until she was fifty-two, Lilian Westall was most often employed as a servant, living in when she was single and living out after her marriage.[25]

Winifred Foley (born 1914), the daughter of a miner, entered service at fourteen. This was "the common lot of every girl in our mining village." There were no other options for her. After her marriage in 1938 she continued doing domestic work, part or full time depending upon how much money she needed or time she had. Both Westall and Foley entered service much as girls had in the past. The circumstances of their families or the limited opportunities of (in Foley's case) a mining village made service a logical choice. Unlike their predecessors, however, the changed nature of domestic service made it an occupation increasingly available to them as married women. No longer the stage between childhood and marriage, domestic service became a lifelong employment.[26]

Jean Rennie (born 1906), the daughter of a Scottish riveter, had not planned to enter service. But when her father became unemployed in 1924 she turned down a scholarship to Oxford because of her family's desperate financial situation and became a maid instead. Older than either Lilian Westall or Winifred Foley when she began work, Jean remembered her mother's hurt and sadness at the fact that "her daughter, her eldest, gawky, clever, talented daughter, was going 'into service' as she herself had done at the age of twelve—without education." At the time Jean thought she would eventually get a better type of job, but she never did. Despite her secondary education and her obvious intelligence, she, too, remained a maid. After her marriage she worked as a cook.[27]

Domestic service still claimed a share of the female work force. But while migrant girls, miners' daughters in regions with no other options, and girls in dire need of money and therefore of readily available employment still might enter service, they did so in declining numbers. In contrast, as we have shown in Chapter 7, the numbers of older, married women servants grew. Domestic service was, by the 1930s, no longer the characteristic form of employment for working-class girls. They "preferred any kind of job in mill or factory, or even a place with rock bottom wages at Woolworth's and freedom . . . to the best that domestic service could offer."[28] This sense of choice, the ability to reject domestic service, was also a form of autonomy.

Not only freedom—greater autonomy at work and outside it—but better wages, less-demanding working conditions, and shorter, more regular hours drew young girls to jobs in factories, mills, and shops. A sense of choice is evident in many descriptions of work from this period. Girls were said to enter shop work, for example, because the status was higher, the work "clean," and the clientele "genteel." Many girls described the job as an alternative to "the monotony of needlework," the occupation followed by their mothers. One critic wrote:

> Like all "clean" jobs, that of the salesgirl seems each year to have more attractions for young girls looking for work. A misplaced "amour propre" prevents many of them from taking work [which would pay better] and leads them to choose this job where they are not workers but demoiselles —demoiselles de magasin.[29]

Yet despite its attraction, salesclerking had some similarities to domestic service. Indeed, an examination of the conditions of work show how limited were the choices of working girls. No skill was required of a shop girl, and an elementary education sufficed. In the past, a shop assistant—male or female—had been formally apprenticed to a retail tradesperson in order to learn the business and set up a shop on his or her own. But the practice of apprenticeship in the retail trades declined by the end of the nineteenth century and the shop assistant was only an unskilled employee. She might dream of owning a shop of her own someday, but there was no guarantee this would ever happen, no necessary relationship between her work and her future.

The work involved running errands and assisting shop owners or other clerks in the larger stores, as well as organizing and shelving stock and keeping the store clean and tidy. Sometimes shop assistants also sold items to customers, but in the larger stores they were permitted to do this only after having gained experience and won a "promotion." Wearing a simple uniform or a smock, the shop girl stood for long hours during most of the day. (Some of the earliest reform legislation—in 1899 —involved the provision of chairs by shop owners on which their sales help might occasionally sit.) The hours of shop employees were not subject to the same regulations as industrial workers until 1911 in England.[30] Only in 1906 were French sales personnel guaranteed one day off in a seven-day week. Unlike factory workers, but like servants, salesgirls in small shops especially were assumed to be involved in a kind of personal service to their employers. The pay was notoriously low. Assistants received an average annual wage of about 900 francs in Paris. One estimate in Paris in 1901 indicated that with a minimum of expenditures a single girl would still have a deficit of some 215 francs.[31] An Englishwoman reported that industrial workers regarded shop girls with scorn, saying they "are paid by the year because their wages are too small to divide by the week."[32] In the department stores in large cities, such as London and Paris, girls were boarded in dormitories provided by their employers. Like earlier industrial arrangements these dormitories disciplined the work force, permitted the recruitment of migrants, and enabled employers to underpay their help. (The system of granting commissions on sales to clerks also stimulated aggressive salesmanship and permitted store owners to pay very low regular wages.)[33]

In small and large shops jobs were often restricted to single women; indeed the practice was so widespread that some critics charged that immorality and licentiousness resulted because salesgirls preferred illicit liaisons to marriage and the loss of their jobs. Furthermore, young women were preferred for these jobs. Older shop assistants were cast aside even after some years of dedicated service, simply because they were too old. Among English shop assistants it was said that a girl was "too old at 21."[34] These hiring policies resulted in a constant turnover in the sales force. Young girls took jobs when they finished school, changed places often, either because they found better-paying opportunities or because an employer found them unsatisfactory, and then left the occupation for good upon marriage. An investigator's comment on the attitudes toward marriage of shop assistants echoed earlier such sentiments expressed by domestic servants:

> It is a significant fact that whereas large numbers of factory girls cannot be prevailed upon to give up their factory work after marriage, the majority of shop assistants look upon marriage as their one hope of release and would, as one girl expressed it, "marry anybody to get out of the drapery business."[35]

(The disastrous marriage of Monica, one of the central characters in George Gissing's novel *The Odd Women*, resulted in part from her overwhelming desire to "get out of the drapery business.")[36]

Like shop assistants, most young girls (even those in factory employment) seem to have looked upon their work as temporary. Wage-earning lasted only until marriage. Paid work was specific to a stage of women's life cycles; it was no longer a lifetime necessity. In part, of course, this resulted from employers' preferences for single women as employees. Like shopkeepers, state and administrative agencies restricted the ages at which women could be hired. French telephone operators had to be single and between the ages of eighteen and twenty-five.[37] Similarly, authorities discouraged schoolteachers from marrying. Until 1900 female teachers in France were forbidden by law to marry. No such formal prohibition existed in England, but in practice local officials often prevented a teacher who married from continuing to teach. This practice was not outlawed until 1944.[38]

Of course, teaching and nursing involved longer-term career commitments for many women than did the more typical forms of white-collar employment. The additional training many women received, the system of salary increments over a period of years, and the development of pension plans encouraged women to devote themselves to a lifelong professional career. In France, more than in England, married women continued to teach, for there were not enough single women to meet the demand for teachers. In fact, by 1922, 56 percent of all women teachers in France were married.[39] But in both countries many professional women remained single. The "old-maid" schoolteacher who had chosen to "mother" society's children rather than have children of her own was a familiar figure. The age structure of the teaching and nursing professions was more mixed than in sales and clerical jobs, turnover was lower, wages and status were higher. Though women's wages in teaching lagged behind men's (until 1919 in France and 1952 in England in primary education), the field had a social and economic status considerably higher than most other female white-collar jobs.[40]

Employer preferences were only one reason that most women left full-time work when they married. Family expectations and family pressures also influenced the pattern of women's work. While families increasingly preferred to keep mothers out of the labor force, daughters were expected, as in the past, to work in the family interest. The shift in occupational opportunity for women did not dramatically alter their family obligations. Compulsory education delayed their entry into the labor market, but when they took jobs, daughters worked in the family interest. As working-class populations settled into cities, more and more children lived at home until they married. The availability of diverse jobs in cities and towns made long-distance migration less likely. The decline of domestic service meant that fewer working girls "lived in." Moreover, as the birth rate dropped among more and more of these families, there was more room in the house for co-residing children. Of course, some salesgirls were boarded, and teachers often had to journey far from home to fill an assigned post. But the more typical jobs were to be found near home. By 1959, the practice was virtually universal; 90 percent of English children still lived at home two years after finishing school. In the same period, Wilmott and Young found that over half of the unmarried people in the sample they studied in Bethnal Green lived with their parents.[41]

Working-class families still counted on children's contributions. "Two or three children out to work and the dream of early marriage days fulfilled at last."[42] One study of French families showed a rise in the importance of children's wages from about 10 percent of the household income in 1907 to 18.5 percent by 1914.[43] Rowntree reported from York in 1899 that children who left home sent money to their families only occasionally, but those living in the household regularly contributed. It became customary in York "for older children to pay to their parents such portion of their wage as they would have had to pay for board and lodgings if not living at home." Whatever money was left over was their own to spend or save as they wished.[44] Similar practices were reported among French miners, textile workers, and clerks. Arrangements for sums to be paid seem to have varied a great deal. In some families children paid a weekly fee to their mothers; in others they turned over their entire wage packet and received pocket money in return. Indeed, a recurring figure in working-class lore is the exemplary daughter or son who refuses to take as much pocket money as the mother offers. Obviously, too, arrangements depended on the extent of family need, the poorest families taking as much as possible, if not all, of a child's earnings. In the 1920s and 1930s, the advent of social welfare measures—unemployment insurance, health and accident compensation, family allocations—alleviated some of the need in working families, some of the dependence on children's earnings. Even with these buffers, however, the earning child living at home contributed to the family fund. Studies of English and French families in the 1950s repeatedly cite the practice. Despite a higher standard of living among the working class, the ethic of mutual economic assistance persisted:

> The money we have is for the kids and whatever the kids can earn is for us. . . . We live for one another and with one another's help.[45]

Yet the total sense of self-abnegation implied in this French worker's statement is misleading. For though economic interdependence existed and though families recognized mutual obligations between parents and children, they also acknowledged the existence of a child's individual needs, needs which were personal and independent of the family interest.

Children were assumed to be entitled to some of the money they earned, and they were autonomous in their use of it. Working daughters, for example, often spent their money on clothes and leisure-time entertainment. One English study estimated that in 1910, about 55 percent of a girl's earnings went to her parents for room and board. Another 14 percent was spent on clothing; 10 percent on amusements, holidays, and picnics. The habit of saving varied greatly.[46] Although some might accumulate a small nest egg for marriage, the old practice of saving all of one's earnings for a dowry virtually disappeared. "The girls never do save," Clara Collet wrote of those in London's match factories. "They buy their clothes and feathers (especially the latter) by forming clubs; 7 or 8 of them will join together paying a shilling a week each and drawing lots to decide who shall spend the money each week."[47] A parliamentary report of 1904 compared working girls and married working women:

> While no doubt young girls and young women often spend a good deal on clothes, the married woman who works for spending money for herself . . . is so rare as to be negligible. . . . [48]

Clothing clubs were quite common among urban working girls. They reflected the growth of consumer interests among these women and they facilitated the purchase of clothing by cooperative savings. While married women became increasingly active in food-buying cooperatives, single women joined clothing clubs. Both kinds of organizations, however, were consumer cooperatives and both reflected the increased importance of "consumerism" among working-class families.

Though some mothers railed at the "coquetterie" of their daughters and criticized their preoccupation with "polishing" themselves, they seem to have accepted their daughters' behavior. First, of course, they had little control over it. As individual wage earners, girls had the right to spend some of their money as they chose. Moreover, those in white-collar jobs were required to dress presentably. In addition, a daughter might learn how to manage money, a skill she would need as a housewife. Indeed, some instances were cited of mothers confiscating most of a son's wages while permitting a daughter to keep her money so the daughter would learn how to budget it.[49] Some mothers, too, must have approved of their daughter's expenditures, knowing how brief would be the period of leisure and self-indulgence. Moreover, they recognized the fact that money had to be spent on things which had not involved expenditure in the past. Whereas girls once had made their Sunday dresses, they now bought their garments, since they neither were trained nor had time to sew and since ready-made clothes were relatively inexpensive. Leisure activities cost money too. In the past most of the socializing of young adults took place under public auspices. The holiday festival in a town square, the *veillées* in a barn, harvest and religious celebrations in fields or churches, and craft-sponsored festivities all were older forms of recreation at which young people had met and courted. Now the pubs or cafés and dance halls which young people frequented were privately owned and so cost money to attend. Hence a daughter's ability to participate in the activities of youth depended on her having some money to spend.

Increasingly, too, the activities of youth were separated from family and community activities. Not only did young people spend some money on themselves, but they spent a great deal of time with their peers, despite the fact that they lived at home for longer periods of their lives. School was one important source of peer-group socializing; work was another. In place of the mixed age structure of farm, craftshop, or household—where education and work took place simultaneously— factories, department stores, and offices tended to group workers homogeneously by age as well as by sex. Of course, shop assistants in small enterprises might, like domestic servants, be isolated employees. Teachers in rural areas often led very lonely lives. Nevertheless, increasingly young women worked in larger-scale establishments where they could form close associations with one another. Savings clubs, social organizations, even trade unions were the forms association might take.

Trade union activity among women was never as extensive or successful as it was among men. In France, where union membership was weak among men and women only 2 percent of all working women belonged to a union in 1906. (About 7 percent of the entire labor force was unionized in 1911).[50] Women also went out on strike less frequently than did men. The reasons for this, of course, lay in different orientations of women to their work and in differences in kinds of working conditions. First, women did not remain at their jobs for long periods of time; frequently they did not think of themselves as permanent workers. Second, there was often a great deal of turnover in women's jobs, making more difficult the establishment of a sense of collective membership and grievance. Third, family pressures often interfered with the ability of single and married women to devote time and money to a union. At the 1877 Trades Union Congress, for example, a male delegate from Oldham told of how "parents wanted to take all their daughters' earnings, and grudged even the small amount of their contribution to the union."[51] In addition, of course, some unions were ambivalent about organizing women. Unions in France and England bitterly debated the question of female members at the end of the nineteenth and beginning of the twentieth centuries. The printers' union, for example, prohibited members from marrying women who were printers. The famous Coriau Affair which began in 1913 involved the expulsion from the printers' union of a man who had violated this regulation. Other trades also rejected the idea of organizing women workers or of securing equal pay for them, preferring instead to drive women out of the labor force. Yet another obstacle to the organization of working women stemmed from the fact that middle-class feminists or socialists sometimes tried to organize working-class women. The goals of the leaders often did not represent the central concerns of their constituents. The Women's Trade Union League in England was founded in 1873 by a group of middle-class feminists who, among other things, opposed protective legislation for working women. It did successfully recruit a following, particularly among textile workers, but the working women did not always fully agree with the leadership's opposition to laws protecting women at work.

Nonetheless, among women in certain occupations there was evidence of growing strike and union activity after the 1880s. By 1889 the Women's Trade Union League had organized 118,000 women, most of them in the textile industry. Textile workers formed a large part of the constituency of the National Federation of Women Workers, founded in 1906. In France, too, textile workers were among the ranks of organized women. The garment, tobacco, and shoe trades also had significant numbers of women either in all-female unions or in "mixed" *syndicats*. In general, the women who organized came from predominantly female trades such as textiles and garment making. Sometimes, too, they were women who shared lodgings as well as worked at the same place. The London match girls who struck in July 1888, for example, tended to live together in boardinghouses near the factory. "The London match girls," wrote one observer, "have always shown a remarkable power of combination."

> Those in the East End are nearly all under one management and therefore live near each other. . . . They are distinguished by a strong *esprit de corps*, one girl's grievance being adopted as the grievance of every girl in the same room. They buy their clothes and feathers . . . by forming clubs. . . . They all work under the same conditions. . . . The difficulties in the way of trade union which would be found in every other industry are therefore much less here.[52]

The 1888 strike was called to protest a cut in wages and it led to the formation of a union of more than 800 women. (Middle-class organizers Annie Besant and Clementina Black assisted the efforts of the girls.)[53] In France, similar strike activity was reported, particularly among textile workers. In both countries, as well, trade associations demanding higher wages and better conditions had formed among teachers, nurses, shop girls, and secretaries by 1914.[54]

COURTSHIP AND MARRIAGE

Trade unions grouped women with their peers at work. In leisure, too, young women spent a good deal of time with friends. Indeed, friends made at school and then at work were also companions in recreation. A few girls who worked together might spend Sundays and holidays or go to a local dance hall with one another. The growth of cities and of neighborhoods in which populations of workers came from many different trades brought with it new forms of recreation and social intercourse. Activities which were individually organized or arranged by small groups of people replaced the large-scale community events more characteristic of rural areas or of urban craft associations. Neighborhood pubs and cafés mixing people of varying occupations substituted for the trade-specific centers which before had combined occupational and social functions. "Formerly, public houses in York were largely used as meeting places at which the business of Football Clubs, Trade Unions, Friendly Societies, etc. was transacted. The use of public houses for these purposes is, however, less general than it was. . . . "[55] Instead the pubs became centers of entertainment and amusement. The context in which young people met and interacted with one another changed. Young people had always formed groups and had had special roles and activities within a community. Now these activities took place in specially designated locations rather than as part of general public recreation. The locations were places apart that were frequented exclusively or predominantly by the young.

Certain bars became gathering spots for young people.

> Boisterous, quarrelsome, teasing, the young people have the same tastes as their parents. But pleasures differ according to age. They [the young] more regularly frequent the wine merchant [and] dances and café-concerts. . . . [56]

Rowntree offered a similar description of public houses in York: "The company is almost entirely composed of young persons, youths and girls sitting round the room at small tables."[57] Young men took their girlfriends to cafés, groups of men and women stopped off at them together after a Sunday picnic or a walk in the woods. The picnics and walks, too, became typically youthful activities.

> Young men and women in pairs, groups and droves went "rambling." Market Street, Manchester, on a Sunday morning was typical of many another city street—one saw what looked like a marching army of youth en route for London Station and the Derbyshire hills.[58]

The imagery of these descriptions and of Zola's in *Au bonheur des dames* are vivid. Amusement and leisure combine with flirtation and sexual implications as young people rest after a week of work and look over the field in search of a spouse.

The dance hall was the quintessential embodiment of this kind of youthful recreation.

> The young from 16 to 25 flocked into the dance halls by the hundred thousands. Some went "jigging" as often as six times a week. . . . At 6d per head (1s on Saturdays) youth at every level of the manual working class from the bound apprentice to the "scum of the slum" foxtrotted through the new bliss in each other's arms.[59]

Men lined up on one side of the hall, women on the other. "A male made his choice, crossed over, took a girl with the minimum of ceremony from in among and slid into rhythm."[60]

It was important for girls to "look nice" at these occasions, for personal appearance was an element in the selection process. Many girls invested the money that once might have been a dowry in cheap and readily available garments to enhance their appeal to men. The assumption that marriage involved the union of two wage-earning capacities, the fact that in any event wage-earning couples brought no endowment to their marriages, meant a greater emphasis on personal attraction and a lessening of the importance of the material resources one brought to a union. This does not mean, however, as Edward Shorter has suggested, that individual emotional considerations completely overcame "instrumental" attitudes toward sex and marriage.[61] The behavior and the looks of an individual, instead of her family's wealth or her father's occupation, did become increasingly important standards by which to assess the character, suitability, and reliability of a future mate. The goal of those standards was nevertheless "instrumental"—each partner sought a mate who would help support and maintain a family.

The context in which couples chose partners had changed in a number of ways. The fact that young people met in places away from home and that these places grouped the young exclusively meant there was less direct parental supervision of and interference with the selection of one's mate. For young women contacts with men depended less on parental networks than on their own friendship groups formed at school and work. If family sponsorship persisted, it was through siblings rather than parents. A brother's friends at work or in a neighborhood were potential suitors for a sister. A sister's friend often became her sister-in-law. Moreover, since parents did not provide a dowry or property, they had little control over the process. The close ties of occupational and geographic communities had disappeared and with them the occupational and geographic endogamy which had characterized earlier marital patterns. Even in a small town like Carmaux in southwestern France, the exclusiveness of the glassworkers' craft and social lives was broken in the 1880s by technological innovation. As the trade was opened to sons of miners and peasants, so marriage patterns changed. Daughters of glassworkers, who once had married men in their fathers' craft, now found husbands among men in a variety of working-class occupations in the city.[62] If marriages increasingly crossed occupational lines, however, they rarely crossed class lines. Though corporate endogamy declined, class endogamy persisted.

The social networks along which young people traveled were based on jobs and neighborhoods and were aspects of a general working-class culture. Except for teachers, who, in France at least, tended to marry other teachers, the new jobs available for working-class daughters offered few opportunities for social mobility.[63] All of this meant that, at least as far as choice of a spouse was concerned, daughters were more autonomous than they had been in the past.

Although parents might have a hand in concluding a marriage for their children their role was much diminished by the twentieth century. The couples themselves usually made the necessary arrangements. One account suggests that "the lead in translating courtship into marriage was normally taken by the woman."[64] Moreover, the large family and community celebrations seem to have waned among urban working-class families. While "a funeral demands special clothes," one observer in London noted in 1911, "a marriage is, by comparison almost unnoticed. . . . It occurs most frequently on a Saturday or Sunday, as it is hardly worthwhile to lose a day's work . . . few attend it outside a small circle of lady friends."[65]

Yet the increased autonomy of working children did not remove them completely from family influences, nor did it create individualistic values which opposed those of the family. Parents seem to have recognized children's needs, to have accepted (if sometimes dubiously) the dance halls and dresses. The changed activities of youth were simply incorporated into the family life cycle. Even though socializing and courtship took place away from home, parental influence affected the activities of their children. "Too early an interest in sex might be condemned by parents just feeling the benefit of a new wage-earning son or daughter."[66] Moral and social codes (the elaboration and function of which need more study) and the threat of expulsion from home governed the behavior of children. A working daughter's potential financial independence was dubious, given the low wages she earned. In addition, being forced to leave home was not a happy experience, for sentimental and emotional ties held her to her family. "The Edwardian slum child," Roberts recalled, "like his forbears, felt an attachment to family life that a later age may find it hard to understand."[67]

Children still sought the approval of their parents for a future partner, and few weddings were arranged before it was secured. Indeed a mother might force the issue and insist, for example, that her son marry a girl who was pregnant with his child. A French worker described the pressure put on him (he was nineteen at the time) by his mother and future mother-in-law in such a situation. His mother-in-law, having learned that her daughter was pregnant, arranged for the wedding. On the day it was to take place, Amedée's mother said to him, "You will marry!" "I'm not getting married," he replied. "If you don't say yes," she threatened, "I will slap your face. . . . " Finally, he recalled, "I said yes." As one might expect, the marriage did not last very long.[68] Nonetheless it exemplified the social and emotional power of family pressure.

The "settling" of working-class populations as well as the longer co-residency of working children within the parental household seems to have changed but not broken family ties. New forms of peer-group activity were absorbed in the family life cycle, and parents, while grumbling and criticizing the freedom of youth, nonetheless expected and permitted young adults to be independent while they still fulfilled family economic responsibilities. There was thus no necessary contradiction between the fulfillment of the needs of single young women and men and the French worker's description of his relations with his children: "We live for one another and with one another's help."

If, during the period of school and work, a daughter enjoyed a degree of independence, marriage brought her back to the family—her own new one and to her family of origin as well. Young couples frequently settled near the wife's parents and became active participants in a family network. Although the most complete descriptions of this phenomenon are contained in studies of working-class families later in the twentieth century, there is evidence to indicate that it was characteristic at the beginning of the century as well. Numerous autobiographies and memoirs refer to continuing contacts between parents and their married children. Whether or not they lived close by, young couples frequently lived in the same city as their parents, which enabled them to maintain contact and to visit.

Ties seem to have been especially close between mothers and daughters in working-class families. Once a daughter married (and particularly when she had a child) "she returns to the woman's world, and to her mother." With the period of full-time work and courtship over, the autonomy of youth was gone. Young women entered a world in which their peers were of varying ages, though of the same sex. It was a "woman's world" in which they shared with their mothers and with other married women the same experiences and "the same functions of caring for home and bringing up children," whether or not they also went out to work.[69]

MARRIED WOMEN'S WAGE LABOR

Within the working-class family married women continued to perform the activities they had in the past. They earned wages when necessary, they managed household activities and expenditures, and they bore and cared for children. Yet, by the first decades of the twentieth century in a growing number of urban families, the relative importance of each of these activities had begun to change as a consequence of economic, demographic, and political developments. Married women's childbearing and domestic responsibilities became more demanding and more time-consuming, while the time they spent in wage-earning activities diminished.

This was not, to be sure, a uniform or universal pattern. On small farms the older form of the family economy continued. Women combined housework and farm work as partners in a family enterprise. In England, of course, few of these farms existed by 1911. In France their numbers were high in contrast to England, but slowly and steadily declining. Nonetheless, as late as the 1950s sociological studies of farm life indicated that the family farm engaged the farm wife in many hours of "productive" work.[70] Her chores and the rhythm of her life would have been familiar to many an eighteenth-century peasant wife. The cities of both countries also had households organized as family labor economies. In the still numerous shops and family businesses of France home and work were one. Consequently, married women's domestic responsibilities merged into their market roles. Though English cities had fewer enterprises organized on a small scale, many existed. The corner shop in Salford, where Robert Roberts grew up, was run jointly by his parents. The family lived in rooms above the store where the mother bore seven children and cared for them while also running the business.[71]

In cities such as Stockport, where the occupational structure created an enduring shortage of steady and well-paying male employment on the one hand, and continuing opportunities for women to work on the other, married women worked in the mills even when they had young children at home. Indeed, in these cities the Child Labor and Education acts passed after the 1870s resulted in an overall increase in the numbers of married women at work. The availability, too, of more appealing white-collar jobs for single women created more openings for married women in factories. In Lille in 1899, 31 percent of all women with children under a year old worked in the mills.[72] (See Figure 7–3 Part B, for the increased proportion of married women working in Roubaix in 1906 as compared to 1872. Increased employment of married women in the British textile industry is discussed above.) These women worked because their families needed their wages; in fact, in many instances they were the family's primary wage earners. A British factory inspector reported in 1904 that the death, unemployment, or low wages of the husband were primary motives for married women's factory work. "The family income in cotton towns," noted one survey in 1911, "frequently consists of both husband's and wife's earning. . . . The wife is most frequently employed when the husband's wage is low. . . . "[73] In textile town after textile town, mill operatives told the French government commission in 1904 that they sent their children to baby minders and endured high infant mortality rates because a wife's work was essential for the "family wage." Still in 1931, an investigation in Lille revealed that the vast majority of married women sought employment in textile factories for the same reasons.[74]

In these towns, too, married women alternated with their children as family workers, withdrawing from full-time factory employment as soon as their children could earn wages. In Armentières, France, in 1906, for example, the percentage of employed married women declined dramatically when there were working children in the household. In the shoemaking center of Fougères, a similar decline in married women's work-force participation occurred as their children became wage earners. Women who entered factories during World War I because their husbands were at war, and because factories recruited their labor, also withdrew from work when their children could substitute for them as family wage earners. "During the war, I was alone with my children, so I worked in a factory," a former metalworker recalled in 1921. "I ruined my health there. When the children began earning their own living, I stayed at home. . . . "[75]

In all cities with diverse occupational structures, the wives of the poorest, and widows were the bulk of full-time workers, whether employed in domestic industry or away from home (usually as casual laborers). Where the family fund depended on a woman's wages, she worked at what jobs she could find. This kind of family wage economy was most prevalent among the poorest families. Most home workers in Birmingham said they toiled long hours because "the husband's wage was either too small or too irregular to keep the home." A large number were widows who "had generally started work when their husbands became invalided."[76] In London, too, "only the widows . . . or those who have invalid or worthless husbands go to work each day."[77] The home workers who worked longest hours in London, too, and who were most exploited were those desperate women who "have others to support." For them, a reporter commented, "life . . . is nothing more than procrastination of death." Their "poverty and misery are caused by the industrial position of the husband, or by the mental and moral defects ... of either husband or wife ... or by sickness or accident."[78]

Most of these women did home work, sewing garments or trimming hats in their households. But, although they worked at home, their lives and jobs differed from those of women in the preindustrial household. Above all, these women had little control over their work. Their competitive position was poor and they had no ability to bargain for better wages. They depended for work on an industry located near their homes and willing to subcontract work to them. The misery of these women stemmed from the fact that they had no choice. Their families' subsistence and its survival demanded that they work. Their desperate circumstances, moreover, left them little choice as to what kind of job they would take and little room to negotiate for wages or decent working conditions. The continuing pressure on these women to earn wages was a sign of need in their households. It is no wonder, then, that working-class culture adopted the image of the married woman at home as the sign of the health, stability, and prosperity of a household. The expression of this ideal was less a result of the *embourgeoisement* of the working class than it was a statement about the realities of working class experience.

Although examples abounded of married women in employment during the first decades of the twentieth century, there was an overall increase in the numbers of them at home, for women continued to withdraw from the labor force when they married, or after the birth of a first child. In both England and France, there were fewer married women than single women in the labor force. In England in 1911, 68.3 percent of single women and only 9.6 percent of married women worked. In France, a far less dramatic contrast existed in 1906; 68 percent of single women over fourteen were employed, as compared with 56 percent of married women. More revealing is the comparison of the nonagricultural female work force in France, which employed 40.8 percent of single women (over fourteen) as compared with 20.2 percent of married women in 1906. The higher rate in France than in England of married women employed outside of agriculture stemmed partly from France's higher nuptiality rate. Other factors were the continued importance of domestic production and small family enterprises, which provided jobs for women which were reconciled easily with domestic tasks. Nonetheless, in both countries there seem to have been fewer married women employed in 1914 than there had been fifty years before.[79]

How can we explain this decline in married women's employment? It stemmed from a combination of structural, economic, and demographic factors. First, the sectors of the economy which had employed the largest numbers of married women were contracting. The garment and shoe trades in England employed 19 percent of all working women in 1851, 15 percent in 1911. In France, the decline began only after 1906. (By 1921 this sector employed 20 percent of all women working outside of agriculture, as compared with 27 percent in 1906. In 1936, the figure was 15.5 percent).[80] Textiles, too, employed a smaller proportion of all working women. The shrinkage of this sector meant an aggregate decline in opportunities for married women. This occurred at the same time that married women continued to work in the textile industry and, indeed, as noted above, made up an increasingly large proportion of female textile operatives. The growth of the tertiary sector, moreover, displaced married women in the distributive trades and opened few new opportunities for them. Clerical and administrative positions as well as jobs in the liberal professions were most often restricted to young single women. Since the supply of single women was ample, married women were usually not hired for these jobs.

The overall decline in opportunities for married women probably meant that more of those who did have to work sought jobs as casual laborers or improvised short-term cash-producing activities for themselves. There is ample evidence for the continuation of some earlier practices. In Birmingham, provision shops, carried on "in an adapted kitchen" were common. "One frequently finds a woman with an empty shop and with the business in abeyance because she cannot buy anything to put in the window."[81] From Salford comes a similar description:

> "Curran cakes! 3 for 2d," advertised one neighbour on a little pile of grey lumps in her house window. Nobody bought. We children watched them growing staler each day until the kitchen curtain fell again on the venture like a shroud.[82]

Yet even though it is impossible to measure changes in this area, since activities of this type were rarely recorded, it is reasonable to conclude that the need for improvised wage earning also decreased. The changes in the organization and the scale of urban markets made the street hawker a less familiar figure. Established neighborhood shops with cheap goods and produce easily competed with a housewife's ad hoc efforts. The prolonged presence of adult children at home and the declining numbers of rural-to-urban migrants made boarding a less common practice. Moreover, the decline in the numbers of married women working and in the numbers of children born created less need for baby minders and nurses in working-class neighborhoods. The numbers of married women who did charring and laundry did increase, but they did not offset losses in other areas. The list of occupations of women in the poorest households in York in 1899 reflects the structure of opportunity for casual labor we have described. Of the 367 women, 165 were charwomen; another 78 did laundry. Only 28 took in lodgers, while two were streethawkers. The rest were dressmakers, field laborers, nurses, small shopkeepers, or unskilled day laborers.[83]

The second factor which decreased married women's work-force participation was the overall increase in men's real wages which occurred between 1880 and 1914 in both countries. Real wages improved in both England and France through the last years of the nineteenth century until about 1910. There was a marked decline in prices in the period, according to both aggregate indices and indices specifically designed to measure working-class living conditions. This meant that even though wage levels remained relatively constant, workers were able to enjoy a higher standard of living. It must be noted, however, that the working-class households with higher than average incomes at the turn of the century all had more than one worker in them.[84]

The British Board of Trade survey of household expenditures of workers in several large towns in 1904 showed the possibility of substantial choice in food purchases. A French index of the cost of living showed a similar decline from 1880 to 1900, then a rise to 1910 and a steeper rise thereafter.[85] With these conditions, French and British working-class wives had more choice about paid employment outside or within the home. Wives' potential salaries were likely to be not a matter of desperately needed pennies but a means to buy small additional "luxuries." A woman's wages were likely to be low, for there continued to be a substantial differential between male and female wages. In 1910, a French economist attributed women's low wages to the fact that they usually were members of units which provided their subsistence; hence according to him they did not demand a living wage from their own earnings. He noted that this suited the purpose of employers, who hired women as cheap labor.[86] British observers also argued that there were two different ways of calculating wages according to sex: men's wages were based on the cost of living; women's wages were "of a supplementary character. If she can add something to the net weekly takings of the family, that is the chief point. . . . A woman considers what it will be worth to add to the family revenue, rather than what her work is really worth."[87] Of course, none of these arguments took into account the possibility of a married woman as an independent earner outside the family context. In the period before World War I, however, they represented the normative situation in which women found themselves. Although real wages increased, then, the differential between male and female wages remained. The choice for married

women, when their husbands were present and working, was not between home and paid jobs with good wages, but between market work
at poor wages and activity in the household in the service of preferred
and better-paid workers. Many wives quite reasonably chose the home
role.

The families of skilled workers benefited earliest from the improvement in real wages.[88] It was among these families especially that the
decline in married women's work was most widespread. In York, Rowntree did find a third of the working-class population in what he termed
"primary poverty" in 1899. The better-off families, however, formed
the largest proportion of the population. (In 1936, when he returned,
he found the standard of living 30 percent higher than it had been in
1899.) Far more families were in the highest economic bracket ("Class
D," earning more than 30 shillings a week) and far fewer were in the
lowest ("Class A," earning under 18 shillings a week.). ("Class C" families had a weekly income of 21 to 31 shillings.) The position of wives in
Class D families he described as more private. "The women, left in the
house all day whilst their husbands are at work, are largely thrown upon
their own resources."[89] The French sociologist Maurice Halbwachs reported in 1914 that fewer wives in working-class families contributed
to the household budget than had done so seven years earlier. (31
percent in 1907; 26 percent in 1914). Moreover, he noted, the wages
of those who did earn some money accounted for a smaller proportion
of the family budget in the later period (11.7 percent in 1907; 5.4
percent in 1914).[90]

A third factor which influenced married women's employment rates
was related to improvements in real wages. The increased standard of
living improved the diet, the health, and the life span of working-class
adults. The decline of incidences of illness and death of a husband thus
drove fewer married women into the labor force. In the course of her
lifetime, a wife faced fewer emergencies which compelled her to
become the family breadwinner. The most dramatic drops in married
women's entries into the labor force occurred in their younger years
and particularly when young children were at home. Life crises tended
to cluster almost exclusively in old age. Many a village and city in
England and France still "had its quota ... of elderly women, broken
like horses, who could be hired to drag a hundredweight of coke in a
wagon a mile or more for three pence."[91] Yet there were fewer examples, on the whole, of struggling young widows with three or four
children to support.

The fourth factor which diminished the need for wage earning by
married women was a decline in family size. Beginning in the 1880s in
both England and France, working-class couples had fewer children

than their predecessors had had. (Of course, family limitation was practiced more or less extensively among different occupational groups, for
reasons which historians and demographers are only beginning to
understand.) Fewer children in a family meant fewer demands on
financial resources and hence fewer demands on mothers to engage in
wage-earning activity. Circumstances, therefore, less often drove married women to work, while fewer opportunities attracted them to the
job market.

A fifth influence on married women's work patterns was the prolonged residence of working children in the household. These children
contributed to the household budget, on the one hand, and so raised
family living standards. Their presence, however, meant increased domestic work for the mother. In York in 1899, Rowntree noted that Class
D families enjoyed a certain financial security because of the contributions of working children. Twenty-one of the forty-eight Class D families he described had working children living at home. (On the other
hand, only one fourth of Class C families had working children at home.)
They ranged in age from fourteen to thirty-five; the average age was
twenty. In a machinist's family, for example, four adult children
worked. A twenty-eight-year-old son was a fitter, a nineteen-year-old
son a machinist, a fifteen-year-old son a pharmacist, and a seventeen-
year-old daughter a tailor. Similarly, a boilersmith had three working
children. One son (twenty-seven) was a fitter; another (twenty-two) was
a fireman; the third (nineteen) was a cleaner. A twenty-five-year-old
daughter also lived in the household, and she was listed as assisting at
home.[92]

The aggregate decline in married women's work ought not to ob-
scure the fact that different patterns of employment existed in different
cities. Figure 8–1 compares patterns of married women's work in Anzin
and Roubaix in 1906. In Anzin, few married women worked in 1906 (far
fewer than in 1872). An increased proportion of male workers were
employed in well-paying administrative and commercial jobs in 1906.
Moreover, the home industries typical of married women's employment in the 1870s had declined by the early twentieth century in
Anzin. In Roubaix, on the other hand, opportunities still existed for
married women to work in the mills, where they were employed in
large numbers. As compared to 1872, more of them worked for longer
periods of their lives. This reflected the decline in employment opportunities for young children and compulsory education until age thirteen. After children were thirteen, the alternating patterns of mother's
and children's work is evident in Roubaix in 1906, as it was in 1872. The
contrast between Anzin and Roubaix reminds us that specific patterns

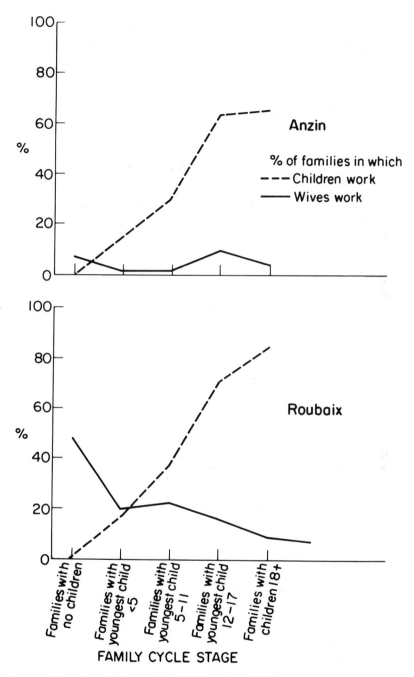

Figure 8.1   Family Patterns of Wives' and Children's Employment;
Anzin and Roubaix, 1906

of married women's employment varied with the economic organization of particular cities.

Although circumstances less often drove married women to work, they did not entirely abandon wage-earning activity. Even for those who could live up to the ideal of the married woman at home, work was always a possibility. In working-class families no one believed that femininity and employment were incompatible. For one thing, women's wage-earning ability was still a kind of insurance; married women were still the family reserve labor supply. "I think it is every woman's place to work and help if the husband is short of work or does not earn sufficient to support the home," an elderly woman in Birmingham told an investigator in 1904. "I think that . . . the woman ought to help only in cases of illness or shortness of work," said another.[93] The imperative remained: married women ought to earn wages if necessary. Life was precarious enough that necessity might call at any time.

Yet even among stable and prosperous families, married women occasionally entered the labor market, not to ensure subsistence, but in order to supplement their family's income; not from necessity, but by choice. The fact that they had a choice made all the difference, for then their work was not a sign of family hard times:

> The majority of [women] of the skilled artisan and shop-keeping class . . . are not ashamed of working, or of working for money, but are most anxious to make it clear that they are only earning pocket-money—pursuing a trade of their own free choice, not because they are obliged.[94]

The greater health and prosperity of their families enabled these women to take on work if they had the time and to control the time they spent in earning money. "Over and over again," reported one observer of the London garment trades, "I have met women in comfortable circumstances who have told me either that they left off taking in work because it did not pay for the trouble, or that they only worked half the week because they had the washing to do and the clothes to mend, and the time was worth more than the money."[95]

No quantitative data exist which show the distribution of the family economic status of women who did piecework at home; but the surveys do mention the wide variety of the women's backgrounds. In London, Collett found home workers from "every grade of society." In Amiens, where three-quarters of the outworkers were married, their husbands' occupations ranged from white-collar jobs to unskilled agricultural laborers. Many of the women, investigators reported, were earning merely *"un salaire d'appoint."*[96]

Even where domestic employment was not available on a large scale, married women took on short-term jobs, charring, doing laundry, picking fruit or canning it in factories during the busy season, in order to add some money to the household budget, often to buy specific items they wanted. Mrs. L., a laborer's wife in York, "does an odd day's charring now and again." Mrs. D. "is glad to do a day's charring, or will do plain sewing at home. . . ." Rowntree's phrasing captures well the desultory nature of their work.[97] As late as the 1950s this practice continued among Irish families in London:

> After marriage the women work only when they need money. If the man is out of work or if they want something in particular, they will take a job for a short time. . . . As soon as the immediate need for money has passed they give it up.[98]

Irregular and episodic forms of employment were most suited to the needs of these women, and so they continued as the most typical form of married women's work. Although the nature of their work—unskilled and temporary—meant that wages and working conditions would never be very good, the fact that these women chose to work often meant they could refuse the most exploitative and lowest-paying jobs. Those jobs were the lot of the destitute, of those who had no choice.

Those married women who chose to work did so not usually from individualistic motives nor from a desire for financial independence. Rather they sought to improve the position and comfort of their families and to raise rather than simply to maintain the family's standard of living. They worked in the interest of the family's economic position, which now took the form of what we have termed the "family consumer economy." The standards and style of life of many working families had begun to demand more expenditures by the early 1900s. Rowntree noted, for example, that the practice of taking short summer vacations was increasing among better-paid working men's families in York in 1899. While commentators often remarked on the lack of thrift in working-class families, they also pointed to the existence of short-term saving clubs (goose clubs, for example, so that the family was guaranteed a Christmas dinner). There was also a form of longer-term saving practiced on a large scale—burial insurance, which guaranteed nothing for the survivors (they presumably had their own labor power to rely on) but did provide a decent funeral for the dead.[99]

While men's wages and those of working children took care of most family necessities, the wages earned by married women helped raise family consumption levels, enabling the purchase of children's clothing, various luxuries, or the accumulation of savings for vacations or children's education.

> Many skilled [women] workers do not work for the bare necessities of life, but their standard of living is relatively high and they often work in order to maintain this standard, especially with regard to their children's clothing.[100]

> The young wife of the clerk ... is glad to add something to the savings which may be useful some day when the children are being educated or started in life.... The wife of the carman with 18s a week may make butter-scotch boxes in order that her children and her rooms and her dress may look as well as those of her sister who is married to a mechanic earning 32s a week. [101]

The mother of a Parisian family continued to do charring several days a week, even when her children, all of whom had jobs, insisted she quit and remain at home. "All right, I will stop," she agreed at last, "but not for another year, because in August I will take you to Le Havre." After the eight-day vacation—the family's first—she stopped working.[102]

In all of these cases the mother's work was undertaken as a supplement to her domestic activities, often only after children were at school or work. Its goal was to improve the family's living standard by making the consumption of more things possible. Whereas other family members often retained a portion of their wages, married women rarely did. Memoirs by workers often recall how a mother would scrimp and save, rarely buying a dress or anything for herself, so that a child could have new clothes.[103] In this sense, married women's work involved a great deal of self-sacrifice. On the other hand, by boosting the spending ability of the family, a married woman enhanced her own position and the amount of money at her disposal even if she spent most of the money on the family rather than on herself. For as the family economy became a family consumer economy, the woman's position as financial manager of the household expanded. The primary source of her status in the family (and in the community) came from the wife's ability to provide for the needs of the household by carefully managing the money contributed by others. Her own occasional wage-earning efforts enabled her to better fulfill her domestic role by providing "extras" which would improve the quality of family life.

> "I could have stopped working much sooner," an old French woman who worked until she was 65 recalled, "but I wanted to continue, to earn

money. I always wanted to have money. . . . And that permitted us many things that we otherwise would not have been able to have."[104]

On the whole, by 1914 fewer married women worked and women spent less time working during their lives. Diminished financial pressure within the family increased their control over the allocation of their time. The choice, however, was not between wage earning and leisure, nor between productivity and nonproductivity. It was between forms of economic and household activity—family-oriented work.

MARRIED WOMEN'S DOMESTIC ACTIVITIES

The household division of labor within working-class families continued as in the past, but the distinction sharpened between male and female tasks. Increasingly, men were the primary, if not the sole, wage earners, their income supplemented by contributions from working children during the period in which those children lived at home. Wives, on the other hand, were more concerned exclusively with home and children.

Most married women had few occupational skills to compare with their husbands' but they became specialists in child rearing and household management, acquiring a store of experience which their husbands never shared. A woman's major domestic responsibility continued to be the management of household finances, a consequence of her role as chief consumer for the family. At all levels of the working class, women held the purse strings, collecting all or some of the earnings of working family members.

> Her purse or pocket is the common fund, and from this she distributes the family income. They are the earners, but she is the spender. . . .[105]

Housewives, a French trade union publication noted in 1912, "are the Finance Ministers of our homes." As such, they not only allocated money, but decided how it was to be spent.

> Any arrangement made by the wife without previous consultation with her husband is nearly always ratified by him, but the converse is by no means true.[106]

In most instances, husbands retained or were given some pocket money for carfare, drink, and tobacco. In some families, the husband paid his wife an agreed-upon "wage." "I'm a blacksmith and I make good money," said a blacksmith to Rowntree in 1936, "and on Friday night after paying the wife, I have between 30s and 35s left in my pocket and it all goes on beer. . . ."[107] As late as the 1950s, this practice was reported among Irish families in Liverpool. Noted one study, "a 'good' dad hands over his entire wages and is given something back."

> A Mum does expect to see her husband's wage packet and to know exactly how much he had earned each week, so that she is in a position to judge for herself whether she has received a fair "wage" or not.[108]

For others payday was marked by bitter dispute, tears, and blows over how much the husband would keep and how much was legitimate for the wife to claim. Describing payday in a working-class suburb of Paris, the wine merchant Leyret wrote:

> On this day, the suburb has a very particuliar atmosphere, a mixture of gaiety and anxiety. . . . The housewives wait at the windows or stand in the doorways, and sometimes in their impatience . . . one sees them walking toward the factory to meet their husband. . . . In the street voices snarl, in the houses insults fly . . . hands are raised, tears flow. . . .[109]

No one pattern seems to have prevailed in working families, although it may be that greater harmony existed in the homes of the better-paid workmen who had more surplus to spend. In any case, there are as many examples of cooperation as there are of contest. A particularly striking example of cooperation comes from an undoubtedly unusual woman, an activist in the English Women's Cooperative Guild. Her exposure to the guild came when her "husband brought me two tickets for a tea and social which he asked me to use. I could not well spare the time, but I did not like to waste the tickets, for I knew it was a big sacrifice out of my husband's little bit of pocket money."[110]

Most of the household money a woman received continued in this period to be spent on food. Various studies estimate that food accounted for some 60 percent of the working-class family budget in France during the period 1880–1914. (Among middle-class families the figure was at most 20 percent.)[111] In England the figure may have been somewhat lower, but not appreciably. Clearly these averages do not capture the economic diversity of working-class families, but they do give some idea of aggregate patterns. Although bread was still a major item in a family's budget, lowered prices on many items of food made for a more varied diet. The poorest families rarely ate meat, but the better-off ate it more frequently. The consumption of sugar, tea, coffee, and chocolate rose steadily in France. In England, the importation of cheap wheat and meat in the 1880s and lowered taxes on imports produced a drop in food prices and a consequent improvement in working-class diet.[112] Milk and fresh fruit and vegetables were most often lacking in the diets of working families in both countries, and a study in 1904 found that 33 percent of English children were undernourished. They rarely drank milk and lived largely on a diet of bread, margarine, jam, and tea.[113] A 1902 survey found that while middle-class families consumed an average of 6 pints of milk per person per week, families of artisans drank only 1.8 pints and laborers .8 pints, per person, per week.[114] There was no dramatic improvement in diet in the prewar period. Until after World War I, malnutrition was a common problem, particularly among women and children. The nutritional problems of working-class families were not easily or quickly solved. Nonetheless, more and a greater variety of food items were evident in these families' budgets. One consequence was that shopping became a more time-consuming process for the housewife, as did the preparation of meals. Although working women might buy cooked meals from pushcarts or shops, "good artisan families never brought cooked food home, 'a mother would have been insulted.' "[115] Moreover, whatever labor-saving devices were used in upper-class homes were too costly for the working-class household.

In addition, activities associated with the purchase of food could demand additional hours of women's time. The growth in England of the cooperative movement and particularly of the Women's Cooperative Guild (founded in 1883) organized housewives into consumer cooperative societies. By 1930, the guild had some 67,000 members many of whom actively participated in meetings, and in the administration of local societies.[116] The very real economic advantages of membership for the individual housewife came as a result of an investment of money (to buy shares) and of some of her time. Those women who did not have the time to walk the extra distance to the cooperative store and to work some hours there, lost an economic advantage for their families.

The cooperative movement, appealing as it did to a permanent interest of married women (as opposed to their temporary involvement in the labor market), also mobilized women politically. The English cooperative movement supported the Labour Party. Women in the guild became advocates on issues of education, health, and maternity care. The success of the guild stemmed from the fact that it spoke directly to married women's major concern with, as one cooperator put it, "The Marketing Basket."[117]

The centrality of food in the woman's household responsibility could still lead her to riot when prices soared and crucial items became scarce.

In France in 1911, housewives in the Nord and the Pas-de-Calais re-
fused to pay high food prices. (The fact that most were wives of miners
and metalworkers may also indicate the impossibility for these women
to find jobs to help the family meet the high cost of living in that year.
Mining and metallurgical centers had few opportunities for women to
work.) They seized and destroyed eggs, milk, and butter in some towns,
in others they stopped wagons and forced farmers to sell their products
at a "just price." Initially a spontaneous outburst, the "housewives'
revolt" spread from town to town with the assistance of trade union
activists, who helped organize boycotts of markets and then set up
housewives' trade unions. Like food riots of the past, the 1911 demonstrations mobilized women as family consumers. The scale of politics in
the early twentieth century and the existence of organized working-
class political institutions, however, gave the protests new form, ideological content, and wider political significance (demonstrators waved
the red flag and sang the *Internationale*). The outbursts were quickly
incorporated into trade union activity and interpreted as an aspect of
ongoing workers' protests against the high cost of living. Nonetheless,
their special character as market-oriented protests was a direct consequence of the fact that they were initiated by women.[118]

A wife's financial responsibilities, in addition to the purchase of food,
included paying the rent, providing clothes for family members, and
furnishing the household. Gareth Stedman Jones has described the increasing importance of home life among English working-class families
at the turn of the century. As a result of shorter work days, increased
leisure time (stemming from legislation which reduced working hours),
and suburban migration, he says, the work-centered culture of an earlier period was replaced by a culture centered around family and home.
Workmen spent more time at home by the early twentieth century.
Sundays became the day for a family outing (in France and England),
when everyone stopped at a café or pub for refreshment. Higher earnings and increased buying power also enabled families to aspire to
higher standards of material comfort. Small decorative items, pictures
on the walls and flowers in the window, like a suit of good Sunday
clothes, helped keep up appearances as well as make the house a more
pleasant place. A woman's ability to add a few luxuries to her home was
an important indication of her housekeeping skill.[119] Sick club or burial
society dues also demanded regular contribution, and in many of the
poorest homes, "the mother managed to pay 1s a week for family burial
insurance." Union subscriptions also came out of household funds. "For
twenty-six years I paid all subscriptions [for my husband's trade union]
and willingly paid a levy of 1£ a year for political purposes. . . ." wrote
one workman's wife.[120]

The effort to meet required payments often took a good deal of juggling of family funds, as indicated by the constant use of the word *managed* to describe a housewife's financial activity. "Papa gave [Mama] what he had and she managed with it," a French worker recalled. An old woman told Rowntree how she had "managed" on her husband's wage of 17s a week. "Each week, . . . as soon as she received the 17s, she put aside the money required for rent, and then planned out exactly how she could spend the remainder to the best advantage."[121]

Paying bills also involved keeping records and dealing with merchants, insurance men, and other representatives of bureaucratic organizations. Married women were the family members who almost exclusively dealt with these people. The extension of the wife's domestic function, in other words, was to be the family's public representative. A visiting nurse in London commented on the wife's expertise in these matters, implicitly comparing middle-class practices with those she observed in the households of working men:

> Although one would imagine that the larger share of worldly experience fell to the husband, it is always the wife who shows most caution with regard to getting bills receipted and so forth.[122]

The wife was the specialist in home management and, as such, handled all strangers who came to the house. "If a stranger calls, [the husband] will leave it to his wife to represent the family interest."[123] Thus, the clergyman, philanthropist, and moral reformer all were met at the door by the mother of the house. Mothers also dealt with school officials, truant officers, and, if children got into trouble, with police and magistrates. All of this took time as well as experience.

Clearly, the economic situation and smooth functioning of the household depended on the woman's ability to "manage." Over and over again accounts refer to the wife as a good or a bad manager. It may well be that the self-denial which seems to have been characteristic of working-class women was related to their sense of themselves as responsible for shortages, particularly food. Rowntree's repeated inquiries among poor housewives in York "as to how they met expenditures for household replacements or for any other special purposes always drew forth a reply to the same effect, namely, 'we have to get it out of the food money and go short.'" It was the women who most frequently "went short." "I have gone without my dinner . . . and just had a cup of tea for the children's sakes," reported a plate layer's wife. "If there's anything extra to buy . . . me and the children goes without dinner . . . but Jim allers takes 'is dinner to work, and I never tell 'im," said a York housewife.[124] Studies well into the 1930s showed that mothers bore the brunt of nutritional deprivation. As wage earners, men had to have the lion's share of food, and, if she could not manage to provide enough for everyone, the manager herself had to do without. Describing working men's wives in Paris, Leyret noted that they often wore *sabots* so their children might have shoes. The woman's sense of competence, her "pride," he added, came from her ability to do her job well. A clean, well-fed, and respectably dressed family testified to her managerial skills.[125]

An informal network of female neighbors and kin often aided a housewife. If she had some time to spend gossiping and chatting, a woman could gain useful information about where, for example, the prices were lowest and the quality highest. "Matrons in converse," Roberts noted, "were both storing and redistributing information that could be important economically to themselves and their neighbors."[126] This network was not only economically useful, it also involved an exchange of services from one household to another, often though not exclusively among relatives. The mother's ability to nurse others who were sick, to assist at childbirth and at the laying out of the dead, guaranteed her family similar help if they needed it. Along these networks, too, passed the growing store of information related to the care and nurture of children.

CHILD CARE

By the first decades of the twentieth century children had assumed an increasingly important place in working-class families. Consequently, the mother's time spent in caring for them increased. There were several reasons for this development. During the last part of the nineteenth century, a decline began in the fertility of working-class families. After 1900, infant mortality also declined as a result of the active campaigns to combat infant death, led usually by doctors and middle-class philanthropists concerned about the scarcity of army recruits and the weakening of the country's population growth. Mothers were taught how to sterilize bottles by visiting nurses or volunteer "ladies." Doctors campaigned to encourage breast feeding. Milk was distributed free to needy families. The new health measures required that mothers spend additional time with young children. The standards of child care rose and so did the time a woman spent in child-rearing activities.

Declining infant mortality contributed to a further effort at family limitation. As more infants lived, families bore fewer children. But as fewer children were born, the value of each particular child increased. Greater care had to be taken to ensure the survival of one's children, who also were dependent and at home for longer periods of time than in the past. Somewhat ironically, as the size of the working-class family declined, the responsibilities of a mother for her children increased.

The health campaigns and the experience of families with wet nurses and baby minders seem to have convinced mothers of their importance to their children's health.

> It is a very general opinion among working women that children put out to mind do not thrive, and after a little experience of this a great many women leave the factory and start as homeworkers in order to watch over their own children.[127]

Mothers insisted that children did not eat as well anywhere as at home.

Mothers were defined as the moral and social as well as the physical guardians of their children. In addition to clothing them, they saw to it that they went to school and later to work. In Birmingham, school attendance was far higher among children with mothers at home than away at work.[128] Apprenticeship and employment arrangements were made by mothers, who then supervised the comings and goings of their working children. Frequently a harsh disciplinarian, the vigilant and watchful mother was seen as the cause of her child's ultimate success.

Success was a relative achievement in the eyes of many working families at the turn of the century. It more often meant getting established in a stable job, acquiring some training and education, than it did moving upward in the social scale. Of course, some families sought that too, but they were the exception. Nonetheless the child's future became a kind of investment for families. "Our ideas for our children," said an English working man's wife, "was to give them the best education, a trade and music that we could afford so they could grow up to be clean, honest, truthful and to go straight in life and become good citizens."[129] Each child in her family chose his own trade and was given music lessons, sometimes at great cost to family finances. But "better prospects for their children" was a widely held goal.

The return on the investment in children was a certain material security for the parents in their old age, but it had its symbolic and emotional aspect as well. The success and improvement of the next generation was a comment on the success of the parents. The crowning achievement of a lifetime was not so much material reward or the accumulation of wealth and property for oneself, but the satisfaction of seeing one's children well established in their lives. Such children were the proof of time and money well spent. They were the recipients of an intangible transfer of resources. Not property or skill or money, but good training, discipline and opportunity were what parents gave children to "start them out in life." And the mother of the family was largely responsible for providing these resources, for it was she who had borne, nurtured, socialized, and then launched her children. In an increasingly complex society, women often served as "job brokers," intermediaries between their children and potential employers. "She it was," wrote one daughter, "who had to start us all out in life."[130] "The happiest possible future for me," an elderly Frenchwoman told an interviewer, "is that my children will be happy."[131]

The importance of the mother in caring for her children, evident in an earlier period, became more pronounced by the early twentieth century. This placed the mother at the center of her children's affections. For one thing, she was still "the most permanent and most important figure in family life."[132] "Naturally," recalled a French worker in his autobiography, "I was closer to maman than to papa. We were with maman more. . . . We rarely saw papa." It is clear from accounts of this sort how important the mother was. Many autobiographies of working-class people focus on the writer's mother, dealing only perfunctorily with the father. At every point in a child's life, frequently even after his or her marriage, the mother's intervention with help, or sometimes only with advice, was crucial. Her activities seem to have been a source of respect and status in her household and, by extension, in her neighborhood. And they were a source, too, of continuing gratitude from her children. In the 1950s the English sociologists Wilmott and Young recorded the memories of working-class family members of their "mums." These portray her position at an earlier period as well:

> "It all broke up when Mum died," said one woman. "There's been no head of the family—no organization." . . ."We used to spend Christmas together until the old lady died," another informant told us, "and then we all separated." One man, a dustman, said of his wife's relatives: "We don't see much of them since Mum died—Mum's used to be the central depot in this family."[134]

All of this is not to glorify married women's life at home. Many observers worried about their isolation, the drudgery and boredom of their existence. Rowntree, for example, questioned the effects on wives of better-off workers of "the deadening monotony of their lives," and the fact that they could become "mere hopeless drudges."[135] These women knew no leisure as they devoted long hours to family concerns. Working-class women, like men, were often discontented with their jobs, whether at home or in the workplace. Yet they seem to have

accepted the necessity for hard work for both spouses and they accepted the division of labor within the family between husband and
wife. We ought not apply middle-class standards of education and leisure to working-class women's activities. Such standards may be worthy
of aspiration; understanding them points up the disparities of wealth,
education, and enjoyment between the upper and lower classes. But
using middle-class standards as a yardstick for comparison also obscures
the nature of the experience of a working-class mother and wife. Although a working-class married woman's life at home was difficult and
time-consuming, it was also of great economic, social, and emotional
importance to her family. It could be as well a source of respect and
status in the eyes of the family she served and a source of some pride
for herself.

By the first decades of the twentieth century married women in
working-class families spent more time at home, less time earning
wages. Household and child care responsibilities demanded a new expertise which in turn required more time than it had in the past. The
expanded role of household manager and guardian of children's health,
education, and future was recognized as an important one by family
members. Over the course of her lifetime, a woman's time increasingly
was segmented. As a single, young adult, a woman spent her time
working. When she married and had children, however, she withdrew
from full time wage earning. Productive activity took less of her time,
while children and household management took more. Wage earning
was an interruption, usually of short duration, of a married woman's
primary occupation, as mother and housewife.

9

Changes in Women's Work Since World War II

The history of women's work does not conform to a simple evolutionary model. The pattern evident by 1900 continued with some variation during the 1920's and 1930's, but after World War II the work-force participation of women in Britain and France differed significantly from what it had been at the beginning of the century. The differences represented not a continuation of, but a departure from, the earlier patterns.

In Britain, rates of female employment were higher in the postwar period than they had been for a century. Virtually all single women worked in the 1950s and 1960s. Although the percentage of employed married women declined immediately after the war, the figure rose again during the 1950s. In 1951 over 20 percent of all Britain's married women were employed as compared to some 10 percent in 1931.[1] In France, on the other hand, the size of the female labor force decreased relative to earlier years. The proportions both of single and of married women in employment declined. By the 1950s, France's female employment was still high from an international perspective, but not as high as it had been. The French level and pattern of women's employment in the 1950s and 1960s more closely resembled Britain's than at any other time in the preceding century.

The timing of these changes in women's employment led some commentators to conclude that the war itself had an important impact on women's work. For Britain, they suggested that exposure to wage earning led married women to redefine their family priorities. In addition, some argued that public attitudes about women's ability to work were

214

changed by the example of the British counterparts of "Rosie the Riveter."[2] (Similar arguments were made to support the erroneous view that French women's employment had also increased.)[3] Of course, levels of women's employment were very high in both countries during the war years, since women were recruited to replace mobilized male workers. But a close examination of evidence from Britain and France suggests that World War II was not the watershed it seemed. Postwar changes in patterns of women's employment stemmed largely from the changes in economy, demography, and family already under way by 1939. The war may have hastened the impact of these changes, but it did not cause them.

In this chapter we shall briefly examine the transformations of economy, demography, and family that took place in Britain and France during the twentieth century. Our analysis here will be neither as full nor as extensive as it was in earlier chapters. For this chapter is an overview rather than a full discussion. As such it has several purposes. First, we want to show that the history of women's work did not continue unchanged after 1914. This chapter will indicate the nature and direction of the changes that did occur. Second, we want to underline the importance of the analysis we have used throughout the book. An understanding of the position of women, in this case of their work-force participation, comes from an understanding of the economic, demographic, and family contexts within which they shape their lives. The history of women's work must be understood in terms of the history of changes in each of these variables and of changes in the relationships among them.

ECONOMIC CHANGE

In both Britain and France most of the new demand for women workers came from the expanding tertiary sector. The growth of this sector, which had begun in the nineteenth century, continued. By far the largest area of new jobs for women was white-collar clerical jobs. These multiplied with the bureaucratization of government services, the differentiation of business organization, and the growth of scale of consumer commerce. In France, according to Jean Daric, the percentage of working women (excluding agriculture) in commerce rose from 18 to 27 percent between 1906 and 1936. Those in the liberal professions increased from 7 to 14 percent in the same period. "Since 1906," he writes, "there has been a constant increase in the proportion of women in commercial activities and the liberal professions, compensated by a particularly clear decline [of working women] in industry."[4]

In both countries the decline in the importance of manufacturing as an employer of women, evident earlier in the century, continued after 1945. In France the percentage of the nonagricultural female labor force engaged in manufacturing fell from 44 percent in 1936 to 40.2 percent in 1947 to 32.5 percent in 1962. Manufacturing accounted for 38.9 percent of all women workers in Britain in 1951, 34.8 percent in 1961.[5]

The war did have some impact on the manufacturing sector. Both Britain and France suffered enormous losses of industrial plants, housing, and public buildings. In the postwar years both countries devoted resources and labor power to reconstruction. These efforts involved heavy industry and the construction trades primarily and, therefore, male labor. The division of labor by sex and the characteristic sexual segregation of occupations did not change. The proportions of women in the metal and machine trades increased a bit. So did the numbers engaged in new light industries such as electronics. But these increases did not affect the proportion of women employed in manufacturing as a whole. Far more important was the continuing decline of the textile and clothing industries, traditionally large employers of women. Increasingly, migrants from nonindustrial nations in Europe filled the diminishing numbers of jobs in these trades. British and French women moved into white-collar jobs.

Despite the similar developments in the manufacturing and tertiary sectors, changes in the levels of female employment were different in France and Britain, as Figures 4–1 to 4–4 show. In Britain, the increased size of the tertiary sector was accompanied by a substantial increase in women's employment. In France there was also increased tertiary employment of women, but overall, female participation in the labor force declined. The explanation for the difference is a familiar one: the organization of French agriculture. After 1945 the least productive, small family farms were abandoned. Concentration and industrialization slowly transformed peasant agriculture. As a result, agriculture declined as an employer of both men and women, but the decline in female employment was much more dramatic.[6] Some of the decline was offset by the movement of women into white-colar jobs, but not all of it. The decline in female labor-force participation in France reflected a reduction in the numbers of peasant farms, the last vestige of the household mode of production.

DEMOGRAPHIC CHANGE

One of the striking postwar changes in the British and French female labor force was an increase in the rate of employment of married women. The figures are different for each country and reflect their different economic organizations.

In France, the percentage of married women listed in censuses as "employed" actually declined. This directly reflected the decline of family farms and, outside of agriculture, of family-run shops. Nonetheless, the proportion of married women in wage-earning activity away from home increased. In 1906, only 37 percent of employed married women were salaried workers; 63 percent were either heads or co-heads of enterprises or worked in their own households. By 1936, the proportion of wage-earning workers among married women had increased by 60 percent.[7] This tendency continued in the 1950s and 1960s. In addition, the proportion of all working women (outside agriculture) who were married also increased in France after 1921.[8]

In Britain, married women represented an increasingly large share of women workers. By 1911 there had been a drop in married women's labor-force participation, as compared to earlier years. Over the course of the twentieth century, however, the pattern changed and married women constituted an increasingly large proportion of women workers. Of all working women in Britain, 14.1 percent were married in 1911, 43 percent in 1951 and 59 percent in 1970.[9]

There were several reasons for the increase in the representation of married women among female wage earners. First, the demand for female workers increased after World War II, in part as a consequence of population growth. During the immediate postwar period both countries experienced a short "baby boom" as couples made up for reproductive time lost during the war years or, possibly, modified their long-range calculations about children. Neither France nor Britain had the kind of baby boom which occurred in the United States, but in both countries fertility rates increased temporarily. The change in fertility was greater in France than in Britain, since French fertility had been especially stationary just before the war. The increase in France's fertility accompanied a decline in peasant farms and the transfer of rural populations to cities. Furthermore, population growth was encouraged by the French government. It paid family allowances based on numbers of children born and also provided additional benefits for families with three or more children. Population growth in both countries contributed to an expansion of the tertiary sector and thus to the demand for female workers. More nurses and teachers were needed, for example, to care for increasingly large numbers of young children in the populations of both countries. As commerce and consumer industries expanded with growing populations, demand for female employees also increased.

As the demand for female employees grew, the pool of available single women—those traditionally hired as wage earners—contracted.

As a result of low fertility rates in the 1930s, the numbers of women arriving at adulthood in the 1950s were small. The pool of young adults who could be employed was further reduced by the extension of school-leaving age in both countries. The supply of single women was diminished even more by increasing nuptiality rates. More and more women were marrying, and were doing so at younger ages, than in the past.

In France, nuptiality had been higher than in Britain at the end of the nineteenth century. French nuptiality rates increased slightly after 1921, and help account for some of the increase in married women wage earners.[10] In Britain, however, the increases were dramatic. In 1968, 57 percent of women aged twenty to twenty-four were married, as compared with only 24 percent of that age group in 1911. Single women represented 46.2 percent of the female population over ten years of age in 1911; by 1970 single women accounted for only 19 percent of all women over fifteen years old. Married women constituted 44.6 percent of all females in 1911; 67 percent in 1970.[11] In addition, there was a substantial drop in the British age of first marriage. (Table 9–1)

All of these factors combined to reduce the supply of single women workers and to increase the numbers of married women drawn into the labor force.[12] Older married women, past childbearing age, tended to fill jobs first. Most evidence from the postwar period shows that wives with young children preferred to remain at home.[13] The need for women workers could be strong enough to lead employers to accommodate married women with children. The Peak Freen biscuit factory in London introduced part-time shifts and flexible hours in the 1950s, for example, in an effort to recruit young mothers.[14]

Other demographic factors influenced the availability of married women as employees. Although fertility increased somewhat after the war, it never reached the heights of earlier years. Families tended to have two or three children in all. Continued improvements in nutrition and health care further reduced infant mortality. The steady improvement in infant life chances meant that women had to have fewer pregnancies to obtain the number of children they wanted. Less of their time, in other words, had to be spent bearing children. In addition,

TABLE 9–1. Mean Age at First Marriage of Females in England and Wales

1936–40	25.38
1951–55	24.18
1960	23.26
1964	22.78

SOURCE: E. A. Wrigley, *Population and History*, p. 228.

improvements in children's health meant fewer demands on mothers for nurture and child care. Indeed, it became possible for parents to assume that children would live to adulthood, and they became increasingly concerned about preparing their children for the future. By the 1950s less of a working-class woman's time was needed for childbearing and child rearing.

CHANGES IN THE FAMILY

Change in the definition of the needs of children was the primary family influence on married women's work in Britain and France after World War II. The change continued a process under way at the turn of the century. By the postwar period child labor had virtually ended. Social pressures and family aspirations recognized the value of at least a minimal education for children. Families now rarely relied on their children as wage earners. The pattern characteristic of the industrializing period was reversed. In the past children had worked so that their mothers could remain at home fulfilling domestic and reproductive responsibilities. Now, when families needed additional income, mothers worked instead of children.

Family need now routinely included children's education. Married women often explained that they worked so that a son or daughter could go to trade school or even a university. Children cost families more than they had in the past, and they contributed less toward their own upkeep. One result of this, of course, was that families decided to have fewer children. A mother's care for her children increasingly involved earning some of the money for their support. The fact that these women had fewer children on the average made such wage earning possible.

The timing of women's work-force participation was thus different after World War II from what it had been in previous periods. It is instructive here to compare the new patterns with earlier patterns of women's employment over the course of the family cycle in Britain and France. In Britain, in 1850, many single women worked (Figure 9–1). Married women did paid work at times of family need, when children were very young, and also in later years, when life crises accumulated. By 1910, the pattern was different. Young single women still did paid work. Married women worked less often. Their work was irregular and episodic in response to family need. Life crises were scattered throughout a family's existence, but many crises were associated with old age. At that point children left home to set up new households of their own; the primary wage earner became sick or died. By 1960, there was again

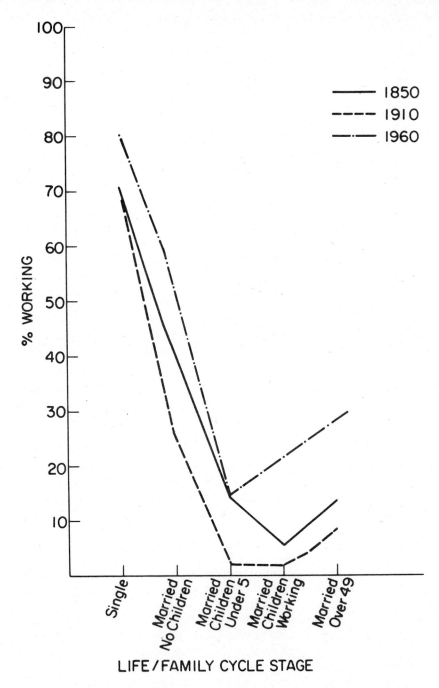

Figure 9.1 Schematic Diagram showing percent women employed by Life/Family cycle stage, France

a new pattern. Children's wage earning was no longer relevant to the family work cycle, and married women were much more likely to do paid work. They were least likely to do such work when their children were very young. The different relationship between wives' and children's work in 1850 and 1960 is striking.

Women's labor-force participation in France differed from that in Britain (Figure 9–2). The small-scale unit of production, the long continuation of household production, lower fertility, and the greater demand for women workers have made married women's work more likely in France since the earliest period. These factors shift the whole curve upward. More married women were counted as workers, but more women were working in small household units than in Britain. This pattern continued in 1910. In 1960, there was, overall, less work by married women because of the decline in the small farms and shops. There was an important parallel to the British situation, however. Children no longer replaced their mothers as family wage earners. Instead, mothers worked to provide support and schooling and thus to improve the future prospects of their children.

The expenditure of more of a married woman's time in wage-earning activity was not a consequence of the "industrialization" of housework. Until very recently, few French or British working-class households could afford to buy labor-saving appliances. Moreover, time-budget studies comparing housework schedules of working and nonworking wives show that working wives continued to spend long hours doing domestic chores. They devoted weekends and evenings to washing and cleaning in an attempt to "catch up" on housework. They rarely owned vacuum cleaners or washing machines. Working wives carried a double burden, since the sexual division of household labor gave them primary domestic responsibility even when they went out to work.[15] (Indeed, the possibility of buying labor-saving appliances may have been a spur to married women's wage-earning activity. They may have worked so that they could buy appliances in order to lessen the burdens of housework.)

In the postwar period the needs of children required additional expenditures of money and less of a mother's household time. In addition, the potential wages a married woman could earn had increased relative to her counterparts in the past. The women entering the labor force after World War II had at least a minimal education. Changes in the economy, and in the demand for trained workers had made the schooling of children a social and familial priority. Extended schooling for working-class children had an important effect on their future employment. The time of an educated female, even one with a minimal education, has higher market value than that of a woman without education.

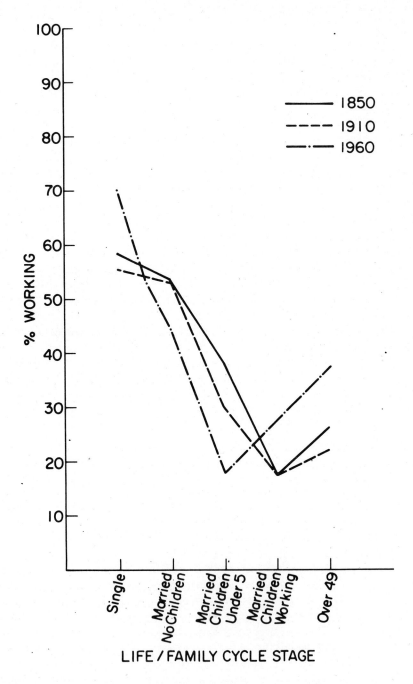

Figure 9.2 Schematic Diagram showing percent women employed by Life/Family cycle stage, France

When girls went to work at an early age with no training or skills, as they did during much of the nineteenth century, they had few skills and their wages were low. Once married, specialization in child and home care made sense, for the alternative use of their time for market work brought very low wages. In the early period poverty and crises were the chief factors that led married women to reenter the labor force, in the episodic manner we have described. By the mid-twentieth century young working-class women had some education and training. There was still a large differential between women's and men's wages and between those of single and married women. Many married women were still forced by desperate need to take low-paying, exploitative jobs. But, as a result of education, married women's wages were on the whole relatively higher than they had been in the past. These women had greater incentive to remain at work after marriage or to return to work once their children entered school. The value of time spent in wage earning had increased.

Children's needs were a primary motive for married women's work, but other reasons existed as well. Some women told investigators that their wages improved the comforts of their families, enabling them "to enjoy luxuries that otherwise would be beyond their means."[16] The patterns of consumer orientation we have described in Chapter 8 became more evident in the postwar period. Married women took part-time or full-time jobs so their families might have a vacation, a radio, better housing, or more furniture.

> The way in which her wages were spent showed that the woman worked neither to meet basic economic needs nor to provide personal pleasures for herself. Money was wanted as a means of raising the family's standard of living. It was used to build up, on a do-it-yourself basis, a more modern and attractive home, to provide more generous food, better footwear and larger wardrobes, to buy durable consumer goods, to give the family a seaside holiday, and to acquire a cheap second-hand car.[17]

Some women, responding to surveys in the 1950s and 1960s, also said that they worked because they liked the companionship and found their jobs more interesting than staying home. A cleaning woman questioned by Viola Klein about why she worked said, "I am bad with nerves and it helps my health. The doctor told me to take a job: I don't really need to do it."[18] Rowntree and Lavers noted that of the 1,278 working wives in their sample from York in 1951 (most of whom worked part-time), some 21 percent claimed they worked "for the pleasure of meeting people instead of being cooped up in their homes all day."[19] The need for sociability followed from the increasing privacy of family life made possible in part by expanded housing facilities. The fact that women expressed this motivation for their work is important. It indicates that married women's work was less often a consequence of family poverty and more often a matter of individual choice. Nonetheless, the women who exercised such choice were a minority. Most of those wives and mothers who worked did so to maintain or improve their families' position. In an age of increased consumption, improving the family's position meant earning money for expenditure on the family's needs.

THE NEW PATTERN OF WOMEN'S EMPLOYMENT

Changes in the economy, in fertility, mortality, and nuptiality, as well as in the needs of children and the value of married women's wage-earning time changed the pattern of women's work over the course of the working-class family's life cycle. Single women continue to work in large numbers. Their work, however, is less often a stage between school and marriage than it was in the past. Increasingly, single women develop skills and experience in jobs that will continue after they are married. Married women still work in the interest of their families. Yet the pattern of their labor-force participation has changed. Employers still pay married women as if they are secondary wage earners and as if their commitment to work is secondary to family concerns. To some extent this is an accurate assessment. Yet, in the past decades family needs have tended to make women's commitment to paid work more stable over the course of their lives. Greater expenses, many of them associated with children, have replaced poverty as an incentive to work. Moreover, married women with skills and education are reluctant to forgo the potential wages they can earn during their married years. Some take part-time jobs. Many withdraw entirely from work while their children are very young. But reduced fertility has dramatically shortened the period of childbearing and child nurture in a married woman's life.

The new pattern of women's work corresponds in some ways to preindustrial patterns. Women do paid work and household work throughout their lives. Productive activity may be temporarily interrupted when children are born, but it is not permanently curtailed. Unlike preindustrial women, however, contemporary working-class wives spend very few years in reproductive activity. Their life expectancy is much greater. Family economic needs continue to require a married woman's wages. Reduced reproductive demands make it possible for her to spend more of her lifetime earning them.

YEARS DEVOTED TO REPRODUCTIVE ACTIVITY, 1750

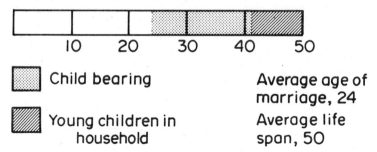

Child bearing

Young children in
household

Average age of
marriage, 24

Average life
span, 50

Figure 10.1

Source: Evelyne Sullerot, *Women, Society and Change*, p. 75.

YEARS DEVOTED TO REPRODUCTIVE ACTIVITY, 1960

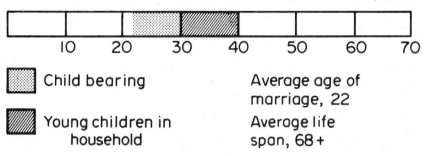

Child bearing

Young children in
household

Average age of
marriage, 22

Average life
span, 68 +

Figure 10.2

Conclusion

What was the impact of industrialization on women's work? There is no simple or single answer. Changes in the mode of production did not immediately or automatically transform women's work. Nor did they directly alter reproductive strategies and family organization, both of which influenced women's productive activities. Yet important changes have occurred. We can best answer the question about the impact of industrialization by conceiving of a process of change which affected the economy, demography and family organization in different ways and which also changed the relationships among them.

Let us review briefly the changing relationships among the economic, demographic and family influences on the work of women of the popular classes in Britain and France since 1700. In the household mode of production typical of the preindustrial economy, the unit of production was small and productivity was low. All household members worked at productive tasks, differentiated by age and sex. We have called this form of organization the *family economy*. Within marriage, fertility was high. High mortality was, however, an involuntary check on net reproduction. Children were potential workers, but they were also potential heirs to limited resources. So households controlled the size of future generations by late marriage and enforced celibacy for some members. Parental control of limited resources limited the autonomy of children. High fertility, high mortality, a small-scale household organization of production, and limited resources meant that women's time was spent primarily in productive activity. Unmarried women worked in their parents' households or in other households if there was

227

no need for their labor at home. Married women were both producers and mothers. The household setting of work facilitated the combination of productive and domestic activities. Married women adjusted their time to meet the demands of production in the interest of the family economy.

During industrialization, the size of productive units grew and productive activity moved out of the household to workshops and factories. Increasingly, people worked for wages. Early industrialization, particularly in the textile industry, relied heavily on the labor of women and children. Families adapted older expectations about work and strategies of reproduction to the new circumstances. The result was the *family wage economy.* Under this organization the family continued to allocate the labor of its members. Now the household's need for wages rather than for labor determined the productive activity of women when they were daughters as well as wives and mothers. Families continued to bear many children, and infant mortality remained very high. This high mortality and the fact that surviving children were potential family wage earners made the continuation of earlier high fertility strategies feasible. Yet high fertility in the new circumstances created problems for married women. As in the past, they had to balance their time between productive and reproductive activities, but work now took them away from home. Under the family wage economy, married women worked when the household needed their wages. A woman's time was not invested exclusively in child care or domestic activity when subsistence had to be earned. But the domestic and reproductive needs of the household also claimed much of her time. So, her work tended to be episodic and irregular. If possible, she improvised cash-producing activities connected to her domestic work. When other family members, particularly children, were available to replace her as wage earners, the married woman withdrew from wage-earning activity. Over the course of her lifetime, a woman alternated productive and reproductive activity. Family needs determined when she worked. As a daughter, a woman was usually a family wage earner. As a mother and wife, the time she spent earning money depended on the need of the family for wages and therefore on the wages and work of other family members.

Technological change, the growth of heavy industry, and the increased scale of industrial organization led to increased productivity and greater prosperity by the end of the nineteenth century. The new organization of manufacturing required an adult male labor force primarily. In the tertiary sector, however, an increasing number of white-collar jobs were available for women. Men's wages in this period increased, and the standard of living of many working-class families rose above the subsistence level. The family economy became a *family consumer economy,* as households specialized in reproduction and consumption. Nonetheless, the family continued to allocate the labor of its members. Children of both sexes were family wage earners, usually after they had completed school. The state now required some schooling for all children and, increasingly, one's ability to find a regular, well-paying job depended on a minimum level of education. Married women, too, worked when their wages were needed, but increasingly this meant finding a temporary job during a family crisis. These crises of unemployment, illness, or death of the primary wage earner tended more and more to cluster in old age. During most of her married life a woman served as a specialist in child rearing and consumer activities for her family. These tasks filled important and economically useful needs for the working-class family. Managing family finances and buying goods and services required time and skill. Moreover, new fertility strategies demanded that women spend more time nurturing children. By the end of the nineteenth century, families had begun to restrict fertility. New health measures and a decline in infant mortality developed only later—in the first decades of the twentieth century. As families bore fewer children it became important to invest more time in their care so they would survive to maturity. Family needs thus allocated the mother's time away from wage earning and toward domestic responsibilities and child care.

After World War II, economic conditions and family needs exerted a different influence on women's work. The tertiary sector expanded and the demand for women in white-collar jobs grew. More part-time work was also available, particularly in Britain. Fertility continued to decline, but new levels of health reduced the fragility of infant and child life. Children remained in school for longer periods of their lives and spent less time as family wage earners. The result was an increase in the time married women spent in wage-earning activity.

The historical record shows a U-shaped pattern of female productive activity—from relatively high in the preindustrial household economy, to a lower level in industrial economies, to a higher level with the development of the modern tertiary sector. Married women's productive work contributed to this pattern. The fact that married as well as single women worked in the household economy and work today in the consumer economy raises the level of female productive activity in these two time periods.

There is no neat complementary curve for reproductive activity. Reproductive patterns have changed in the following manner: from relatively low nuptiality, high marital fertility, and high infant and child mortality; to high nuptiality, lower fertility, and lower infant and child mortality (dependent on women's increased investment of time in child nurture); to low fertility and low infant mortality (no longer dependent exclusively on a mother's time). Yet at any point in time, patterns of female productive activity have influenced and been influenced by the prevailing family fertility strategies.

DETERMINANTS OF WOMEN'S PRODUCTIVE ACTIVITY

In this book we have compared aggregate features of two nation states over a 250-year period. We have compared several cities with special economic and ecological characteristics. We also have studied women in families in their roles as daughters, wives, and mothers. The comparative examination of women and work at several different levels permits us to offer some general explanations of changes in patterns of women's work.

At the most general level we conclude that the interplay between a society's productive and reproductive systems within the household influences the *supply* of women available for work. The characteristics of the economy and its mode of production, scale of organization, and technology influence the *demand* for women as workers.

Historically, the likelihood of women participating in production is strongly correlated with the household mode of production. The closer in time that a given household is to the experience of household production, the more likely it is that women will do productive work and that they will subordinate time spent in reproductive activity to that work. During the entire nineteenth century the French economy was marked by the continuing importance of a small-scale, household organization of production. Britain, on the other hand, early developed a large-scale, factory-based system. As a result, French rates of female work-force participation were consistently higher than British rates.

Once the industrial mode of production predominates, once people work for wages outside of households, aggregate and local economic organization influence the demand for women in paid employment. An important constraint operates here: the almost universal segregation of occupations by sex. The degree of occupational segregation has varied somewhat over time, but there has been a continuing tendency for societies, employers, and workers to accept sex-typing of occupations. Women, then, are most likely to work when the demand for workers in female occupations is high. When there is a shortage of the supply of male workers (during or after a war, for example) more women will be drawn into nonfemale occupations. The analysis of the economic structure of the different cities demonstrated that levels of female employment were highest where female jobs were most numerous.

The supply of female workers, of course, is shaped in part by demographic, social, and economic factors. Single women are best able to work, since they have few other claims on their time. Married women, on the other hand, must adjust reproductive and domestic activity with paid employment. The difficulties of such an adjustment were evident during the early period of industrialization, particularly in textile towns. Then the economic need for women workers and the family's need for wages led to high levels of married women's employment at high costs to themselves and, even more, to their infants. Even in the textile towns, however, the demographic situation—the proportions in the population of married and single women—shaped the supply of women workers. In later periods, when demand for women was great and the supply of single women small, employers might change work conditions to accommodate the special needs of married women.

Household needs also influence the supply of women workers. The division of labor within the household is based on the family's economic needs. Under the household mode of production, the labor needs of the unit defined the work of all members. For wage-earning families, subsistence requirements replaced labor needs. Poor households sent as many members as possible into wage-earning employment. When possible, however, the family division of labor allocated time for domestic and child care activity to married women. Increased productivity and higher male wages permitted a sharper division of labor and a differentiation of activity within the household. Single women became preferred wage earners, while married women were preferred as child-care and consumer specialists.

Of course, household needs were not simply economic. The emphasis placed on children and childcare also influenced the supply of women, particularly of married women, to the labor market. In the earliest period of high fertility and high mortality there was no notion that infants and children required special care. Beyond time spent in childbirth and suckling an infant, little time was spent on children. With the decline in fertility and improved prospects for children to survive to adulthood, there developed a new emphasis on the needs of children. Mothers were assumed to be responsible for children's physical, mental, and moral health. The time they spent caring for children was considered valuable by the family. Indeed the value of time spent at home began to outweigh time spent in wage-earning activity. After the Second World War, yet another change in conceptions of child care occurred. Continuing low fertility and dramatically improved prospects for infant and child survival mean that there are less demands on a mother's time for the nurture and care of young children. Not the physical survival, but the social and economic future of the child, his or her education and training, have become increasingly important. This kind of investment in children requires additional funds from the family and, increasingly, married women have sought paid employment to help earn those funds.

By looking not only at work, but at workers as members of households, we have been able to assess the role of the family. We have found that the family provided a certain continuity in the midst of economic change. Values, behavior, and strategies shaped under one mode of production continued to influence behavior as the economy changed. The older practices only slowly were adapted to the new circumstances. In the period we have examined, the family economy was modified from a productive unit to a wage unit. Yet membership in a family continued to define the work roles and relationships of parents and children. Our study challenges an older view which held that industrialization separated the family and work, isolating one sphere from another. We have found that industrialization did deprive the family unit of its productive activity. Nonetheless, the family continued to influence the productive activities of its members. That point was well understood by the three commentators we cited at the beginning of this book. Despite the vastly different conclusions they drew, Jules Simon, Jules Turgan, and Friedrich Engels all agreed that women's work had to be assessed in terms of the family.

Throughout this book we have described and analyzed changes in patterns of women's productive activity. Our analysis has been enriched by the insights of other disciplines, particularly economics, anthropology, and demography. Although we have focused on the history of women in Britain and France since 1700, our conclusions have wider applicability. In the past, as in the present, patterns of women's work are shaped by the intersection of economy, demography, and family. Specific historical contexts differ and so do the experiences, attitudes and choices women make in different situations. The excitement and interest of social history lies in exploring and specifying the differences. The use of an interdisciplinary perspective yields important insights both for those seeking to understand women's position in the past and for those seeking to change and improve it in the present and future.

Notes

Introduction

1. Jules Turgan, *Les Grandes usines en France,* 8 vols. (Paris: Bourdilliet, 1860–1868), vol. 4, p. 20.

2. Ibid., vol. 1, p. 124.

3. Jules Simon, *L'Ouvrière* (Paris: Hachette, 1871), pp. iv, vi.

4. Friedrich Engels, *The Origin of the Family, Private Property and the State* (New York: International Publishers, 1971), p. 66.

5. See for example, Ivy Pinchbeck, *Women Workers and the Industrial Revolution,* (New York: A. Kelley, 1969) p. v; see also William Goode, *World Revolution and Family Patterns* (New York: Free Press, 1963), p. 56.

6. Sydel Silverman, "The Life Crisis as a Clue to Social Functions," *Anthropological Quarterly* 40 (1967): 127–138.

7. See the essay on this subject by Elizabeth Pleck, "Two Worlds in One: Work and Family," *Journal of Social History* 10 (Winter 1976): 178–195.

8. Alice Clark, *The Working Life of Women in the Seventeenth Century* (London: Routledge, 1919), p. 4.

9. Cynthia Lloyd, ed., *Sex, Discrimination and the Division of Labor* (New York: Columbia University Press, 1975), p. 9.

10. Ibid., pp. 10–11.

11. Philippe Ariès, *Centuries of Childhood: A Social History of Family Life,* trans. by Robert Baldick (New York: Vintage, 1965).

12. Pierre Goubert, *Beauvais et le Beauvaisis de 1600 à 1730* (Paris: S.E.V.P.E.N., 1960); Peter Laslett, *The World We Have Lost* (New York: Scribner's, 1965); Peter Laslett and Richard Wall, eds., *Household and Family in Past Time* (Cambridge: At the University Press, 1972); E. A. Wrigley, *Population and History* (New York: McGraw-Hill, 1969), and *Industrial Growth and Population Change* (Cambridge: At the University Press, 1961).

Chapter One

1. Cited in J. H. Clapham, *The Economic Development of France and Germany, 1815–1914* (Cambridge: At the University Press, 1966), pp. 8–10.

2. J. F. C. Harrison, ed., *Society and Politics in England, 1780–1960* (New York: Harper and Row, 1965), p. 23.

3. David Davies, "The Case of Labourers in Husbandry, 1795," in Harrison, p. 39.

4. Samuel Bamford, "Early Days, 1849," in Harrison, p. 54.

5. Carlo Cipolla, *Before the Industrial Revolution: European Society and Economy, 1000–1700* (New York: Norton, 1976), p. 74.

6. Cited in Robert Forster and Elborg Forster, *European Society in the Eighteenth Century* (New York: Harper Torchbooks, 1969), p. 113.

7. René Baehrel, *Une Croissance: La Basse Provence rurale (fin du XVIe siècle–1789)* (Paris: S.E.V.P.E.N., 1961), pp. 109–120; Pierre Goubert, "The French Peasantry of the Seventeenth Century: A Regional Example," in Trevor Aston, ed., *Crisis in Europe, 1540–1660: Essays from Past and Present* (London: Routledge and Kegan Paul, 1965), p. 148, and idem, *Beauvais et le Beauvaisis;* Olwen Hufton, *The Poor of Eighteenth Century France, 1750–1789* (Oxford: Clarendon Press, 1974), and idem, "Women and the Family Economy in Eighteenth Century France," *French Historical Studies* 9 (Spring 1975): 1–22.

8. Daniel Thorner, Basile Kerblay, and R. E. F. Smith, eds., *A. V. Chayanov on the Theory of Peasant Economy* (Homewood, Ill.: Richard D. Irwin, 1966), p. 54; Jean-Louis Flandrin, *Familles: Parenté, maison, sexualité dans l'ancienne société* (Paris: Hachette, 1976), p. 103.

9. Lutz Berkner, "The Stem Family and the Developmental Cycle of the Peasant Household: An Eighteenth Century Austrian Example," *American Historical Review* 77 (April 1972); 398–418; Ann Kussmaul-Cooper, "Servants and Laborers in English Agriculture," unpublished paper, University of Toronto, 1975 (cited with author's permission); Alan Macfarlane, *The Family Life of Ralph Josselin* (Cambridge: At the University Press, 1970), p. 209.

10. See Edward P. Thompson, *Whigs and Hunters* (London: Allen Lane, 1975), and Douglas Hay *et al.*, *Albion's Fatal Tree* (New York: Pantheon, 1975), for details.

11. E. J. Hobsbawn, *Industry and Empire: An Economic History of Britain since 1750* (London: Weidenfeld and Nicolson, 1968), p. 15.

12. Davies, in Harrison, p. 39.

13. Ibid., p. 40.

14. James Raine, "Historic Towns" (1893), pp. 204–206, quoted in Benjamin Seebowm Rowntree, *Poverty: A Study of Town Life* (London: Nelson, 1901), pp. 22–23.

15. Pierre Deyon, *Amiens, Capitale provinciale. Etude sur la société urbaine au 17e siècle* (Paris, The Hague: Mouton, 1967), p. x.

16. K. J. Allison and P. M. Tillot, "York in the Eighteenth Century," in P. M. Tillot, ed., *A History of Yorkshire* (London: The Institute of Historical

Research, 1961), p. 219; see also George Benson, *An Account of the City and County of York from the Reformation to the Year 1925* (York: Copper and Swan, 1925), pp. 84–85.

17. Deyon, p. 546.

18. Cipolla, p. 75.

19. Hufton, "Women and the Family Economy," p. 4; Cissie Fairchilds, *Poverty and Charity in Aix-en-Provence, 1640–1789* (Baltimore: Johns Hopkins University Press, 1976), p. 10.

20. Jeffry Kaplow, *The Names of Kings: The Parisian Laboring Poor in the Eighteenth Century* (New York: Basic Books, 1972), p. 45; Allison and Tillot, p. 216.

21. David Landes, *The Unbound Prometheus* (Cambridge: At the University Press, 1969), p. 44.

22. Henri Mendras, *The Vanishing Peasant: Innovation and Change in French Agriculture*, trans. by Jean Lerner (Cambridge, Mass.: M.I.T. Press, 1970), p. 76.

23. R.-J. Bernard, "Peasant Diet in Eighteenth-Century Gevaudan," in Forster and Forster, eds., *Diet from Pre-Industrial to Modern Times* (New York: Harper and Row, 1975), p. 30.

24. Deyon, pp. 7–10.

25. Pierre Goubert, *Beauvais et le Beauvaisis,* p. 344. See also Hufton, *The Poor in Eighteenth Century France.*

26. Deyon, p. 357.

27. Fairchilds, pp. 85–86.

28. Rudolph Braun, "The Impact of Cottage Industry on an Agricultural Population," in David Landes, ed., *The Rise of Capitalism* (New York: Macmillan, 1966), p. 56; see also Flandrin, pp. 180–181.

29. André Armengaud, *La Famille et l'enfant en France et en Angleterre du XVIe au XVIIIe siècle. Aspects démographiques* (Paris: Société d'édition d'enseignement supérieur, 1975), p. 145.

30. Pierre Goubert, "Recent Theories and Research on French Population between 1500 and 1700," *Population in History: Essays in Historical Demography*, ed. by D. V. Glass and D. E. C. Eversley (Chicago: Aldine, 1965); Louis Henry, "The Population of France in the Eighteenth Century" in Glass and Eversley; John Hajnal, "European Marriage Patterns in Perspective," in Glass and Eversley; E. A. Wrigley, "Family Limitation in Pre-Industrial England," *Economic History Review*, 2nd Series, 19 (April 1966): 89–109.

31. David Levine, "The Demographic Implications of Rural Industrialization; A Family Reconstitution Study of Shepshed, Leicestershire, 1600–1851," *Social History* (May 1976), pp. 177–196; see also Braun, "Impact of Cottage Industry."

32. Fairchilds, p. 33.

33. Deyon, p. 254.

34. Armengaud, *La Famille et l'enfant,* p. 30; Deyon, p. 42; see also John Knodel and Mary Jo Maynes, "Urban and Rural Marriage Patterns in Imperial Germany," *Journal of Family History* 1 (Winter 1976).

35. Armengaud, *La famille et l'enfant* p. 52; E. A. Wrigley, *Population and History,* p. 124; Flandrin, p. 197.

36. Wrigley, "Family Limitation in Pre-Industrial England," p. 123.

37. Emmanuel Le Roy Ladurie, "L'Amenorrhée de famine (XVIIIe–XXe siècles)," *Annales: ESC,* 24e Année (November–December 1969), pp. 1589–1601; Jean Meuvret, "Demographic Crisis in France from the Sixteenth to the Eighteenth Century," in Glass and Eversley.

38. Armengaud, *La famille et l'enfant* p. 53.

39. Carlo Cipolla, *The Economic History of World Population,* rev. ed. (Baltimore: Penguin, 1964), p. 77; and L. A. Clarkson, *The Pre-Industrial Economy in England, 1500–1750* (London: Batsford, 1971), pp. 28–29.

40. Goubert, "Recent Theories," p. 468.

41. Armengaud, *La famille et l'enfant* pp. 74–77; Peter Laslett, "Parental Deprivation in the Past: A Note on the History of Orphans in England," *Local Population Studies* 13 (Autumn 1974): 11–18; Jean Fourastié, "De la vie traditionnelle à la vie 'tertiare,' " *Population* 14 (1959): p. 427.

42. Deyon, p. 39.

43. Mohammed El Kordi, *Bayeux au XVIIe et XVIIIe siècles* (Paris, The Hague: Mouton, 1970) p. 64. See also Fourastié, p. 425; Micheline Baulant, "The Scatterred Family: Another Aspect of Seventeenth-Century Demography," in Robert Forster and Orest Ranum, eds., *Family and Society* (Baltimore: Johns Hopkins, 1976), p. 105; Marcel Couturier, *Recherches sur les structures sociales de Châteaudun, 1525–1789* (Paris: S.E.V.P.E.N., 1969), p. 64; Hufton, *The Poor in Eighteenth Century France,* p. 116; François Lebrun, *Les Hommes et la mort en Anjou aux 17e et 18e siècles* (Paris, The Hague: Mouton, 1971), p. 190.

44. Armengaud, *La famille et l'enfant* p. 79. For an overview of the demographic history of this period see Jacques Dupaquier, "Les Caractères originaux de l'histoire démographique française au XVIIIe siècle," *Revue d'histoire moderne et contemporaine* 23 (April–June 1976).

Chapter 2

1. On women's wages, see Henri Hauser, *Ouvriers du temps passé* (Paris: Alcan, 1927); Hufton, "Women and the Family Economy."

2. T. H. Hollingsworth, *Historical Demography* (London: The Sources of History Limited in Association with Hodder and Stoughton Ltd., 1969), pp. 160–168.

3. Quoted in Frances Collier, *The Family Economy of the Working Classes in the Cotton Industry, 1784–1833* (Manchester: Manchester University Press, 1964), p. 2.

4. Joan Thirsk, "Industries in the Countryside," in *Essays in the Economic and Social History of Tudor and Stuart England, in Honor of R. H. Tawney,* ed. by Jack Fisher (Cambridge: University Press, 1961), p. 87.

5. Maurice Garden, *Lyon et les lyonnais au XVIIIe siècle* (Paris: Les Belle-Lettres, 1970); Armengaud, *La Famille et l'enfant,* p. 36.

6. Goubert, *Beauvais et le Beauvaisis,* p. 344.

7. Clark, *The Working Life of Women,* p. 195.

8. Couturier, *Recherches,* p. 181.

9. Rétif de la Bretonne, quoted in Emmanuel Le Roy Ladurie, "De la crise ultime à la vraie croissance, 1660–1789," in *L'Age classique des Paysans, 1340–1789* (Paris: Seuil, 1975), p. 460.

10. Clark, p. 194; Hufton, "Women and the Family Economy," p. 9.

11. Clark, pp. 115–16.

12. Jean-Claude Perrot, *Genèse d'une ville moderne: Caen au XVIIIe siècle* (Paris, The Hague: Mouton, 1975), p. 425; Macfarlane, *The Family Life of Ralph Josselin,* p. 209.

13. Hufton, "Women and the Family Economy," p. 3; Le Roy Ladurie, "De la crise ultime," p. 477.

14. Ann Kussmaul-Cooper, "The Mobility of English Farm Servants in the Seventeenth and Eighteenth Centuries," unpublished paper, University of Toronto, 1975, p. 6. (Cited with permission.)

15. Hufton, "Women and the Family Economy," p. 5.

16. Ivy Pinchbeck and Margaret Hewitt, *Children in English Society,* vol. 1 (London: Routledge and Kegan Paul, 1969), p. 99.

17. Song contributed by Michael Hanagan.

18. Flandrin, *Familles,* p. 106.

19. Deyon, *Amiens,* p. 340.

20. Hufton, "Women and the Family Economy," pp. 7–9.

21. El Kordi, *Bayeux au XVIIe et XVIIIe siècles* p. 125; Armengaud, *La Famille et l'enfant,* p. 36; Couturier, pp. 132, 137; Jean-Marie Gouesse, "Parenté, famille et mariage en Normandie aux XVIIe et XVIIIe siècles," *Annales: Economies, Sociétés, Civilisations* 27 (1972) p. 1145.

22. P. E. H. Hair, "Bridal Pregnancy in Rural England in Earlier Centuries," *Population Studies* 20 (November 1966) pp. 233–243; Hollingsworth, p. 194.

23. Peter Laslett and Karla Oosterveen, "Long-term Trends in Bastardy in England: A Study of the Illegitimacy Figures in the Parish Registers and in the Reports of the Registrar General, 1461–1960," *Population Studies* 27 (1973) p. 284.

24. David Levine and Keith Wrightson, "The Social Context of Illegitimacy in Early Modern England," in Peter Laslett, ed., *Bastardy and Its Comparative History,* forthcoming from Cambridge University Press.

25. John R. Gillis, *Youth and History* (New York: Academic Press, 1974), p. 29; Natalie Davis, "The Reasons of Misrule: Youth Groups and Charivaris in Sixteenth-Century France," *Past and Present* 50 (1971) pp. 41–75.

26. Edward Shorter, *The Making of the Modern Family* (New York: Basic Books, 1975), p. 219.

27. Ernest Cadet, *Le Mariage en France* (Paris: Guillamin, 1870), citing S. Daubie, p. 118.

28. Armengaud, *La Famille et l'enfant,* p. 144; Lawrence Stone, "The Rise of the Nuclear Family in Early Modern England," in Charles Rosenberg, ed., *The Family in History* (Philadelphia: University of Pennsylvania Press, 1975), pp. 48–49.

29. Martine Segalen, *Nuptialité et alliance: Le Choix du conjoint dans une commune de l'Eure* (Paris: G. P. Maisonneuve Larose, 1972), p. 104.

30. Armengaud, *La famille et l'enfant* p. 144.

Chapter 3

1. Gouesse, "Parenté, famille et mariage," pp. 1146–1147.

2. Deyon, *Amiens,* p. 341.

3. El Kordi, *Bayeux,* p. 257.

4. Deyon, p. 254.

5. Armengaud, *La Famille et l'enfant, p. 75.*

6. Le Roy Ladurie, "De la crise ultime," p. 447.

7. Sebastien Le Prestre de Vauban, cited in Michel Morineau, "Budgets populaires en France au XVIIIe siècle," *Revue d'histoire économique et sociale* 50 (1972) p. 236; see also Flandrin, *Familles,* p. 113.

8. Pinchbeck, *Women Workers,* p. 203; Clark, *The Working Life .of Women,* p. 97.

9. Madeleine Guilbert, *Les Fonctions des femmes dans l'industrie* (Paris, The Hague: Mouton, 1966), pp. 30–31.

10. Garden, *Lyon,* p. 324.

11. Clark, p. 61.

12. Pinchbeck, p. 20.

13. Flandrin, p. 113.

14. Bernard, "Peasant Diet," p. 30.

15. Pinchbeck, p. 157.

16. Ibid., p. 127.

17. Clark, p. 156; see also Hufton, "Women and the Family Economy," p. 12.

18. Pinchbeck, p. 284–85.

19. Deyon, *Amiens,* p. 39.

20. Guilbert, pp. 21–22.

21. Clark, p. 194.

22. Pinchbeck, p. 295.

23. Clark, pp. 150, 290; Hufton, *The Poor of Eighteenth Century France.*

24. Kaplow, *The Names of Kings,* p. 45.

25. Clark, p. 135.

26. Morineau, "Budgets populaires en France," pp. 210, 221.

27. Pinchbeck, Women Workers, pp. 284–285.

28. Baulant, "The Scattered Family," p. 106.

29. Hufton, *The Poor of Eighteenth Century France,* p. 116.

30. Baulant, p. 104.

31. Couturier, *Recherches,* p. 139.

32. Hufton, *The Poor of Eighteenth Century France,* p. 117.

33. Cited in ibid., p. 38.

34. This is the position of Eileen Power, *Medieval Women* (Cambridge: University Press, 1975), p. 34.

35. Le Roy Ladurie, "De la crise ultime," p. 481.

36. Olwen Hufton, "Women in Revolution, 1789–1796," *Past and Present* 53 (1971) p. 92.

37. Le Pelletier cited in Morineau, "Budgets populaires en France," p. 210; Georges Lefebvre, *Etudes Orléannaises,* vol. 1 (Paris: CNRS, 1962), p. 218; Hufton, *The Poor of Eighteenth Century France,* pp. 46–48.

38. Roderick Phillips, "Women and Family Breakdown in Eighteenth Century France: Rouen 1780–1800," *Social History* 2 (May 1976) pp. 197–218; Nicole Castan, "La Criminalité familiale dans le ressort du Parlement de Toulouse, 1690–1730," in André Abbiateci et al., *Crimes et criminalité en France, XVIIe–XVIIIe siècles,* (Paris: Colin, 1971); Yves Castan, *Honnêteté et relations sociales en Languedoc (1715–1780)* (Paris: Plon, 1974).

39. E. P. Thompson, "The Moral Economy of the English Crowd in the Eighteenth Century," *Past and Present* 50 (1971) p. 115. Other work on bread riots can be found cited in Louise A. Tilly, "The Food Riot as a Form of Political Conflict in France," *Journal of Interdisciplinary History* 2 (1971) pp. 23–57.

40. Thompson, "The Moral Economy," p. 82.

41. Natalie Zemon Davis, "Women on Top," in Natalie Zemon Davis, *Culture and Society in Early Modern Europe* (Stanford: Stanford University Press, 1975).

42. Thompson, "The Moral Economy," p. 82.

43. Olwen Hufton, "Women and Marriage in Pre-Revolutionary France," unpublished paper, University of Reading (England), 1974, p. 16.

44. Archives Departementales, Cher, Cote 1, MI 23. This reference was given to us by Nancy Fitch of UCLA. We are grateful for her help.

45. Hufton, "Women and Marriage," p. 14.

46. Garden, *Lyon,* p. 324; Hufton, *The Poor of Eighteenth Century France,* p. 318; George Sussman, "The Wet-Nursing Business in Nineteenth Century France," *French Historical Studies* 9 (Fall 1975) pp. 304–323.

47. Pinchbeck and Hewitt, *Children in English Society,* p. 8.

48. Ibid., p. 7.

Chapter 4

1. Wanda F. Neff, *Victorian Working Women* (New York: Columbia University Press, 1929), p. 42.

2. On British Industrialization see: Phyllis Deane, "The Industrial Revolution in Great Britain," *The Emergence of Industrial Societies,* ed. by Carlo M. Cipolla. Vol. 4 of *The Fontana Economic History of Europe* (London: Collins/ Fontana Books, 1973); H. J. Perkin, "The Social Causes of the British Industrial Revolution," *Transactions of the Royal Historical Society,* Series V, vol. 18 (1968); Elizabeth Gilboy, "Demand as a Factor in the Industrial Revolution" in *Facts and Factors in Economic History* (Cambridge, Mass.: Harvard University Press, 1932); E. J. Hobsbawm, *Industry and Empire* (London: Weidenfeld and Nicolson, 1968); David Landes, *The Unbound Prometheus;* Neil J. Smelser, *Social Change in the Industrial Revolution* (Chicago: University of Chicago Press, 1959).

3. Landes, p. 124, citing Phyllis Deane and François Perroux.

4. Deane, "The Industrial Revolution in Great Britain," p. 177.

5. Claude Fohlen, "The Industrial Revolution in France, 1700–1914," in *The Emergence of Industrial Societies,* ed. by Carlo Cipolla, p. 26. See also Maurice Agulhon, Gabriel Desert, and Robert Speckin, *Apogée et crise de la civilisation paysanne, 1789–1914* (Paris: Seuil, 1976), p. 71; Tom Kemp, *Economic Forces in French History* (London: Dobson, 1971); Landes, *Prometheus.*

6. All aggregated national labor force data in graphs and text (unless otherwise noted) are based on tables in T. Deldycke, H. Gelders, and J. M. Limbor, *La Population active et sa structure* (Brussels: Institut de Sociologie, 1969).

7. On domestic industry, see Tom Kemp, *Industrialization in the Nineteenth Century* (London: Longmans, 1961), p. 62; Albert Aftalion, *Le Développement de la fabrique et le travail à domicile dans les industries de l'habillement* (Paris: Sirey, 1906), p. 37; Emile Dorchies, *L'Industrie à domicile de la confection des vêtements pour hommes dans la campagne lilloise* (Lille: Imprimerie centrale du Nord, 1907), pp. 6–7, 151–52. On domestic service, see Theresa McBride, *The Domestic Revolution* (London: Croom Helms, 1976).

8. Clara Collet, "The Collection and Utilization of Official Statistics Bearing on the Extent and Effects of the Industrial Employment of Women," *Journal of the Royal Statistical Society* 61 (1898), p. 224.

9. Pinchbeck, *Women Workers,* p. 37.

10. Ibid., p. 109.

11. Ibid., p. 110. See J. P. D. Dunbabin, *Rural Discontent in Nineteenth Century Britain* (New York: Holmes and Meier, 1974), pp. 134–135, for a description of the need for women workers in agriculture, arrangements for obtaining women's labor, and how this changed in the nineteenth century.

12. Roger Thabault, *Education and Change in a Village Community: Mazières-en-Gâtine, 1848–1914* (New York: Schocken, 1971), p. 21; Gordon Wright, *Rural Revolution in France* (Stanford, Calif.: Stanford University Press, 1964), p. 6.

13. Karl Marx, *The Eighteenth Brumaire of Louis Napoleon Bonaparte,* in *On Revolution,* ed. by Saul K. Padover (New York: McGraw-Hill, 1971), pp. 320–321.

14. Alfred Cobban cited in Wright, p. 1.

15. Eileen Yeo and E. P. Thompson, *The Unknown Mayhew* (London: Merlin Press, 1971), p. 272.

16. See Aftalion, *Développement,* and Clara E. Collet, "Women's Work," in *Life and Labor of the People of London,* ed. by Charles Booth, Series, I, vol. 4 (London: Macmillan, 1902).

17. Quoted in J. F. C. Harrison, *Society and Politics in England,* p. 145.

18. The question of occupational segregation by sex is discussed in Lloyd, *Sex, Discrimination and the Division of Labor;* Edward Gross, "*Plus ça change . . .*? The Sexual Structure of Occupations Over Time," *Social Problems* 16 (Fall, 1968) pp. 198–208; and in a special issue of *Signs,* ed. by Martha Blaxall and Barbara B. Reagan, vol. 1 (Spring 1976), part 2.

19. Adna Ferrin Weber, *The Growth of Cities in the Nineteenth Century* (Ithaca, N. Y.: Cornell University Press, 1967), p. 144.

20. George Benson, *An Account of the City and County of York from the Reformation to the Year 1925* (York: Cooper & Swan, 1925), pp. 88–91.

21. Alan Armstrong, *Stability and Change in an English Country Town. A Social Study of York, 1801–51* (Cambridge: At the University Press, 1974), pp. 43–45.

22. Alberic de Calonne d'Avesne, *Histoire de la Ville d'Amiens,* vol. 3 (Amiens: Piteux, 1906), pp. 4–8, 114–115.

23. Armand Audiganne, *Les Populations ouvrières et les industries de la France* (Paris: Capelle, 1860), pp. 34–35.

24. Claude Fohlen, *L'industrie textile au temps du Second Empire* (Paris: Plon, 1956), p. 162.

25. Louis Reybaud, *La Laine* (Paris: Levy, 1867), pp. 236, 223–224; idem, *Le Coton. Son Regime, ses problèmes. Son Influence en Europe.* (Paris: Levy, 1863), p. 222.

26. Archives municipales d'Amiens (hereafter AMA), 2F38.1 "Situation industrièlle, 4e semestre, 1859" and 2F38.3 "Situation industrièlle, 1er trimestre, 1887."

27. AMA 1F 2.36–37: Census summary of occupations, 1851. See also Howard P. Chudacoff and R. Burr Litchfield, "Towns of Order and Towns of Movement: The Social Structure of Variant Types," unpublished paper, Brown University, 1973. (Cited with permission).

28. Quoted in Gaston Motte, *Roubaix à travers les âges,* (Roubaix: Société d'Emulation, 1946), dedication.

29. Theodore Leuridan, *Histoire de la Fabrique de Roubaix* (Roubaix: Beghin, 1864), pp. 156–157.

30. Reybaud, *Le Coton,* p. 179.

31. Leuridan, pp. 151–152, 163–164.

32. Jacques Prouvost, "Les Courées a Roubaix," *Revue du Nord* 51 (April-June 1969) p. 316.

33. City occupational and demographic characteristics for Roubaix 1861, 1872, and 1906; Anzin, 1861, 1872, and 1906; and Amiens, 1906, are based on a 10 percent systematic sample of households drawn from the nominative lists found in the municipal archives of each city for each of the above years. (Anzin 1906 was filmed from the copy in the Archives départementales du Nord.) Individual level data were coded, put into machine-readable form, and analyzed by computer. The sampling method, code book, and occupational code were derived from R. Burr Litchfield and Howard Chudacoff, "Comparative Cities Project" (Brown University). We thank Professor Litchfield also for sharing his methodological expertise, unpublished papers, and data.

34. Friedrich Engels, *The Condition of the Working Class in England,* trans. by W. O. Henderson and W. H. Chaloner (Oxford: Blackwell, 1958), pp. 51–52.

35. Michael Anderson, "Household Structure and the Industrial Revolution. Mid-Nineteenth Century Preston in Comparative Perspective," in Peter Laslett and Richard Wall, eds., *Household and Family in Past Time* (Cambridge: At the University Press, 1972), p. 215.

36. Michael Anderson, *Family Structure in Nineteenth Century Lancashire* (Cambridge: At the University Press, 1971), p. 75.

37. R. Burr Litchfield, "Cotton Mill Work and the Fertility of Working Class Families in Mid-Victorian Stockport," unpublished paper, Brown University, 1975, p. 5.

38. Anderson, *Family Structure*, pp. 84–85.

39. Audiganne, *Les Populations ouvrières*, vol. 2, p. 100.

40. Poem by Lucien Lucas, from mimeographed brochure "La Ville d'Anzin," available at Anzin City Hall. On the development of the French coal fields of the Nord, see E. A. Wrigley, *Industrial Growth and Population Change* (Cambridge: At the University Press, 1961), p. 24; and Marcel Gillet, *Les Charbonnages du nord de la France au XIXe siècle* (Paris, The Hague: Mouton, 1973).

41. Archives départementales du Nord (hereafter ADN), M473.27: Summary of 1866 census for Anzin. Information on housing from E. Vuillemin, *Enquête sur les habitations, les écoles et le degré d'instruction de la population ouvrière des mines de houille des bassins du Nord et du Pas-de-Calais* (Comité des Houillères du Nord et du Pas-de-Calais, 1872), pp. 11, 13; Reed Geiger, *The Anzin Coal Company, 1800–1833* (Newark, Del.: University of Delaware Press, 1974).

42. Emile Zola, *Germinal* (London: Everyman's Library, 1933), p. 31.

43. Margaret Hewitt, *Wives and Mothers in Victorian Industry* (London: Rockliff, 1958), p. 17.

44. Anderson, *Family Structure*, p. 71.

Chapter 5

1. For discussion of these developments, see Wrigley, *Population and History*. See also Carlo Cipolla, *The Economic History of World Population*, rev. ed. (Baltimore: Penguin, 1964), p. 85.

2. Phyllis Deane, *The First Industrial Revolution* (Cambridge: At the University Press, 1967), p. 32; Joseph J. Spengler, "Demographic Factors and Early Modern Economic Development," *Daedalus. Historical Population Studies* (Spring, 1968), p. 436; age-specific death rates in Wrigley, *Industrial Growth*, pp. 102–109.

3. André Armengaud, "Population in Europe, 1700–1914," in Carlo Cipolla, ed., *The Industrial Revolution* (London: Collins/Fontana, 1973), pp. 54–56.

4. Ibid.

5. Wrigley, *Population and History*, p. 223.

6. See chapter 9.

7. Pierre Bourdieu, "Célibat et condition paysanne," *Etudes rurales*, 5 & 6 (1962–63); Emmanuel Le Roy Ladurie, "A System of Customary Law: Family Structures and Inheritance Customs in Sixteenth-Century France," in Forster and Ranum, *Family and Society*; Martine Segalen, *Nuptialité et alliance: Le Choix du conjoint dans une commune de l'Eure* (Paris: Maisonneuve et Larose, 1972). Katherine Gaskin, "An Analysis of Age at First Marriage in Europe before 1850," unpublished paper, University of Michigan, does a most thorough job in reviewing the literature dealing with age of marriage. We thank her for letting us read her paper.

8. Arnold Van Gennep, *Manuel de folklore français contemporain*, vol. 1, part 2 (Paris: Picard, 1943), p. 257.

9. Alain Corbin, *Archaisme et modernité en Limousin au XIXe siècle* (Paris: Revière, 1975) I, p. 563.

10. Anderson, *Family Structure,* pp. 132–134.

11. Pierre Bourdieu, "Marriage Strategies as Strategies of Social Reproduction," in Forster and Ranum, especially pp. 129–131.

12. Louis-Rene Villermé, *Tableau de l'état physique et morale des ouvriers employés dans les manufactures de coton, de laine et de soie* (Paris: J. Renouard, 1840), I, p. 190.

13. Rudolph Braun, "The Impact of Cottage Industry on an Agricultural Population," in *The Rise of Capitalism,* ed. by David Landes (New York: Macmillan, 1966), p. 57.

14. Ibid., p. 59.

15. Segalen, pp. 106, 60.

16. Pierre Guillaume, "Le Comportement au mariage de differents groupes sociaux bordelais," in *Sur la population française au XVIIIe et au XIXe siècles* (Paris: Société de démographie historique, 1973), pp. 326–328.

17. R. Burr Litchfield with David Gordon, "A Close Look at Manuscript Vital Registration: Illegitimacy in Mid-Nineteenth Century Amiens," unpublished paper, Brown University, 1976.

18. Frédéric Le Play, *Les Ouvriers européens. Etudes sur les trauvaux, la vie domestique et la condition morale des population ouvrières de l'Europe* (Paris: Imprimerie impériale, 1855), V, p. 442; VI, p. 202.

19. Armstrong, *Stability and Change,* p. 165.

20. Anderson, *Family Structure,* pp. 132–34.

21. Villermé, *Tableau,* I, p. 51.

22. Material calculated by Louise A. Tilly from Roubaix, Anzin census samples; Amiens, *Bulletin Municipal de la Ville d'Amiens* (Amiens: Progrès de la Somme, 1887), Annexe 5, 16; and Armstrong, p. 162.

23. Villermé, I, p. 33.

24. Ibid., p. 228.

25. Gerard Duplessis-Le Guelinel, *Les Mariages en France* (Paris: Colin, 1954), p. 130.

26. Edward Shorter, "Illegitimacy, Sexual Revolution and Social Change in Modern Europe," *Journal of Interdisciplinary History* 1 (Autumn 1971), pp. 231–272.

27. AN (Archives nationales) C998: Assemblée nationale Comité de l'Assistance publique. Note sur le mariage des indigents (1848); Societé charitable de St.-François-Régis de Paris, *Circulaire de cette société de charité à toutes les Sociétés de Saint-Régis de France et l'Etranger* (Paris, 1844); *L'Oeuvre charitable de Saint-François-Régis de Marseille, 1838–1938* (Marseille, 1938), pp. 33, 57; Material in Archives Municipales of Roubaix (Series ZIIIF.1), Archives départementales of the Nord (Series M222.373), and Roubaix, *Rapport du Maire* (Roubaix, annual series from 1863) on Society of Saint-François-Régis; Ernest Cadet, *Le Mariage en France* (Paris: Guillaumin, 1870), pp. 49, 167.

28. Helene Berguès et al., *La Prévention des naissances dans la famille. Ses origines dans les temps modernes,* I.N.E.D. Cahier no. 35 (Paris: Presses

Universitaires de France, 1960) reviews information on contraception in France.

29. Fertility strategy and its connection to mortality and life expectancy are discussed in Charles Tilly, "Population and Pedagogy," *History of Education Quarterly* (1973), pp. 113–128.

30. R. Felhoen, *Etude statistique sur la mortalité infantile à Roubaix et dans ses cantons Wattrelos-Croix-Wasquehal comparée avec celle de Lille et Tourcoing, 1871–1905* (Paris: Vigot, 1906).

31. Peter Uhlenberg, "Changing Configurations of the Life Course," unpublished paper, University of North Carolina, 1975.

Chapter 6

1. Audiganne, *Populations ouvrières,* I, p. 198.

2. Agricole Perdiguier, *Mémoires d'un compagnon* (Moulins: Editions des cahiers du centre, 1914), p. 33.

3. Le Play, *Les Ouvriers européens;* see for example III, p. 8; V, p. 45; VI, p. 109.

4. M. E. Loane, *From Their Point of View* (London: Edward Arnold, 1908), p. 52.

5. Louis Reybaud, *Le Coton* (Paris: Levy, 1863), p. 115.

6. Hewitt, *Wives and Mothers,* p. 187.

7. Jennie Kitteringham, "Country Work Girls in Nineteenth-Century England," in *Village Life and Labour,* ed. by Raphael Samuel (London: Routledge and Kegan Paul, 1975), p. 82; Hewitt, pp. 187–188.

8. Antoine Prost, *Histoire de l'enseignement en France, 1800–1967* (Paris: A. Colin, 1968), pp. 94–101.

9. Charles Robert, *De l'ignorance des populations ouvrières* (1863), cited in Georges Duveau, *La Pensée ouvrière sur l'éducation pendant la Seconde République et le Seconde Empire* (Paris: Domat-Montchrestien, 1948), pp. 178–179; E. Anthoine, *L'Instruction primaire dans le département du Nord, 1868–1877* (Lille: Robbe, 1878); ADN M605.14.

10. Diane Theodore, "Travail des enfants dans les manufactures amienoises au XIXe siècle," unpublished paper, University of Amiens, 1972. See also Eugene Tallon and Maurice Gustave, *Legislation sur le travail des enfants dans les manufactures* (Paris: J. Baudry, 1875).

11. AN F17 12203 (1847).

12. AN F17 12203 (1847).

13. John W. Shaffer, "Occupational Expectations of Young Women in Nineteenth Century Paris," unpublished paper, U.C.L.A., 1976, p. 16.

14. Marthe-Juliette Mouillon, "Un Example de migration rurale: De la Somme dans la capitale. Domestique de la Belle Epoque à Paris (1904–1912)," *Etudes de la région parisienne* 44 (July 1970) pp. 3–4.

15. E. Royston Pike, *Human Documents of the Victorian Golden Age (1850–1875)* (London: Allen and Unwin, 1967), p. 156; and John Burnett, ed., *The Annals of Labour: Autobiographies of British Working Class People, 1820–1920* (Bloomington: Indiana University Press, 1974), pp. 135–174.

16. Abel Chatelain, "Migrations et domesticité féminine urbaine en France, XVIIIe siècle-XXe siècle," *Revue d'histoire économique et sociale* 47 (1969) p. 521; Theresa McBride, *The Domestic Revolution* (London: Croom Helms, 1976), pp. 40–41.

17. Mouillon, *passim.*

18. LePlay, V, pp. 374–379.

19. McBride, *The Domestic Revolution,* pp. 34–47; Chatelain, p. 508.

20. For examples, see Yeo and Thompson, *The Unknown Mayhew,* pp. 116–180, and Evelyne Sullerot, *Histoire et sociologie du travail féminin* (Paris: Gonthier, 1968), p. 100.

21. David Mindock, of Northwestern University, sent us a copy of a section of the nominal census list for 1872. The original is in the Archives municipales de Toulouse. We are grateful for Mr. Mindock's willingness to share this piece of information with us.

22. Louis Reybaud, quoted in Abel Chatelain, "Les Usines internats et les migrations féminines dans la région lyonnaise," *Revue d'histoire économique et sociale 48 (1970): p. 381.*

23. Michelle Perrot, *Les Ouvriers en grève* (Paris, The Hague: Mouton, 1974), I, pp. 213, 328; Paul Le Roy Beaulieu, *Le Travail des femmes au XIXe siècle* (Paris: Charpentier, 1873), pp. 414ff; Cadet, *Le Mariage en France,* p. 119. See also Jules Simon, *L'Ouvrière* (Paris: Hachette, 1871), pp. 53–54; Frédéric Monnier, *De l'organisation du travail manuel des jeunes filles: Les Internats industriels* (N.P.: Chaix et cie., 1869).

24. Samuel Richardson, *Pamela* (New York: W. W. Norton, 1958), p. 4.

25. Le Play, V, p. 422.

26. R. H. Hubscher, "Une Contribution à la connaissance des milieux populaires ruraux au XIXe siècle: Le Livre de compte de la famille Flahaut, 1811–1877," *Revue d'histoire économique et sociale* 47 (1969) pp. 395–396.

27. Villermé, *Tableau,* I, p. 270.

28. Frances Collier, *The Family Economy of the Working Classes in the Cotton Industry, 1784–1833* (Manchester: Manchester University Press, 1964), p. 3.

29. Braun, "The Impact of Cottage Industry," pp. 61–63.

30. Pinchbeck, *Women Workers,* p. 185.

31. Collier, p. 15.

32. Ibid., p. 43.

33. ADN M581.143: "Tableau renferment les renseignements par lettre de M. le Prefet du Nord . . ." (1853).

34. Theodore, "Travail des enfants," *passim.*

35. Charles L. Livet, "Enseignment professionnel. Oeuvre des apprentis," Article clipped from proceedings of the Société industriel d'Amiens, 1863, p. 19.

36. France, AN, F12 4709 (1865).

37. Litchfield, "Cotton Mill Work." See also Pinchbeck, *Women Workers,* p. 185.

38. Anderson, *Family Structure,* p. 131.

39. Le Play, III, p. 325.

40. Charles Benoist, *Les Ouvrières de l'aiguille a Paris: Notes pour l'étude de la question sociale* (Paris: Chailley, 1895), p. 37.

41. Turgan, *Les Grandes usines,* vol. 6, p. 467.

42. Villermé, I, p. 113.

43. Le Play, III, p. 275; V, p. 122.

44. Shaffer, "Occupational Expectations," pp. 22–26.

45. Benoist, *Les Ouvrières,* p. 115.

46. A. J. B. Parent-Duchatelet, *De la prostitution dans la ville de Paris* (Paris: J. B. Baillière, 1836), pp. 73–75, 93–94.

47. Yeo and Thompson, *The Unknown Mayhew,* pp. 141, 148, 169; E. M. Sigsworth and J. J. Wylie, "A Study of Victorian Prostitution and Venereal Disease," in Martha Vicinus, ed., *Suffer and Be Still* (Bloomington: Indiana University Press, 1972), p. 81.

48. Le Play, V, pp. 333–334.

49. This account is condensed from Jeanne Bouvier, *Mes mémoires; ou, 59 années d'activité industrielle, sociale et intellectuelle d'une ouvrière* (Paris: L'Action Intellectuelle, 1936), pp. 1–54.

50. AN BB 30.380 (1866). This reference was given to us by J. Harvey Smith of Northern Illinois University. We appreciate his help.

51. Philippe Ariès, *Histoire des populations française set de leurs attitudes devant la vie depuis le XVIIIe siècle* (Paris: Editions du Seuil, 1971), pp. 235–236.

52. Anderson, *Family Structure,* pp. 131–132.

53. Cited in ibid., p. 131.

54. F. Lassale, "La Famille ouvrière," *La Réforme sociale* (May 1, 1904), p. 710.

55. Gabriel d'Haussonville, *Etudes sociales. Misères et Remèdes* (Paris: Calmann Levy, 1900), pp. 268–269.

56. Kitteringham, "Country Work Girls," p. 73.

57. McBride, *The Domestic Revolution* pp. 86–91.

58. Alain Lottin, "Naissances illégitimes et filles-mères à Lille au XVIIIe siècle," *Revue d'histoire moderne et contemporaine* 17 (1970) p. 309.

59. Jacques Depauw, "Amour illégitime et société à Nantes au XVIIIe siècle," *Annales. E.S.C.,* 27e année (1972), pp. 1163–1166.

60. Cissie Fairchilds, "Sex and the Single Woman in Eighteenth Century France," unpublished paper, University of California/San Diego, 1976; and Richard Cobb's notes from Declarations de Grossesse, Lyons, an II–III [1793–95], transmitted by Olwen Hufton.

61. Yeo and Thompson, p. 148.

62. Mouillon, p. 7.

63. McBride, *The Domestic Revolution* pp. 82–98.

64. Collier, pp. 17, 33.

65. Pinchbeck, p. 237.

66. From census of 1851, cited in Pike, *Human Documents,* p. 156.

67. Le Play, III, p. 325.

68. Lynn Lees, "Migration and the Irish Family Economy," unpublished paper, University of Pennsylvania, 1975.

69. Collet, in Booth, p. 312.

70. Anderson, *Family Structure,* pp. 18, 23, 34–41, 147–148.

71. Collet, in Booth, p. 258.

72. John Burnett, ed., *The Annals of Labour,* p. 285.

73. Ibid., p. 77.

74. Collet, in Booth, p. 259.

75. Ada Heather-Bigg, "The Wife's Contribution to the Family Income," *Economic Journal* 4 (1894): p. 58.

76. Simon, *L'Ouvrière,* p. 12.

77. Le Play, III, p. 8, and VI, p. 109.

78. Pinchbeck, p. 59.

79. Hewitt, p. 193.

80. Patricia Branca, "Image and Reality: The Myth of the Idle Victorian Woman," in Mary Hartman and Lois W. Banner, eds., *Clio's Consciousness Raised* (New York: Harper Torchbooks, 1974), pp. 179–189.

81. Morineau, "Budgets populaires," p. 464.

82. *La Politique des Femmes,* June 18–24, 1848. This newspaper extract was sent to us by Laura Strumingher, State University of New York, College at Fredonia. We thank her for it.

83. Louis Reybaud, *Le Fer et la houille* (Paris: Levy, 1874), p. 203; Emile Vuillemin, *Enquête sur les habitations, les écoles et le degré d'instruction de la population ouvrière des mines de houille du Nord et du Pas-de-Calais* (N.P.: Comité des houillères du Nord et du Pas-de-Calais, 1872), p. 20; see also Georges Duveau, *La Vie ouvrière en France sous le Second Empire* (Paris: Gallimard, 1946), pp. 369–370.

84. Reybaud, *Le Fer,* p. 203.

85. H. Stanley Jevons, *The British Coal Trade* (London: Kegan Paul, Trench, Trubner and Co., Ltd., 1920) p. 618; see also M. Davies, ed., *Life as We Have Known It* by Cooperative Working Women (New York: Norton, 1975) p. 26

86. Wage information for Amiens from AMA 2F38.1, "Salaires industriels dans la ville chef lieu du Departement de la Somme pendant l'année 1862."

87. On the decline of artisanal trades see Bernard Moss, *The Origins of the French Labor Movement* (Berkeley, Calif.: University of California, 1975), chap. 1; Gareth Stedman Jones, "Working Class Culture and Working Class Politics: Notes on the Remaking of a Working Class," *Journal of Social History* 7 (1974) pp. 484–485.

88. Ellen Barlee, *A Visit to Lancashire in December 1862* (London: Seely, 1863), p. 32.

89. Engels, *The Condition of the Working Class,* cited in Hewitt, p. 190.

90. Hewitt, p. 193.

91. AN C7321, Enquête textile, 1904.

92. Hewitt, p. 193.

93. Anderson, *Family Structure,* p. 74.

94. See the works of Jean-Baptiste-Firmin Marbeau for early discussion of the need for *crèches: Des crèches, ou moyen de diminuer la misère en augment- ant la population* (Paris: Imprimeurs-Unis, 1845) and *Des crèches pour les petits*

enfants des ouvrières (Paris: Amyot, Guillaumin et Le Clere, 1863). For Roubaix, the history of *crèches* can be followed in the Municipal Archives (Q III a 1–7) and in the annual *Rapports du Maire.* Other discussion in Assemblée Nationale, *Annales,* T.XXXII, 5 juin-7 juillet, 1874 (Annexe 2446), pp. 48–130; AN F15 3812–13; Andre-Theodore Brochard, *L'Ouvrière mère de famille* (Lyon: Joserand, 1874); E. Anthoine, "L'Instruction primaire," pp. 28–29.

95. Hewitt, pp. 116–117.

96. Villermé, I, pp. 242, 271, 394.

97. Hewitt, p. 179.

98. Cited in Elizabeth Leigh Hutchins and A. Harrison, *A History of Factory Legislation* (London: F. Cass, 1966), p. 47.

99. AN F12 4709, 4772, 4723.

100. AN F12 4709 (8 November 1853).

101. Jules Mousseron, quoted in E. Decaillon, *Essai sur la vie et l'oeuvre du poète de la mine* (Centième anniversaire de la naissance de Jules Mousseron) (Denain: Musée de Denain, 1971), p. 6.

102. M. Dournel, *Questions sociales: De Bourses de travail et des Associations populaires et économiques d'alimentation et de consommation* (Amiens: Jeunet, 1879), pp. 47–48.

103. Morineau, "Budgets populaires," *passim.*

104. John Burnett, *Plenty and Want: A Social History of Diet in England from 1815 to the Present Day* (London: Penquin Books, 1966), pp. 44–47.

105. Robert Roberts, *The Classic Slum* (Manchester: Manchester University Press, 1971), p. 107.

106. Anderson, *Family Structure,* p. 77.

107. Ibid.; see also Hufton, "Women and Revolution," pp. 91–93; Laura Oren, "The Welfare of Women in Laboring Families: England, 1860–1950," *Feminist Studies* 1 (1973) pp. 107–125.

108. Duveau, *La Vie ouvrière,* pp. 421, 436; Vuillemin, p. 31; Charles Benoist, *Les Ouvrières de l'aiguille a Paris: Notes pour l'étude de la question sociale* (Paris: Chailley, 1895), pp. 36–38; M. E. Loane, "The Position of the Wife in the Working-Class Home," in *An Englishman's Castle* (London: Edward Arnold, 1909), pp. 183–184.

109. Le Play, III, pp. 161, 281, 325.

110. Duveau, *La Vie ouvrière,* p. 301.

111. Le Play, VI, pp. 110–111. See also Marie-José Chombart de Lauwe, Paul-Henry Chombart de Lauwe, et al., *La Femme dans la société: Son image dans differents milieux sociaux* (Paris: Centre National de la Recherche Scientifique, 1967), p. 158.

112. Le Play, V, p. 427. See also IV, p. 198.

113. Denis Poulot, *Le Sublime ou le travailleur comme il est en 1870 et ce qu'il peut être* (Paris: A. Lecroix, Verboeckhoven, 1872), cited in Duveau, *La Vie ouvrière,* pp. 54–55.

114. Emile Zola, *L'Assomoir* (London: H. Hamilton, 1951); Duveau, *La Vie ouvrière,* pp. 505–510; Michael R. Marrus, "Social Drinking in the *Belle Epoque,*" *Journal of Social History* 7 (1974) pp. 115–141.

115. On the role of cafés, see Michelle Perrot, *Les Ouvriers en grève*, II, pp. 589–592 and *passim.*; Michael Hanagan, "Artisans and Industrial Workers; Work Structure, Technological Change, and Worker Militancy in Three French Towns," doctoral dissertation, University of Michigan, 1976; Marrus, "Social Drinking;" Jones, "Working Class Culture," p. 487.

116. Anderson, *Family Structure*, p. 85.

117. Wrigley, *Population and History*, p. 184.

118. Collet, in Booth, p. 325.

119. Bouvier, *Mes mémoires*, p. 24; Shaffer, p. 23.

120. Anderson, *Family Structure*, p. 77.

121. Margaret Llelwelyn Davies, ed. *Life as We Have Known It*

122. Anderson, *Family Structure*, p. 78.

123. Burnett, *The Annals of Labor*, p. 290.

124. Anderson, *Family Structure*, pp. 150–161. See also the life histories in Davies for descriptions of this kind of exchange of help.

Chapter 7

1. George Gissing, *The Odd Women* (London: Anthony Blond, 1968).

2. Deldycke et al. *La Population active*, Sections E and F.

3. Amy A. Bulley and Margaret Whitley, *Women's Work* (London: Methuen, 1894), p. 111. See also Clementina Black, *Sweated Industry and the Minimum Wage* (London: Duckworth, 1907).

4. Burnett, *Annals of Labour*, pp. 139–140; McBride, *The Domestic Revolution*, pp. 112–113.

5. Leslie Page Moch, "Domestic Service in Paris: An Avenue into the City," unpublished paper, University of Michigan, 1974, p. 17; McBride, *The Domestic Revolution* pp. 113–114.

6. McBride, *The Domestic Revolution* pp. 113–115.

7. Jean Daric, *L'Activité professionnelle des femmes en France. Etude statistique: évolution—comparisons internationales*, I.N.E.D., Cahier no. 5 (Paris: Presses Universitaires de France, 1947), p. 39; McBride, p. 113. See also Jean Fourastié, ed., *Migrations professionnelles. Données sur leur évolution en divers pays de 1900 à 1955*, I.N.E.D., Cahier no. 31 (Paris: Presses Universitaires de France, 1958), p. 159, and Collet, "Women's Work," p. 311.

8. Paul Gemähling, *Travailleurs au rabais. La Lutte syndicale contre les sous-concurrences ouvrières* (Paris: Bloud, 1910); R. Briquet, "Le Travail des femmes en France," *Le Mouvement socialiste*, August 15, 1902; Lewinski, "La Maternité et l'évolution Capitaliste," *Revue d'économie politique* 23 (1909) pp. 521–597.

9. Fédération des travailleurs du livre, *9e Congrès national tenu à Lyon* (Paris: Imprimerie nouvelle, 1905); Gustave Rouanet, "Le Travail des enfants et des femmes," *Le Revue socialiste* (1886), pp. 210–211; Fernand and Maurice Pelloutier, "La Femme dans la société moderne," *Le Revue socialiste* (1894), pp. 285–312; Madeleine Guilbert, *Les Femmes et l'organisation syndicale avant*

1914 (Paris: Centre National de la Recherche Scientifique, 1966), *passim;* L. M. Compain, *Les Femmes dans les organisations ouvrières* (Paris: Girard et Brière, 1910).

10. Daric, pp. 36–37; Alva Myrdal and Viola Klein, *Women's Two Roles: Home and Work* (London: Routledge and Kegan Paul, 1956), pp. 48–49.

11. Lee Holcombe, *Victorian Ladies at Work* (Newton Abbot: David and Charles, 1973), p. 105.

12. Pierre Giffard, *Paris sous la Troisième République: Les Grands Bazars* (Paris: V. Howard, 1882); Henriette Vanier, *La Mode et ses métiers; frivolités et luttes de classes, 1830–1870* (Paris: A. Colin, 1960); Michael B. Miller, "The Department Store and Social Change in Modern France: The Case of the Bon Marché, 1869–1920," doctoral dissertation, University of Pennsylvania, 1976, chap. 1.

13. Holcombe, *Victorian Ladies,* p. 103; noted in Shaffer, "Occupational Expectations."

14. Michel Crozier, *The World of the Office Workers* (Chicago: University of Chicago, 1965), p. 16; Roberts, *The Classic Slum,* p. 201; Holcombe, p. 146; Burnett, *Annals of Labour,* p. 142.

15. Mathilde Dubesset, Françoise Thébaud, and Catherine Vincent, "Quand les femmes entrent à l'usine . . .Les ouvrières des usines de guerre de la Seine, 1914–1918," Maîtrise d'histoire, University of Paris VII, 1974, p. 377.

16. Jeanne Bouvier, *Histoire des dames employées dans les postes, télégraphes et téléphones de 1714 à 1929* (Paris: Presses Universitaires de France, 1930), p. 159; Shaffer, "Occupational Expectations," p. 10; Holcombe, p. 164; Susan Bachrach, "The Feminization of French Urban Post Offices: Women's Work as Postal Clerks, 1892–1914," unpublished paper, University of Wisconsin, Madison, 1976.

17. Bachrach, pp. 17–19.

18. Holcombe, pp. 34, 203.

19. Bouvier, *Histoire des dames,* pp. 159, 234–251; Holcombe, pp. 163–171.

20. Holcombe, pp. 34, 203.

21. Prost, *Histoire de l'enseignement,* p. 378; Ida Berger, *Les Maternelles; étude sociologique sur les institutrices des écoles maternelles de la Seine* (Paris: Centre National de la Recherche Scientifique, 1959), p. 24; Jacques Ozouf, "Les Instituteurs de la Manche," *Revue d'histoire moderne et contemporaine* 13 (1966): p. 99; Ida Berger and Roger Benjamin, *L'Univers des instituteurs* (Paris: Editions de Minuit, 1964).

22. Berger, *Les Maternelles,* pp. 55–65; idem, "Sur l'origine sociale de trois generations d'instituteurs et d'institutrices de la Seine," *Bullétin de la Société d'études historiques, géographiques et scientifiques de la région parisienne* (1954), pp. 3, 8. Berger and Benjamin find that in each department of France "industrialization correlates with the feminization of the teaching corps. By the 1960's almost 75 percent of Parisian teachers were women." Cited by Barnett Singer, "The Teacher as Notable in Britanny, 1880–1914," *French Historical Studies* 9 (Fall 1976) p. 646.

23. Holcombe, pp. 36–37.

24. Ibid., p. 34.

25. Ibid., p. 203; Ozouf, p. 99.

26. Holcombe, p. 78.

27. Ibid., pp. 77, 78, 204–205.

28. Daric, p. 33; Holcombe, p. 216.

29. Rowntree, *Poverty*, p. 32.

30. Benjamin Seebohm Rowntree, *Poverty and Progress. A Second Social Survey of York* (London, New York: Longmans, Green, 1941), p. 9.

31. Rowntree, *Poverty*, p. 33.

32. Calculated from *Census of England and Wales, 1911*, vol. 10, *Occupations and Industries*, part 2 (London, 1913), pp. 689–690.

33. Daniel Bertin, "La Population amienoise de 1880 à 1914 (d'après les listes nominatives de rencensement)," Travail d'études et de recherches, University of Amiens, n.d., pp. 20–21.

34. France, Office du Travail, *Enquête sur le travail à domicile dans l'industrie de la lingerie* (Paris, 1907–1911), III, pp. 213, 218.

35. Ibid., *passim.*

36. Calculated from sample of households from 1906 nominative list.

37. Ethel M. Elderton, *Report on the English Birthrate. Part I. England North of the Humber* (Galton Eugenics Laboratory Publication, 1914), p. 214.

38. Stockport proportions calculated from published census tables for 1851 and 1911; Roubaix figures based on sample from nominative list, census of 1906.

39. Clara Collet, "The Collection and Utilization of Official Statistics Bearing on the Extent and Effects of the Industrial Employment of Women," *Journal of Royal Statistical Society* 61, part 2 (June 1898), p. 242.

40. Ibid.

41. Wrigley, *Population and History*, pp. 195–198; Ansley Coale, "The History of Human Populations," *Scientific American* (September 1974), pp. 41–51.

42. Alexandre Faidherbe, "Etude statistique et critique sur le mouvement de la population de Roubaix (1469–1744–1893), *Mémoires de la Société d'Emulation de Roubaix*, Troisième série, II (1894–1895), p. 147.

43. AN C 7321, Enquête Textile, 1904. Evidence for the use of birth control in England was compiled using lying-in claims to an artisan benefit society: Sidney Webb, *The Decline in the Birth-rate*, Fabian Tract 131 (London: The Fabian Society, 1907), pp. 6–8.

44. Elderton, *Report on the English Birthrate.*

45. Angus McLaren, "Abortion in England: 1890–1914," unpublished paper, University of Victoria, 1975.

46. Norman Himes, *A Medical History of Contraception* (Baltimore: Williams and Wilkins, 1936), pp. 209–259.

47. Ibid.; Peter Fryer, *The Birth Controllers* (London: Seeker and Warburg, 1965); J. A. Banks, *Prosperity and Parenthood* (New York: Humanities, 1954), p. 168, Rosanna Ledbetter, *A History of the Malthusian League, 1877–*

1927 (Columbus: Ohio State University Press, 1976). Professor Richard Soloway of the University of North Carolina at Chapel Hill is at work on a book on the British birth control movement. We are grateful for his willingness to share ideas and bibliographic references with us.

48. Francis Ronsin, "Mouvements et courants Néo-malthusiens en France," Thèse du IIIᵉ cycle, Université de Paris, VII, 1974; André Armengaud, "Mouvement ouvrier et Néo-malthusianisme au début du XXe siècle," *Annales de démographie historique* (1966).

49. Elderton, p. 212.

50. Ibid., pp. 234–235.

51. Women's Industrial Council, *Maternity: Letters from Working Women Collected by the Women's Cooperative Guild* (London: Bell, 1915), pp. 113–114.

52. The recent work of economists Gary Becker, Jacob Mincer, and others is discussed and summarized in Cynthia Lloyd, *Sex, Discrimination and the Division of Labor,* chap. 1. See also Richard Easterlin, "An Economic Framework for Fertility Analysis," *Studies in Family Planning* 6 (1975) pp. 54–63.

53. Elderton, pp. 234–235.

54. Nicole Quillien, "La Main d'oeuvre féminine textile dans l'arrondissement de Lille, 1890–1914," unpublished thesis, University of Lille, 1969, p. 22. See also Robert Pierreuse, "La Situation économique et sociale à Roubaix et à Tourcoing de 1900 à 1914," doctoral dissertation (IIIe cycle), University of Lille, 1972.

55. Etienne van de Walle, *The Female Population of France in the Nineteenth Century* (Princeton, N. J.: Princeton University Press, 1974), pp. 170–198, 204; John Knodel, "Infant Mortality and Fertility in Three Bavarian Villages: An Analysis of Family Histories from the Nineteenth Century," *Population Studies* 22 (1968) pp. 293–318; and John Knodel and Etienne van de Walle, "Breastfeeding, Fertility and Infant Mortality: An Analysis of Some Early German Data," *Population Studies* 21 (1967) p. 130.

56. Aline Lesaege-Dugied, "La Mortalité infantile dans le Departement du Nord de 1815 à 1914," in Marcel Gillet, ed., *L'Homme, la vie et la mort dans le Nord au 19e siècle* (Paris: Editions universitaires, 1972), pp. 85–86, 104; Rowntree, *Poverty,* p. 230.

57. "Report of the Interdepartmental Committee on Physical Deterioration," British Parliamentary Papers, Cd. 2175, LXXII, 1904, p. 28.

58. Gertrude Tuckwell et al., *Women in Industry from Seven Points of View* (London: Duckworth, 1908), pp. 90–91.

59. Lesaege-Dugied, pp. 119–120.

60. AN F15 3812–13.

61. Lesaege-Dugied, p. 120.

62. Felhoen, *Etude statistique,* pp. 167–208; AMR, QII d6.

63. G. F. McCleary, *Infantile Mortality and Infants' Milk Depots* (London: P. S. King, 1905).

64. Lesaege-Dugied, pp. 85–86, 123.

65. Rowntree, *Poverty and Progress,* pp. 286–287.

Chapter 8

1. Henri Boisgontier, *Les Syndicats professionels féminins de l'Abbaye et l'Union Centrale des syndicats féminins* (Paris: Thèse de doctorat, Faculté de droit de Lyon, 1927), p. 97.

2. John R. Gillis, *Youth and History: Tradition and Change in European Age Relations, 1770–Present* (New York, London: Academic Press, 1974), p. 124; Elderton, *Report on the English Birthrate*, p. 233; W. C. Marshall, "The Effect of Economic Conditions on the Birth-rate," *Eugenics Review* 5 (1913) pp. 118–120.

3. Prost, *Histoire de l'enseignement*, p. 101.

4. Geoffrey Best, *Mid-Victorian Britain, 1851–1871* (New York: Shocken Books, 1971), p. 110; Franchomme, "Roubaix de 1870 à 1900 (Etude démographique, économique, sociale et politique)," unpublished thesis (D.E.S.), University of Lille, 1960, pp. 112–113.

5. P. W. Musgrave, *Society and Education in England since 1800* (London: Methuen, 1968).

6. Charles Booth, "Occupations of the People of the United Kingdom, 1801–1881," *Journal of the Royal Statistical Society* 49 (1886) p. 371; see also Inter-departmental Committee on the Employment of School children, *Report* (British Parliamentary Papers, cd. 1849, 1902, XXV, pp. 261–276).

7. Prost, pp. 95, 97.

8. M. Bodin, "L'Institutrice," in *Bibliothèque sociale des métiers*, ed. by G. Renard (Paris: G. Doin, 1922), p. 60.

9. Gillis, p. 125.

10. Prost, p. 275.

11. Collet in Booth, p. 281.

12. Gillis, pp. 124–25.

13. Rowntree, *Poverty*, 117.

14. Ibid., pp. 117–118, 154.

15. Jacques Caroux-Destray, *Une Famille ouvrière traditionnelle* (Paris: Anthropos, 1974), p. 218.

16. Peter Willmott and Michael Young, *Family and Kinship in East London* (London: Penguin Books, 1957), p. 180.

17. Prost, p. 294; see also depiction of importance of education in Georges Emmanuel Clancier, *Le Pain Noir* (Paris: R. Laffont, 1956).

18. Henry Leyret, *En Plein faubourg; moeurs ouvrières* (Paris: Charpentier, 1895), p. 118.

19. Prost, p. 310.

20. Rowntree, *Poverty*, p. 89.

21. Ibid., 164.

22. Ibid., p. 105.

23. Roberts, *The Classic Slum*, p. 144.

24. Rowntree, *Poverty and Progress*, pp. 294, 447.

25. Burnett, *The Annals of Labour*, pp. 214–220.

26. Ibid., pp. 226–234.

27. Ibid., pp. 243–245.

28. Roberts, p. 222. See also Rowntree, *Poverty,* p. 103.

29. André Lainé, *La Situation des femmes employées dans les magasins de vente à Paris* (Paris: Rousseau, 1911), p. 30.

30. Holcombe, *Victorian Ladies,* pp. 128–132

31. Auguste Bessé, *L'Employé de commerce et d'industrie* (Lyon: E. Nicolas, 1901), p. 52; Lainé, p. 30. See also Shaffer, "Occupational Expectations."

32. Holcombe, p. 111.

33. Ibid., pp. 112–114; Leon Bonneff and Maurice Bonneff, *La Classe ouvrière: Les Employés de magasin* (Paris: "Guerre Sociale," 1912), p. 43; Lainé, p. 30; Giffard, *Paris sous la Troisième République,* pp. 24, 89.

34. Holcombe, p. 114.

35. Ibid., p. 117.

36. Gissing, *The Odd Women.*

37. Cited in Shaffer, p. 9.

38. Holcombe, p. 146.

39. Ozouf, "Les Instituteurs," p. 99.

40. Holcombe, pp. 21–67; Ozouf, pp. 100–101; Prost, p. 193.

41. Wilmott and Young, *Family and Kinship,* p. 81. See also Gillis, *Youth and History,* p. 193.

42. Roberts, p. 28.

43. Maurice Halbwachs, "Revenus et dépenses de ménages de travailleurs. Une Enquête officielle d'avant guerre," *Revue d'économie politique* 35 (January–February 1921) pp. 52–53.

44. Rowntree, *Poverty,* p. 56. See also John Condevaux, *Le·Mineur du Nord et du Pas-de-Calais: Sa psychologie, ses rapports avec le patronat* (Lille: Danel, 1928), p. 12; Madeline Kerr, *The People of Ship Street* (London: Routledge and Kegan Paul, 1958); Gillis, p. 130.

45. Caroux-Destray, *Une Famille,* p. 217.

46. Peter Stearns, "Working Class Women in Britain, 1890–1914," in Martha Vicinus, ed., *Suffer and Be Still* (Bloomington: Indiana University Press, 1972), p. 111.

47. Collet, in Booth, pp. 287, 314.

48. Hewitt, *Wives and Mothers,* p. 193.

49. M. E. Loane, "The Position of the Wife," p. 183; Michaud, *J'avais vingt ans: Un jeune ouvrier au début du siècle* (Paris: Editions syndicalistes, 1967), p. 39.

50. Madeleine Guilbert, *Les Femmes et l'organisation syndicale,* pp. 28–29; idem, "Le Travail des femmes," *Revue française du travail* (1946), p. 665. See also G. Dupeux, *La Société française 1789–1970* (Paris: Librarie Armand Colin, 1974), pp. 179–180.

51. B. Drake, *Women in Trade Unions* (London: Labour Research Department, 1924), pp. 17–18; Anne Locksley, "Speculation on Working Women, Resources, and Collective Action," unpublished paper, University of Michigan, 1974.

52. Collet, in Booth, p. 287.

53. Locksley, "Speculation." See also A. Stafford, *A Match to Fire the Thames* (London: Hodder and Stoughton, 1961).

54. Michelle Perrot, *Les Ouvriers en grève,* pp. 323–326; Bouvier, *Histoire des dames,* p. 286; Boisgontier, *Les Syndicats,* pp. 48, 138; Guilbert, "Le travail des femmes," p. 665.

55. Rowntree, *Poverty,* p. 366.

56. Leyret, *En Plein faubourg,* p. 98.

57. Rowntree, *Poverty,* p. 368.

58. Roberts, *The Classic Slum,* p. 235.

59. Ibid., p. 232.

60. Ibid., p. 233.

61. Shorter, *The Making of the Modern Family, passim.*

62. Gillis, p. 121; Joan W. Scott, *The Glassmakers of Carmaux* (Cambridge, Mass.: Harvard University Press, 1974), p. 203.

63. Ozouf, p. 99.

64. Jones, "Working Class Culture," p. 491.

65. Ibid.

66. Roberts, p. 52.

67. Ibid., p. 53.

68. Caroux-Destray, p. 70.

69. Wilmott and Young, p. 61.

70. Alain Girard and Henri Bastide, "Le Budget-temps de la femme mariée à la campagne," *Population* 14 (1959) pp. 253–284.

71. Roberts, pp. 81–83.

72. Lesaege-Dugied, "La Mortalité infantile," p. 107.

73. Elderton, *Report on the English Birthrate,* pp. 222–223.

74. AN C7319 Enquête Textile, 1904; Mathilde Decouvelaere, *Le Travail industriel des femmes mariées* (Paris: Rousseau, 1934), pp. 222–223. See also Eliane Delesalle, *Le Travail de la femme dans l'industrie textile et du vêtement de l'arrondissement de Lille* (Lille: Danel, 1952), and Juliette Minces, *Le Nord* (Paris: Maspero, 1967).

75. Dubesset, Thebaud, and Vincent, "Quand les femmes entrent à l'usine," p. 378. Material on Armentières from William Reddy, "Family and Factory: French Linen Weavers in the Belle Epoque," *Journal of Social History* 8 (Winter 1975) p. 111; on Fougères, from the dissertation research of Allen Binstock, University of Wisconsin.

76. Edward Cadbury, M. Cecile Matheson, and George Shann, *Women's Work and Wages: A Phase of Life of an Industrial City* (Chicago: University of Chicago Press, 1907), p. 147.

77. Alexander Patterson, *Across the Bridges or Life by the South London Riverside* (London: Edward Arnold, 1911), p. 29.

78. Collet, in Booth, pp. 310–311.

79. British figures are from Deldycke et al., *La Population active,* p. 185. French figures for total female labor force are from Henri Nolleau, "Les Femmes dans la population active de 1856 à 1954," *Economie et politique* 7 (1960) p. 7. Figures for French nonagricultural labor force are estimated from data in Jean Daric, "L'Activité professionnelle des femmes en France," I.N.E.D., Cahier No. 5 (Paris: P.U.F., 1947), pp. 15, 24; and Brian Mitchell,

European Historical Statistics. 1750–1970 (New York: Columbia University Press, 1975), p. 36.

80. Guilbert, "Le Travail des femmes," p. 758; Nolleau, p. 14.

81. Cadbury, et al., p. 176.

82. Roberts, p. 19.

83. Rowntree, *Poverty*, p. 156. See also Cadbury, et al., p. 210. For the United States, see John Modell and Tamara Hareven, "Urbanization and the Malleable Household: An Examination of Boarding and Lodging in American Families," *Journal of Marriage and the Family* (1973), pp. 467–479.

84. Board of Trade, *Consumption and Cost of Food in Workmen's Families in Urban Districts in the United Kingdom*, British Parliamentary Papers, 84, Cd. 2337, 1905.

85. Jeanne Singer-Kerel, *Le Coût de la vie à Paris de 1840 à 1954* (Paris: Colin, 1961); François Simiand, *Le Salaire, L'évolution sociale et le monnaie; essai de théorie experimentale du salaire, introduction et étude globale* (Paris: Alcan, 1932), p. 5;

86. Gemähling, *Travailleurs au rabais*, pp. 139–140.

87. Bulley and Whitley, *Women's Work*, p. 113.

88. Singer-Kerel, pp. 452–453.

89. Rowntree, *Poverty*, p. 108.

90. Maurice Halbwachs, "Revenus et dépenses de ménages de travailleurs," *Revue d'économie politique* 35 (1921): p. 52.

91. Roberts, p. 80.

92. Rowntree, *Poverty*, p. 98.

93. Cadbury, Matheson, and Shann, p. 212.

94. Ibid., p. 297.

95. Collet, in Booth, pp. 310–311.

96. Office du Travail, *Enquête sur le travail à domicile dans l'industrie de la lingerie* (Paris, 1907) III, p. 218.

97. Rowntree, *Poverty*, pp. 273, 276.

98. Kerr, *The People of Ship Street*, p. 30.

99. Michaud, *J'avais vingt ans*, p. 22; Rowntree, *Poverty*, p. 391; Cadbury, Matheson, and Shann, p. 174; Jones, "Working Class Culture," pp. 473–475.

100. Cadbury, Matheson, and Shann, pp. 148.

101. Collet, in Booth, pp. 295–296.

102. Caroux-Destray, p. 47; Rowntree, *Poverty*, p. 330. This use of the mother's wages to secure "extras" for her family did not diminish during the twentieth century. When Rowntree returned to York in 1936 he found that "only an insignificant handful" of women supplemented their husbands' earnings by going out to work. This was apparently partially due to the depressed state of the economy and a lack of jobs, for in 1950 Rowntree was struck by the number of women who had formed "the habit" of working, especially among "the best-off sections of the working class." Most of these women worked part-time and few had children under fifteen. (Rowntree and Lavers, p. 56.) Married women working at London's Peak Freen biscuit factory in 1962 usually worked part-time to gain extras for their families: Pearl Jephcott, with Nancy Secar and

John H. Smith, *Married Women Working* (London: Allen and Unwin, 1962), p. 165.

103. For examples see Davies, *Life as We Have Known It*, and Burnett, *The Annals of Labour, passim.*

104. Caroux-Destray, p. 99.

105. Patterson, *Across the Bridges*, p. 32. See also Rowntree, *Poverty and Progress*, p. 332; Jones, p. 486.

106. Jean-Marie Flonneau, Crise de la vie chère, 1910–1914, unpublished paper (Diplome d'Etudes Supérieures), University of Paris, 1966, p. 138. (Quoting *Le Travailleur*, August 26, 1911.)

107. Rowntree, *Poverty and Progress*, p. 357. See also Condevaux, *Le Mineur*, p. 10; Caroux-Destray, p. 47; Rowntree, *Poverty*, p. 91.

108. Kerr, p. 48.

109. Leyret, pp. 49–50. See also Roberts, p. 200.

110. Davies, p. 39.

111. Marguerite Perrot, *La Mode de la vie des familles bourgeoises, 1873–1953* (Paris: Colin, 1961), p. 262; Yves Boulinguiez, "Aspects de la vie économique, politique et sociale du XIXe et XXe siècles," *Revue du Nord* 54 (1972) p. 322.

112. Maurice Halbwachs, *L'Evolution des besoins dans les classes ouvrières* (Paris: Alcan, 1933), pp. 120–22; Burnett, *Plenty and Want*, p. 132.

113. Burnett, *Plenty and Want*, pp. 132, 243–245.

114. Ibid., p. 157.

115. Roberts, p. 107.

116. Davies, p. xi.

117. Ibid.

118. Flonneau, pp. 138–151.

119. Jones, pp. 473–475, 486. See also Leyret, p. 60.

120. Davies, p. 38; Cadbury, et al., p. 174.

121. Caroux-Destray, p. 47; Rowntree, *Poverty*, p. 71; Condevaux, p. 10.

122. Loane, "The Position of the Wife," p. 184.

123. Jones, p. 486.

124. Rowntree, *Poverty*, p. 86; Stearns, "Working Class Women," p. 106.

125. Leyret, p. 122; Burnett, *Plenty and Want*, p. 272.

126. Roberts, p. 43. See also Paul-Henri Chombart de Lauwe, *La Vie quotidienne des familles ouvrières* (Paris: Centre de la Recherche Scientifique, 1956), who writes (p. 56): "Women can build in their neighborhoods, and throughout working class life, an information network which gives them a very important role . . . it's a way for women to have influence despite the obstacles which surround them. . . ."

127. Cadbury, et al., p. 175.

128. Ibid., p. 221.

129. Davies, pp. 63–64.

130. Burnett, *Annals of Labour*, p. 7.

131. Caroux-Destray, p. 46.

132. Patterson, p. 32.

133. Caroux-Destray, p. 46.

134. Wilmott and Young, p. 78.

135. Rowntree, *Poverty,* p. 108.

Chapter 9

1. Viola Klein, *Britain's Married Women Workers* (London: Routledge and Kegan Paul, 1965), p. 27.

2. Myrdal and Klein, *Women's Two Roles,* pp. 3, 39–40. On the American situation, see William H. Chafe, *The American Woman: Her Changing Social, Political and Economic Roles, 1920–1970* (New York: Oxford University Press, 1972).

3. These are discussed in J.-J. Carré, P. Dubois, and E. Malinvaud, *French Economic Growth,* trans. by John P. Hatfield (Stanford, Calif.: Stanford University Press, 1975), p. 37.

4. Daric, *L'activité professionelle,* p. 37.

5. Ibid., p. 24.

6. Gordon Wright, *Rural Revolution in France* (Stanford, Calif.: Stanford University Press, 1964), *passim.;* Carré, Dubois, and Malinvaud, pp. 170–173. Some of the decline in female agricultural employment was probably due to changing definitions of employment in family farms. See Carré et al., pp. 48–54.

7. Daric, p. 62; Françoise Guelaud-Léridon, *Le Travail des femmes en France,* I.N.E.D., Cahier no. 42 (Paris: Presses Universitaires de France, 1964), p. 23.

8. Daric, pp. 28, 40.

9. Holcombe, *Victorian Ladies,* p. 217; Myrdal and Klein, p. 52.

10. Daric, p. 27; Guelaud-Leridon, p. 42–43.

11. Holcomb, p. 217.

12. Klein, pp. 84–86.

13. Rowntree and Lavers, *Poverty and the Welfare State,* p. 56; Guelaud-Leridon, pp. 14–23; Marie-José Chombart de Lauwe, Paul-Henri Chombart de Lauwe, Michèle Huguet, Elia Perroy, and Noelle Bissert, *La Femme dans la Société. Son image dans differents milieux sociaux* (Paris: Centre national de la recherche scientifique, 1967), pp. 80–81; Klein, p. 54.

14. Pearl Jephcott, Nancy Secar, and John H. Smith, *Married Women Working*

15. Myrdal and Klein, p. 80; Klein, p. 16; Joann Vanek, "Time Spent in Housework," *Scientific American* 231 (November 1974): pp. 116–120; Alexander Szalai, ed., *The Use of Time: Daily Activities of Urban and Suburban Populations in Twelve Countries* (Paris, The Hague: Mouton, 1972), *passim.*

16. Rowntree and Lavers, p. 57.

17. Jephcott, Secar, and Smith, p. 165.

18. Klein, p. 43.

19. Rowntree and Lavers, p. 56.

Bibliography

The following is a guide to books and articles readily available in university libraries. It is by no means comprehensive, and it contains many more references to books in English than in French. The list is meant primarily for undergraduates beginning a research paper. Students wishing a more extensive bibliography should consult the notes for each chapter. Those notes contain complete references to many of the primary and secondary sources the authors consulted. A complete bibliography of works consulted may be obtained from the authors.

Abensour, Léon. *Le Féminisme sous le règne de Louis-Phillippe et en 1848.* Paris: Plon-Nourrit, 1913.

Agulhon, Maurice; Desert, Gabriel; and Specklin, Robert. *Apogée et crise de la civilisation paysanne, 1789–1914.* Vol. 3 of *Histoire de la France rurale.* Paris: Seuil, 1976.

Allison, K. J., and Tillot, P. M., "York in the Eighteenth Century." In *A History of Yorkshire,* edited by P. M. Tillot. London: The Institute of Historical Research, 1961.

Anderson, Michael. *Family Structure in Nineteenth Century Lancashire.* Cambridge: At the University Press, 1971.

———. "Household Structure and the Industrial Revolution: Mid-Nineteenth Century Preston in Comparative Perspective." In *Household and Family in Past Time,* edited by Peter Laslett and Richard Wall. Cambridge: At the University Press, 1972.

Ariès, Philippe. *Centuries of Childhood: A Social History of Family Life,* translated by Robert Baldick. New York: Vintage, 1965.

Armengaud, André. *La Famille et l'enfant en France et en Angleterre du XVIe au XVIIIe siècle. Aspects démographiques.* Paris: Société d'édition d'enseignement supérieur, 1975.

————. "Population in Europe. 1700–1914." In *The Industrial Revolution*, edited by Carlo M. Cipolla. Vol. 3 of *The Fontana Economic History of Europe*. London: Collins/Fontana Books, 1973.

Armstrong, Alan. *Stability and Change in an English Country Town. A Social Study of York, 1801–51*. Cambridge: At the University Press, 1974.

Bairoch, Paul. "Agriculture and the Industrial Revolution, 1700–1914." In *The Industrial Revolution*, edited by Carlo M. Cipolla. Vol. 3 of *The Fontana Economic History of Europe*. London: Collins/Fontana Books, 1973.

Baker, Elizabeth. *Technology and Woman's Work*. New York: Columbia University Press, 1964.

Banks, Joseph A. *Prosperity and parenthood. A Study of Family Planning Among the Victorian Middle Classes*. London: Routledge and Kegan Paul, 1954.

Baulant, Micheline. "The Scattered Family: Another Aspect of Seventeenth Century Demography." In *Family and Society*, edited by Robert Forster and Orest Ranum. Baltimore: Johns Hopkins University Press, 1976.

Berger, Ida. *Les Maternelles; étude sociologique sur les institutrices des écoles maternelles de la Seine*. Paris: Centre National de la Recherche Scientifique, 1959.

Berguès, Helene; Ariès, Philippe; Helin, Etienne; Henry, Louis; Piquet, R. P. Michel; Sauvy, Alfred; and Sutter, Jean. *La Prévention des naissances dans la famille. Ses origines dans les temps modernes*. I.N.E.D. Travaux et Documents, Cahier no. 35. Paris: Presses Universitaires de France, 1960.

Berkner, Lutz K. "The Stem Family and the Developmental Cycle of the Peasant Household: An Eighteenth Century Austrian Example." *American Historical Review* 77 (April 1972): 398–418.

Bernard, R. -J. "Peasant Diet in Eighteenth-Century Gevaudan." In *European Diet from Pre-Industrial to Modern Times*, edited by Elborg Forster and Robert Forster. New York: Harper and Row, 1975.

Black, Clementina, ed. *Married Women's Work*. London: G. Bell and Sons, 1915.

————. *Sweated Industry and the Minimum Wage*. London: Duckworth, 1907.

Blackburn, Helen, and Vynne, Nora. *Women Under the Factory Act*. London: Williams and Norgate, 1903.

Bondfield, Margaret Grace. *A Life's Work*. London: Hutchinson, 1948.

Booth, Charles. "Occupations of the People of the United Kingdom, 1801–1881." *Journal of the Royal Statistical Society* 49 (1886): 314–435.

————, ed. *Life and Labour of the People in London*. First Series. *Poverty*. London: Macmillan, 1902.

Bott, Elizabeth. *Family and Social Network; Roles, Norms and External Relationships in Ordinary Urban Families*. London: Tavistock Publications, 1957.

Bourdieu, Pierre. "Marriage Strategies as Strategies of Social Reproduction." In *Family and Society*, edited by Robert Forster and Orest Ranum. Baltimore: Johns Hopkins University Press, 1976.

————. "Social and Biological Determinants of Human Fertility in Nonindustrial Societies." *Proceedings of the American Philosophical Society* 3 (1967): 160–163.

Bouvier, Jeanne. *Histoire des dames employées dans les postes, télégraphes et téléphones de 1714 à 1929*. Paris: Presses Universitaires de France, 1930.

Branca, Patricia. "Image and Reality: The Myth of the Idle Victorian Woman." In *Clio's Consciousness Raised*, edited by Mary Hartman and Lois W. Banner. New York: Harper Torchbooks, 1974: 179–189.

Braun, Rudolph. "The Impact of Cottage Industry on an Agricultural Population." In *The Rise of Capitalism*, edited by David Landes. New York: Macmillan, 1966.

Brown, Judith K. "A Note on the Division of Labor by Sex." *American Anthropologist* 72 (1970): 1073–1078.

Burnett, John. *Plenty and Want: A Social History of Diet in England from 1815 to the Present Day*. London: Penguin Books, 1966.

——, ed. *The Annals of Labour: Autobiographies of British Working Class People, 1820–1920*. Bloomington: Indiana University Press, 1974.

Cadbury, Edward; Matheson, M. Cecile; and George Shann. *Women's Work and Wages: A Phase of Life of an Industrial City*. Chicago: University of Chicago Press, 1907.

Carré, J. -J.; Dubois, P.; and Malinvaud, E. *French Economic Growth*, translated by John P. Hatfield. Stanford, Calif.: Stanford University Press, 1975.

Chafe, William H. *The American Woman: Her Changing Social, Political and Economic Roles, 1920–1970*. New York: Oxford University Press, 1972.

Charles-Roux, Edmonde, et al. *Les Femmes et le travail du Moyen-Age à nos jours*. Paris: Editions de la Courtille, 1975.

Chatelain, Abel. "Migrations et domesticité féminine urbaine en France, XVIIIe siècle-XXe siècle." *Revue d'histoire économique et sociale* 47 (1969): 506–528.

——. "Les Usines internats et les migrations féminines dans la région Lyonnaise, seconde moitié du XIXe siècle et au début du XIXe siècle." *Revue d'histoire économique et sociale* 48 (1970): 373–394.

Chevalier, Louis. *La Formation de la population parisiènne au XIXe siècle*. Paris: Presses Universitaires de France, 1950.

——. *Laboring Classes and Dangerous Classes in Paris in the First Half of the Nineteenth Century*, translated by Frank Jellinek. New York: H. Fertig, 1973.

Chombart de Lauwe, Marie-Josè; Chombart de Lauwe, Paul Henry; et al. *La Femme dans la société: Son image dans differents milieux sociaux*. Paris: Centre National de la Recherche Scientifique, 1967.

Cipolla, Carlo. *Before the Industrial Revolution: European Society and Economy, 1000–1700*. New York: W. W. Norton, 1976.

Clapham, J. H. *The Economic Development of France and Germany, 1815–1914*. Cambridge: At the University Press, 1966.

Clark, Alice. *The Working Life of Women in the Seventeenth Century*. London: G. Routledge and Sons, 1919. (Reissued by Frank Cass, 1968.)

Clark, Frances Ida. *The Position of Women in Contemporary France*. London: P. S. King and Sons, 1937.

Coale, Ansley J. "Age Patterns of Marriage." *Population Studies* 25 (1971): 193–214.

————. "The Decline of Fertility in Europe from the French Revolution to World War II." In *Fertility and Family Planning*, edited by S. J. Behrmann, Leslie Corsa, and Ronald Freedman. Ann Arbor: University of Michigan Press, 1967.

————. "Factors Associated with the Development of Low Fertility: An Historical Summary." In *Proceedings of the World Population Conference 1965*. 2 vols. New York: United Nations, 1967.

————. "The History of Human Populations." *Scientific American*, September 1974: 411–51.

Cohen, Miriam. "Italian-American Women in New York City, 1900–1950: Work and School." In *Class, Sex, and the Woman Worker*, edited by Milton Cantor and Bruce Laurie, Westport, Conn.: Greenwood Press, 1977.

Collet, Clara E. "Women's Work." In *Life and Labour of the People in London*. First series, vol. 4, edited by Charles Booth. London: Macmillan, 1902.

Collier, Frances. *The Family Economy of the Working Classes in the Cotton Industry, 1784–1833*. Manchester: Manchester University Press, 1964.

Daric, Jean. *L'Activité professionnelle des femmes en France. Etude statistique: évolution—comparaisons internationales*. I.N.E.D., Cahier no. 5. Paris: Presses Universitaires de France, 1947.

Davies, M. L. *Life As We Have Known It by Cooperative Working Women* (New York: Norton, 1975).

Davis, Kingsley, and Blake, Judith. "Social Structure and Fertility: An Analytic Framework." *Economic Development and Cultural Change* 4 (1956): 211–235.

Davis, Natalie Zemon. "The Reasons of Misrule: Youth Groups and Charivaris in Sixteenth-Century France." *Past and Present* 50 (1971): 41–75.

————. "Women on Top." In Natalie Zemon Davis *Culture and Society in Early Modern Europe*. Stanford, Calif.: Stanford University Press, 1975.

Deldycke, T.; Gelders, H.; and Limbor, J. M. *La Population active et sa structure*. Brussels: Institut de sociologie, 1969.

Delesalle, Eliane. *Le Travail de la femme dans l'industrie textile et du vêtement de l'arrondissement de Lille*. Lille: Imprimerie Danel, 1952.

Depauw, Jacques. "Amour illégitime et société à Nantes au XVIIIe siècle." *Annales. Economies, Sociétés, Civilisations*, 27e Année (1972): 1155–1182.

Deyon, Pierre. *Amiens, Capitale provinciale. Étude sur la société urbaine au 17e siècle*. Paris, the Hague: Mouton, 1967.

Dingle, A. E. "Drink and Working-Class Living Standards in Britain, 1870–1914." *Economic History Review* 25 (1972): 608–622.

Drake, Barbara. *Women in Trade Unions*. London: Labour Research Department, 1924.

Dunham, Arthur L. *The Industrial Revolution in France (1815–1848)*. New York: Exposition Press, 1955.

Dupâquier, Jacques. "Les Caractères originaux de l'histoire démographique française au XVIIIe siècle." *Revue d'histoire moderne et contemporaine*, 23 (April-June 1976): 182–202.

Duplessis-Le Guelinel, Gérard. *Les Mariages en France*. Paris: Colin, 1954.

Duveau, Georges. *Les Instituteurs*. Paris: Editions du Seuil, 1957.

————. *La Pensée ouvrière sur l'éducation pendant la Seconde République et le Second Empire*. Paris: Domat-Montchrestien, 1948.

————. *La Vie ouvrière en France sous le Second Empire*. Paris: Gallimard, 1946.

Easterlin, Richard. "An Economic Framework for Fertility Analysis." *Studies in Family Planning* 6 (March 1975): 54–63.

Engels, Friedrich. *The Origin of the Family, Private Property and the State*. New York: International Publishers, 1972.

Fairchilds, Cissie. *Poverty and Charity in Aix-en-Provence, 1640–1789*. Baltimore: Johns Hopkins University Press, 1976.

Flandrin, Jean-Louis. *Familles: Parenté, maison, sexualité dans l'ancienne société*. Paris: Hachette, 1976.

Fohlen, Claude. *L'industrie textile au temps du Second Empire*. Paris: Plon, 1956.

Forster, Edward Morgan. *Marianne Thornton: A Domestic Biography, 1797–1887*. New York: Harcourt, Brace, 1956.

Forster, G. C. F., "York in the Seventeenth Century." In *A History of Yorkshire*, edited by P. M. Tillot. London: The Institute of Historical Research, 1961.

Fourastié, Jean. "De la vie traditionelle à la vie 'tertiare.'" *Population* 14 (1959): 417–432.

————, ed. *Migrations professionnelles. Données sur leur évolution en divers pays de 1900 à 1955*. I.N.E.D., Cahier no. 31. Paris: Presses Universitaires de France, 1958.

Friedlander, Dov. "Demographic Characteristics of the Coal Mining Population in England and Wales in the Nineteenth Century." *Economic Development and Cultural Change* 22 (1973): 39–51.

Fryer, Peter. *The Birth Controllers*. London: Soeker and Warburg, 1965.

Garden, Maurice. *Lyon et les lyonnais au XVIIIe siècle*. Paris: Les Belles-Lettres, 1970.

Gauldie, Enid. *Cruel Habitations: a History of Working Class Housing, 1780–1918*. London: Allen and Unwin, 1974.

George, Mary Dorothy. *London Life in the XVIIIth Century*. New York: Alfred A. Knopf, 1925.

Gillis, John R. *Youth and History: Tradition and Change in European Age Relations, 1770-Present*. New York, London: Academic Press, 1974.

Gissing, George. *The Odd Women*. London: Anthony Blond, 1968.

Glass, David Victor. *Population Policies and Movements in Europe*. Oxford: Clarendon Press, 1940.

Goode, William J. *World Revolution and Family Patterns*. New York: Free Press of Glencoe, 1963.

Goody, Jack. "Class and Marriage in Africa and Eurasia," *American Journal of Sociology* 76 (1971): 585–603.

————. "Inheritance, Property and Marriage in Africa and Eurasia." *Sociology* 3 (1969): 45–76.

————. "Strategies of Heirship." *Comparative Studies in Society and History* 15 (1973): 3–20.

————, ed. *The Character of Kinship*. Cambridge: At the University Press, 1973.

Goubert, Pierre. *Beauvais et le Beauvaisis de 1600 à 1730. Contribution à l'histoire sociale de la France du XVIIe siècle*. Paris: S.E.V.P.E.N., 1960.

————. "Legitimate Fecundity and Infant Mortality in France during the Eighteenth Century: A Comparison." *Daedalus. Historical Population Studies* (Spring 1968): 593–603.

Gross, Edward. "Plus ça change . . .? The Sexual Structure of Occupations Over Time." *Social Problems* 16 (Fall 1968): 198–208.

Gueland-Léridon, Françoise. *Le Travail des femmes en France*. I.N.E.D., Cahier no. 42. Paris: Presses Universitaires de France, 1964.

Guilbert, Madeleine. *Les Femmes et l'organisation syndicale avant 1914*. Paris: Centre National de la Recherche Scientifique, 1966.

————. *Les Fonctions des femmes dans l'industrie*. Paris, The Hague: Mouton, 1966.

Haines, Michael R. "Fertility and Occupation: Coal Mining Populations in the Nineteenth and Early Twentieth Centuries in Europe and America." *Western Societies Program Occasional Papers, No. 3*. Cornell University, Ithaca, New York, 1975.

Hair, P. E. H. "Bridal Pregnancy in Rural England in Earlier Centuries." *Population Studies* 20 (November 1966): 233–243.

Hajnal, John "European Marriage Patterns in Perspective." In *Population in History: Essays in Historical Demography*, edited by D. V. Glass and D. E. C. Eversley. Chicago: Aldine, 1965.

Hartwell, R. M. "The Service Revolution: The Growth of Services in the Modern Economy." In *The Industrial Revolution*, edited by Carlo M. Cipolla. Vol. III of *The Fontana Economic History of Europe*. London: Collins/Fontana, 1973.

Heather-Bigg, Ada. "The Wife's Contribution to the Family Income." *Economic Journal* 4 (1894): 51–58.

Hewitt, Margaret. *Wives and Mothers in Victorian Industry*. London: Rockliff, 1958.

Himes, Norman. *A Medical History of Contraception*. Baltimore: Williams and Wilkins, 1936.

Holcombe, Lee. *Victorian Ladies at Work*. Hamden, Conn.: Archon Books, 1973.

Hollingsworth, T. H. *Historical Demography*. London: The Sources of History Limited in Association with Hodder and Stoughton Ltd., 1969.

Hufton, Olwen. *The Poor of Eighteenth Century France, 1750–1789*. Oxford: Clarendon Press, 1974.

————. "Women and the Family Economy in Eighteenth Century France." *French Historical Studies* 9 (Spring 1975): 1–22.

————. "Women in Revolution, 1789–1796," *Past and Present* 53 (1971): 90–108.

Hunt, E. H. *Regional Wage Variations in Britain, 1850–1914*. Oxford: Clarendon Press, 1973.

Hutchins, Elizabeth Leigh, and Harrison, A. *A History of Factory Legislation.* London: F. Cass, 1966.

Innes, John W. *Class Fertility Trends in England and Wales, 1876–1934.* Princeton, N. J.: Princeton University Press, 1938.

Jephcott, Pearl, with Nancy Secar and John H. Smith. *Married Women Working.* London: Allen and Unwin, 1962.

Jones, Gareth Stedman. "Working Class Culture and Working Class Politics: Notes on the Remaking of a Working Class." *Journal of Social History* 7 (1974): 460–508.

Kerr, Madeline. *The People of Ship Street.* London: Routledge and Kegan Paul, 1958.

Kitteringham, Jennie. "Country Work Girls in Nineteenth Century England." In *Village Life and Labour,* edited by Raphael Samuel. London: Routledge and Kegan Paul, 1975.

Klein, Viola. *Britain's Married Women Workers.* London: Routledge and Kegan Paul, 1965.

Knodel, John. "Infant Mortality and Fertility in Three Bavarian Villages: An Analysis of Family Histories from the Nineteenth Century." *Population Studies* 22 (1968): 293–318.

————, and Maynes, Mary Jo. "Urban and Rural Marriage Patterns in Imperial Germany." *Journal of Family History* 1 (Winter 1976).

————, and van de Walle, Etienne. "Breastfeeding, Fertility and Infant Mortality: An Analysis of Some Early German Data." *Population Studies* 21 (1967): 109–131.

Langer, William L. "Europe's Initial Population Explosion." *American Historical Review* 69 (October 1963): 1–17.

Laslett, Barbara. "The Family as a Public and Private Institution: An Historical Perspective." *Journal of Marriage and the Family* 35 (1973): 480–492.

Laslett, Peter. *The World We Have Lost.* New York: Scribner's 1965.

————, and Osterveen, Karla. "Long-term Trends in Bastardy in England: A Study of the Illegitimacy Figures in the Parish Registers and in the Reports of the Registrar General, 1461–1960," *Population Studies* 27 (1973): 255–286.

Le Play, Frédéric. *Les Ouvriers européens. Etudes sur les trauvaux, la vie domestique et la condition morale des populations ouvrières de l'Europe.* Paris: Imprimerie impériale, 1855.

Levine, David. *Family Formation in an Age of Nascent Capitalism.* New York: Academic Press, 1977.

Lloyd, Cynthia B., ed. *Sex, Discrimination and the Division of Labor.* New York: Columbia University Press, 1975.

Macfarlane, Alan. *The Family Life of Ralph Josselin.* Cambridge: At the University Press, 1970.

McBride, Theresa. *The Domestic Revolution.* London: Croom Helms, 1976.

McKendrick, Neil. "Home Demand and Economic Growth: A New View of the Role of Women and Children in the Industrial Revolution." *Historical*

Perspectives: Studies in English Thought and Society in Honour of J. H. Plumb. London: Europa, 1974.

Meillassoux, Claude. *Femmes, greniers et capitaux.* Paris: Maspero, 1975.

Mendras, Henri. *The Vanishing Peasant. Innovation and Change in French Agriculture,* translated by Jean Lerner. Cambridge, Mass.: M. I. T. Press, 1970.

Morineau, Michel. "Budgets populaires en France au XVIIIe siècle." *Revue d'histoire économique et sociale* 50 (1972): 203–237, 449–481.

Myrdal, Alva, and Klein, Viola. *Women's Two Roles: Home and Work.* London: Routledge and Kegan Paul, 1956.

Neff, Wanda F. *Victorian Working Women.* New York: Columbia University Press, 1929.

Oakley, Ann. *Housewife.* London: Allen Lane, 1974.

———. *Woman's Work: The Housewife, Past and Present.* New York: Pantheon, 1974.

Oppenheimer, Valerie Kincade. "Demographic Influence on Female Employment and the Status of Women." *American Journal of Sociology* 78 (1973): 946–961.

———. *The Female Labor Force in the United States.* Berkeley: University of California Press, 1970.

Oren, Laura, "The Welfare of Women in Laboring Families: England, 1860–1950." *Feminist Studies* 1 (1973): 107–125.

Ozouf, Jacques. "L'Enquête d'opinion en histoire un exemple: l'instituteur français 1900–1914." *Le Mouvement social* 44 (1963): 3–22.

———. "Les Instituteurs de la Manche." *Revue d'histoire moderne et contemporaine* (1966): 98–106.

Peller, Sigismund. "Births and Deaths among Europe's Ruling Families since 1500." In *Population in History: Essays in Historical Demography,* edited by D. V. Glass and D. E. C. Eversley. Chicago: Aldine, 1965.

Perrot, Michelle. *Les Ouvriers en grève. France 1871–1890.* Paris, The Hague: Mouton, 1974.

Phillips, Roderick. "Women and Family Breakdown in Eighteenth Century France: Rouen 1780–1800." *Social History* 2 (May 1976): 197–218.

Pike, E. Roysten. *Human Documents of the Victorian Golden Age (1850–1875).* London: Allen and Unwin, 1967.

Pinchbeck, Ivy. *Women Workers and the Industrial Revolution, 1750–1850.* New York: G. Routledge, 1930; A. Kelley, 1969.

———, and Hewitt, Margaret. *Children in English Society.* vol. 1. London: Routledge and Kegan Paul, 1969.

Prost, Antoine. *Histoire de l'enseignement en France, 1800–1967.* Paris: A. Colin, 1968.

Reddy, William. "Family and Factory: French Linen Weavers in the Belle Epoque." *Journal of Social History* 8 (Winter 1975): 102–112.

Ritter, Kathleen V., and Hargens, Lowell L. "Occupational Positions and Class Identification of Married Working Women." *American Journal of Sociology* 80 (1975): 934–948.

Roberts, Robert. *The Classic Slum.* Manchester: Manchester University Press, 1971.

Roubin, Lucienne A. "Espace masculin, espace féminin en communauté provençale." *Annales. E.S.C.* 26 (March-April 1970).

Rowntree, Benjamin Seebohm. *English Life and Leisure.* London: Longmans, Green, 1951.

———. *Poverty: A Study of Town Life.* London: Nelson, 1901.

———. *Poverty and Progress: A Second Social Survey of York.* London, New York: Longmans, Green, 1941.

———, and Kendall, May. *How the Laborer Lives: A Study of the Rural Labor Problem.* London: T. Nelson and Sons, 1913.

———, and Lavers, G. R. *Poverty and the Welfare State.* London: Longmans, Green, 1951.

Rubinstein, D. *School Attendance in London, 1870–1904.* New York: Kelley, 1972.

Sanderson, Michael. "Education and the Factory in Industrial Lancashire, 1780–1840." *Economic History Review* 20 (1967): 266–279.

Scott, Joan W., and Tilly, Louise A. "Women's Work and the Family in Nineteenth Century Europe." *Comparative Studies in Society and History* 17 (1975): 36–64.

Segalen, Martine. *Nuptialité et alliance: Le Choix du conjoint dans une commune de l'Eure.* Paris: G. -P. Maisonneuve et Larose, 1972.

Shorter, Edward. "Female Emancipation, Birth Control, and Fertility in European History." *American Historical Review* 78 (June 1973): 605–640.

Sigsworth, E. M., and Wylie, J. J. "A Study of Victorian Prostitution and Venereal Disease." In *Suffer and Be Still,* edited by Martha Vicinus. Bloomington: Indiana University Press, 1972.

Smelser, Neil J. *Social Change in the Industrial Revolution: An Application of Theory to the British Cotton Industry.* Chicago: University of Chicago Press, 1959.

Stearns, Peter. "Working Class Women in Britain, 1890–1914." In *Suffer and Be Still,* edited by Martha Vicinus. Bloomington: Indiana University Press, 1972.

Stone, Lawrence, "The Rise of the Nuclear Family in Early Modern England." In *The Family in History,* edited by Charles H. Rosenberg. Philadelphia: University of Pennsylvania Press, 1976.

Sullerot, Evelyne. *Histoire et sociologie du travail féminin.* Paris: Gonthier, 1968.

Sussman, George. "The Wet-Nursing Business in Nineteenth Century France." *French Historical Studies* 9 (Fall 1975): 304–323.

Thabault, Roger. *Education and Change in a Village Community. Mazières-en-Gâtine, 1848–1914,* translated by Peter Tragear. New York: Schocken Books, 1971.

Thompson, E. P. "The Moral Economy of the English Crowd in the Eighteenth Century." *Past and Present* 50 (1971): 71–136.

———. "Rough Music: Le Charivari anglais." *Annales E.S.C.* 27 (1972): 285–312.

Thorner, Daniel; Kerblay, Basile; and Smith, R. E. F., eds. *A. V. Chayanov on the Theory of Peasant Economy.* Homewood, Ill.: Richard D. Irwin, 1966.

Tilly, Charles. "Population and Pedagogy." *History of Education Quarterly* 2 (1973): 113–128.

Tilly, Louise A.; Scott, Joan W.; and Cohen, Miriam. "Women's Work and European Fertility Patterns." *Journal of Interdisciplinary History* 6 (Winter 1976): 447–476.

Van de Walle, Etienne. *The Female Population of France in the Nineteenth Century.* Princeton, N. J.: Princeton University Press, 1974.

Vanek, Joann. "Time Spent in Housework." *Scientific American,* November 1974: 116–120.

Watson, C. "Birth Control and Abortion in France since 1939." *Population Studies* 5 (1952): 261–286.

Willmott, Peter, and Young, Michael. *Family and Kinship in East London.* London: Penguin Books, 1957.

Wrigley, E. A. "Family Limitation in Pre-Industrial England." *Economic History Review,* 2nd Series, 19 (April 1966): 89–109.

Yeo, Eileen, and Thompson, E. P. *The Unknown Mayhew.* London: Merlin Press, 1971.

Index